Can the Media Serve Democracy?

Can the Media Serve Democracy?

Essays in Honour of Jay G. Blumler

Edited by

Stephen Coleman
University of Leeds, UK

Giles Moss
University of Leeds, UK

and

Katy Parry
University of Leeds, UK

First published 2015 by
PALGRAVE MACMILLAN

Palgrave Macmillan in the UK is an imprint of Macmillan Publishers Limited, registered in England, company number 785998, of Houndsmills, Basingstoke, Hampshire, RG21 6XS

Palgrave Macmillan in the US is a division of St Martin's Press LLC, 175 Fifth Avenue, New York, NY 10010.

Palgrave is the global academic imprint of the above companies and has companies and representatives throughout the world.

Palgrave® and Macmillan® are registered trademarks in the United States, the United Kingdom, Europe and other countries

ISBN: 978–1–137–46791–1 hardback

This book is printed on paper suitable for recycling and made from fully managed and sustained forest sources. Logging, pulping and manufacturing processes are expected to conform to the environmental regulations of the country of origin.

A catalogue record for this book is available from the British Library.

A catalog record for this book is available from the Library of Congress.

Contents

Acknowledgements

We are very grateful to all our contributors, who immediately expressed their support for this project, and have produced splendid, thought-provoking chapters. Thanks are due to regular participants in the Political Communication Research Group at the University of Leeds with whom we have shared many enjoyable hours debating the themes and preoccupations of this book. We are especially indebted to Lone Sorenson, who painstakingly checked each chapter for corrections and formatting, and whose thoughtful work went beyond the usual proofreading duties. We also thank Felicity Plester and Chris Penfold at Palgrave Macmillan for their patience and assistance over the final months of preparations.

Notes on Contributors

W. Lance Bennett is a professor of political science and Ruddick C. Lawrence is a professor of communication at the University of Washington, Seattle, USA, where he directs the Center for Communication and Civic Engagement (www.engagedcitizen.org). The focus of his work is on how communication processes affect citizen engagement with politics. His most recent book is *The Logic of Connective Action: Digital Media and the Personalization of Contentious Politics* (with Alexandra Segerberg, 2013). He has received the Ithiel de Sola Pool and Murray Edelman career awards from the American Political Science Association, and the National Communication Association has recognized him as a Distinguished Scholar for lifetime achievement in the study of human communication.

Menahem Blondheim teaches in the Department of History and the Department of Communication and Journalism at the Hebrew University of Jerusalem, where he holds the Karl and Matilda Newhouse Chair in Communications. He also serves as the head of the Harry S. Truman Research Institute for the Advancement of Peace. In researching the history of communications and communications in history, he focuses on the United States and on the Jewish experience. He also explores communication technologies, old and new, and is engaged in big-data studies analyzing the representation of our contemporary world in international online news.

Jay G. Blumler is emeritus professor of public communication at the University of Leeds and emeritus professor of journalism at the University of Maryland. He is a leading, internationally recognized figure in political communication, having published numerous books, including *The Crisis of Public Communication* (with Michael Gurevitch, 1995). He is a fellow and former president of the International Communication Association. In 2006, he was given a lifetime achievement award by the American Political Science Association.

Kees Brants is an honorary professor at the University of Amsterdam's School of Communication Research and professor emeritus of political communication at Leiden University. Before reading political science and mass communication, he studied journalism and worked as a reporter for local and national newspapers in the Netherlands. He has published extensively, and his latest English-language book being *Political Communication in Postmodern Democracy* (edited with Katrin Voltmer, 2011). With his wife, he shares what some call a morbid fascination for the social construction in memory, history and lieux de mémoires of the First World War, about which they wrote two books.

Stephen Coleman is a professor of political communication at the University of Leeds. He has published several articles and books, the most recent of which is *How Voters Feel* (2013). He is also an honorary professor of political science at the University of Copenhagen and a research associate at the Oxford Internet Institute, University of Oxford. His book *The Internet and Democratic Citizenship* (with Jay Blumler, 2009) was winner of the American Political Science Association Award for best book on politics and information technology.

John Corner is a visiting professor in the School of Media and Communication at the University of Leeds and emeritus professor of the University of Liverpool. He has written widely on media and culture in books and journals. Among his major publications are *The Art of Record* (1996), *Critical Ideas in Television Studies* (1999), *Public Issue Television* (with Peter Goddard and Kay Richardson, 2007) and *Theorising Media: Power, Form and Subjectivity* (2011, paperback 2014). He is an editor of the journal *Media, Culture and Society*.

James Curran is director of Goldsmiths Leverhulme Media Research Centre and a professor of communications at Goldsmiths, University of London. He has written or edited over twenty books about the media, including most recently *Misunderstanding the Internet* (with Natalie Fenton and Des Freedman, 2012), *Media and Democracy* (2011), *Power Without Responsibility* (with Jean Seaton, 7th edition, 2010), *Media and Society* (5th edition, 2010). He is a fellow of the International Communication Association in recognition of his lifetime research on the media, and has been a visiting professor at California, Pennsylvania, Stanford, Stockholm and Oslo Universities.

Stephen Cushion is a senior lecturer at the Cardiff School of Journalism, Media and Cultural Studies. He is co-author of *The Rise of 24-Hour News Television: Global Perspectives* (2010), and sole author of *Television Journalism* (2011) and *The Democratic Value of News: Why Public Service Media Matter* (2012).

William H. Dutton is the Quello Professor of Media and Information Policy in the College of Communication Arts and Sciences at MSU, where he is director of the Quello Center. Bill was the first professor of internet studies at the University of Oxford, where he was founding director of the Oxford Internet Institute, and a fellow of Balliol College. He has recently edited the *Oxford Handbook of Internet Studies* (2013), four volumes on *Politics and the Internet* (2014), and a reader entitled *Society and the Internet* (with Mark Graham, 2014).

Frank Esser is a professor of international and comparative media research at the University of Zurich. There he also co-directs an 80-person strong National Research Center on the Challenges to Democracy in the 21st Century (*NCCR Democracy*). His research focuses on cross-national studies of news journalism and political communication. His co-edited books include *Comparing Political Communication* (2004), *Handbook of Comparative Communication Research* (2012), and *Mediatization of Politics* (2014).

Bob Franklin is a professor of journalism studies at Cardiff University, UK. He is the editor of *Digital Journalism, Journalism Practice* and *Journalism Studies*. He edits the book series *Journalism Studies: Theory and Practice* and co-edits a series, *Journalism Studies: Key Texts*. His recent books include *The Future of Journalism: Developments and Debates* (2013); *Journalism, Sources and Credibility: New Perspectives* (with Matt Carlson, 2011) and *Journalism Education, Training and Employment* (with Donica Mensing, 2011). He was a visiting professor at the Manship School of Journalism and Mass Communications, Louisiana State University, in 2008.

Elihu Katz is the Distinguished Trustee Professor at the Annenberg School for Communication, University of Pennsylvania and emeritus professor of Sociology and Communication at the Hebrew University of Jerusalem. He was the first director of the Israeli Television, founded Hebrew University's Communication Institute, and served as former director of the Institute of Applied Social Research in Israel. He has authored many books, including the influential *Uses of Mass Communications* (with Jay Blumler, 1974), and *Media Events* (with Daniel Dayan, 1992). He is an elected member of the American Academy of Arts and Sciences.

Sonia Livingstone is a professor in the Department of Media and Communications at LSE. Taking a comparative, critical and contextualised approach, she asks how the changing conditions of mediation are reshaping everyday practices and possibilities for action, identity and communication rights, with a focus on children and youth. She is author or editor of eighteen books, including *Media Consumption and*

Public Engagement (with Nick Couldry and Tim Markham, 2010), *Media Regulation: Governance and the Interests of Citizens and Consumers* (with Peter Lunt, 2012); *Meanings of Audiences: Comparative Discourses* (edited with Richard Butsch, 2013) and *Digital Technologies in the Lives of Young People* (edited with Chris Davies and John Coleman, 2014).

Paolo Mancini is a professor in the Dipartimento di Scienze Politiche, Università di Perugia. His research focuses mostly on political communication in a comparative dimension. Mancini's major publications include *Politics, Media and Modern Democracy* (with David Swanson, 1996) and *Comparing Media Systems: Three Models of Media and Politics* (with Dan Hallin, 2004). This book won the 2005 Goldsmith Book Award from Harvard University, the 2005 Diamond Anniversary Book Award of the National Communication Association and the 2006 outstanding Book Award of the International Communication Association.

Gianpietro Mazzoleni is a professor of political communication at the University of Milan, Italy. His research focuses on media-politics relations, pop politics and sociology of communication. His work has been published in *Political Communication* and *European Journal of Communication* and in the edited volume, *Mediatization of Politics* (2014). He is general editor of the *International Encyclopaedia of Political Communication* (forthcoming).

Denis McQuail is emeritus professor at the University of Amsterdam and honorary fellow of the Amsterdam School of Communication Research. He started his career at the Television Research Unit of the University of Leeds in 1959. His work has covered several different aspects of communication research, including political communication, audience research, media policy and media performance. He was a founding editor with Jay Blumler of *European Journal of Communication*. His most recent publication was *Journalism and Society* (2013).

David Morrison is emeritus professor at the Institute of Communication Studies (renamed the School of Media and Communication in August 2014), University of Leeds. He was one of the very early figures involved in the establishment of the Institute through the development of social science research. Supported by endowment monies raised by Jay Blumler, his activity offers itself as a continuous link to Blumler's older 'Centre for Television Research'. His work has involved large-scale survey research on both social and political issues, including voting, along with historical writing on communication research, notably a biography of Paul Lazarsfeld.

Giles Moss is a lecturer in media policy in the School of Media and Communication, University of Leeds. His research focuses on various aspects of the relationship between new media and politics, including not just the politics that goes on through these media but also the politics that surrounds them and shapes how they are structured and used. His work has appeared in a range of academic journals including *British Journal of Politics & International Relations*, *Convergence*, *Political Studies*, and *New Media & Society*.

Katy Parry is a lecturer in media and communication at the University of Leeds. Her work focuses on visual politics and how 'frames of war' circulate in public culture. She is a co-author of *Pockets of Resistance: British News Media, War and Theory in the 2003 Invasion of Iraq* (with Piers Robinson, Peter Goddard, Craig Murray and Philip Taylor, 2010), and *Political Culture and Media Genre: Beyond the News* (with Kay Richardson and John Corner, 2012).

Winfried Schulz is emeritus professor of mass communication and political science and an associate lecturer at the University of Erlangen-Nuremberg, Germany. He formerly held positions at the universities of Mainz and Muenster and visiting appointments at several European universities as well as at the University of California at Berkeley. He has published extensively in various areas of political communication. Schulz is doctor *honoris causa* of the Charles University Prague and a fellow of the International Communication Association.

James Stanyer is a reader in comparative political communication in the Department of Social Sciences at Loughborough University. He has authored three books and co-edited three collections, and has published in a range of leading journals in the field of communication and media studies. He has been a principal investigator on projects funded by the BBC Trust, the UK government and third-sector organizations. He serves on the editorial boards of various journals, and is a member of the COST Action network on Populist Political Communication and the Network of European Political Communication Scholars.

David H. Weaver is a distinguished professor and the Roy W. Howard Research Professor Emeritus in the School of Journalism at Indiana University. He has published thirteen books, including *Media Agenda-Setting in a Presidential Election* (1981), *The American Journalist* (1986), *The Formation of Campaign Agendas* (1991), *The American Journalist in the 1990s* (1996), *The American Journalist in the 21st Century* (2007), and *The Global Journalist in the 21st Century* (2012), as well as numerous articles and book chapters about journalists, the agenda-setting role of media, voter learning in political campaigns, newspaper readership, foreign news coverage, and journalism education. He is past president of AEJMC (Association for Education in Journalism & Mass Communication) and a Fellow of ICA (International Communication Association).

1

Introduction: Can the Media Serve Democracy?

Stephen Coleman, Giles Moss and Katy Parry

The problem

There has arguably never been a time when so many opportunities have been available for 'the people' to contribute to the democratic process, yet political participation seems to be in decline...
(McHugh, D. and Parvin, P. *Neglecting Democracy: Participation and Representation in 21st Century Politics*, London, Hansard Society, 2005: pp. 7–8)

The general argument for a free press as a means of free communication...has to do with a number of different things. These include the ability to give a powerful voice in the public domain to those unable to do so effectively for themselves... Importantly, it is also to do with the constitution by the media in their own right of a public forum, where information, ideas and entertainment are both circulated and held up to scrutiny.
(Report of the Leveson Inquiry into the Culture, Practices and Ethics of the Press, 2012: Vol. I, p. 62, para 3.4)

It is sometimes said that the media is accountable daily through the choice of readers and viewers. That is true up to a point. But the reality is that the viewers or readers have no objective yardstick to measure what they are being told. In every other walk of life in our society that exercises power, there are external forms of accountability, not least through the media itself...I do believe this relationship between public life and media is now damaged in a manner that requires repair. The damage saps the country's confidence and self-belief; it undermines its assessment of itself, its institutions; and above all, it reduces our capacity to take the right decisions, in the right spirit for our future.

(Speech to Reuters by British Prime Minister Tony Blair, 12 June 2007, available at http://news.bbc.co.uk/1/hi/uk_politics/6744581. stm, date accessed 14 June 2014)

Something seems to be wrong. Talk of decline, disengagement and disenchantment dominates the debate about the state of contemporary democracy. All too often, such talk leads on to expressions of ill-concealed frustration about 'apathetic' citizens who have forgotten their civic 'duty' and 'irresponsible' media failing to serve the public interest. Avoiding these well-rehearsed lamentations, the aim of this book is to reflect upon the ways in which one of the key institutional actors in the public domain – the media in their various forms – both serve and undermine democratic objectives. Let us take the Leveson Report's call for the media: 'to give a powerful voice in the public domain to those unable to do so effectively for themselves' and to provide 'a public forum, where information, ideas and entertainment are both circulated and held up to scrutiny' as a normative benchmark. To what extent do the media in developed political democracies reach that benchmark? How realistic is it to expect them to do so?

We start from the assumption that for the media to serve democracy they must enter into a positive relationship with their readers, viewers and listeners as citizens. To address people as citizens is to acknowledge that they are more than consumers who buy things, audiences who gaze upon spectacles, or isolated egos, obsessed with themselves. To act as a citizen is to engage in public situations of various kinds with people one might not know, who might not share one's interests, tastes, values, or even language. Sometimes the interaction will involve relations with governments, authorities, or employers. At other times, it involves ways of living alongside neighbours and strangers. At all times, the work of citizenship is geared towards the sustenance and invigoration of shared political communities. Without strong and prevalent civic attitudes, the binding ties of social solidarity and the amicable co-existence of cultural differences are likely to be at risk.

But the work of being an active citizen can be complex and time-consuming. Firstly, it involves being sufficiently informed to know what's going on in the world; what matters personally and what matters globally; how government works and how language is used both to illuminate and obfuscate political realities; where to access reliable information and how to compare sources so that rival perspectives can be transformed into useful knowledge. Secondly, active citizens need to arrive at judgements about who and what can be trusted. Can one party or politician be trusted more than another? Are elected representatives and governments able to do what they promise at election time? How far can friends, neighbours and strangers be depended upon to engage in the kind of collective action that might bring about desired changes? Can the existing constitutional system be trusted to serve the interests of all people, or should active citizens be thinking about working around the system, creating their own rules of engagement? Thirdly, active citizens need to make their voices heard and their presence felt. This involves using whatever skills and resources are available to develop networks of collective self-organisation, contributing to the political discourse and making a tangible impact upon the ways in which political power is exercised.

Most people find these challenges overwhelming. They know little about formal politics (Carpini, 1996; Eveland et al., 2005), rarely trust politicians or political processes (Norris, 2011; Hardin, 2013) and feel that they have little or no voice in policy formation and decision-making (Kenski and Stroud, 2006; Karp and Banducci, 2008). It is little wonder that many citizens seem to have given up on politics, believing that participation will probably result in confusion, manipulation or frustration.

The media have a crucial role to play here. Whether in the form of daily newspapers, radio discussion programmes, television news bulletins and issue documentaries, or the vast range of channels of public expression that have emerged online, it is the media's first task to remind people that they are inhabitants of a world in which they can make a difference. By enabling citizens to encounter and make sense of events, relationships and cultures of which they have no direct experience, the media constitute a public arena in which members of the public come together as more than passing strangers. As media theorist Michael Schudson has argued,

> When the media offer the public an item of news, they confer upon it public legitimacy. They bring it into a common public forum where it can be discussed by a general audience. They not only distribute the report of an event or announcement to a large group, they amplify it. An event or speech or document in one location becomes within a day, or within hours, or instantaneously, available to millions of people all over a region or country or the world. This has enormous effects. (1995: p.19)

How can the media perform this vital function in ways that might enable citizens to become better informed, more confident about making political judgements and more able to communicate in meaningful and influential ways? In short, how might the media play a role in nurturing and stimulating active democratic citizenship?

Many professional media producers would respond rather defensively by saying that they are already performing this role perfectly well. Their job, they would say, is to provide objective and balanced information to citizens who are free to decide what they want to do with it. They could point to numerous opportunities for the public to express themselves via newspaper letters' columns, phone-ins, studio-based discussions in which politicians face direct questioning from the public, user-generated content that helps to shape and enrich media agendas – not to mention the numerous new forms of public expression afforded by social media. They would argue that it is not their job to persuade citizens to participate, but to provide them with a trusted guide to what's going on and how they could, if they so wished, engage in various forms of civic activity.

Critics of the contemporary media argue that there is an element of self-delusion at play here: that by persistently presenting politics as a cynical game and politicians as manipulators who must be exposed, the media have become 'complicit in a process which is degrading democracy's institutions and undermining political representatives' (Barnett, 2002: p. 400). This critique has taken a number of forms. Jay Blumler (1983b: p. 67) has argued that the media stand 'accused of denigrating the political sphere instead of serving and invigorating it, encouraging opinion manipulation, and sapping participatory dispositions'. John Lloyd (2004: p. 1) has argued that 'the British media are destructive...of public communication and democratic practice'. His argument is that the media have become 'ravenous for conflict, scandal, splits, rows and failure' and have turned politics into 'a spectator sport' (ibid., p. 89). For all of these critics, the consequence of the media's obsession with the Westminster bubble and the exposure of ignominious political behaviour is mass public disenchantment with both the people and institutions that claim to represent them.

How might the media better serve democracy?

But there are signs that this mediated relationship between the public and their representatives is changing in at least two highly significant ways. Firstly, the old tripartite model of political communication involving a fixed pyramid of relationships between politicians, journalists and citizens is not nearly as clear-cut as it once was. While many aspects of this model continue to prevail, they do so within an expanded media ecology that includes many more platforms for public communication, offering variety, while threatening fragmentation. The idea of the public as an audience that receives information and entertainment from vast industry-like transmission centres is still highly relevant to mass broadcasters and advertisers, but it must now compete with new forms of mediation which, in some contexts and for certain demographic groups, changes the terms of public communication. The rise and ubiquity of digital media makes it possible for messages, images and sentiments to circulate within social networks that lack centres and are characterized by many-to-many polylogue rather than monological one-to-many transmission. In this new media ecology, the gatekeeping role of editors and journalists is undermined by the prevalence of user-generated news content and digital networks with agendas that are no longer susceptible to elite management. Regardless of the extent to which one believes the balance between old and new media is currently weighted in favour of the former, there is little doubt that the latter have a capacity to disrupt the flow of the former; the hegemony of national media centres is atrophying.

Alongside this reconfiguration of the media ecology is a second significant change. Whereas the meaning of the term 'political' in political communication seemed pretty self-evident half a century ago, when scholars like Jay Blumler, Denis McQuail and Elihu Katz began to consider the impact of television on political life, it is no longer as simple as that. Politics was taken to refer to a narrow set of institutions and practices: national parliaments and executives; local government; mainstream parties; a political agenda that, while changing from week to week, tended to revolve around a fixed range of issues, policies and ideologies. The study of political communication, therefore, was mainly interested in the ways that political institutions disseminated messages to the public via the mainstream media; the strategic operations involved in election campaigning and government information initiatives; attempts by the media to set agendas and frame events; and attempts by party 'spin doctors' to influence or resist such priming and framing. Indeed, much contemporary political communication revolves around precisely these themes. But in recent decades political governance has moved on to a number of different and often competing levels: local, regional and transnational institutions vie with national polities for legitimacy, while unaccountable global organisations wield power that no government can control. The locus of political power and decision-making is no longer as apparent as it once seemed to be. Alongside this so-called 'decentering' of political power, there has been a profound sense in which the self-referential language and customs of institutional politics are giving way to new forms of public expression and popular accountability. Politics has become more personal, in the sense that power relationships are increasingly acknowledged to be taking place at the mundane, micro level of everyday experience. Political language has become more vernacular, as power is increasingly rehearsed, performed and resisted in terms that shun the exclusivity of institutional elites. Daily struggles over power, authority and norms, whether they take place in the home, the workplace, the playground or the pub, are increasingly recognized as political. People who do not think of themselves as acting politically frequently find themselves employing democratic discourses and principles in order to pursue what they might prefer to think of as personal campaigns for a better life (Eliasoph, 1998).

These two changes in the communication ecology and political culture are forcing the media to rethink their relationship to their audiences. Large, authoritative, regulated media organisations, such as broadcasting networks, newspapers and press agencies, can no longer hope to manage the production of news and its dissemination to mass national populations. The interruptive force of digital media places pressure on them to gather and tell their stories in different ways. Notions of democratic citizenship as a set of obligatory, somewhat ritualized practises, upon which politicians once based a thin and irregular conception of political representation, begin to look unsustainable in the face of public disenchantment. An urge to 'do politics differently' has led parties and media organisations to adopt a number of experimental strategies in recent years, ranging from online 'conversations' with supporters and well-rehearsed attempts to show their leaders being 'ordinary' and 'spontaneous' in the case of parties, to conspicuous audience feedback loops and satirical performances of political infotainment in the case of the mainstream media. But few of these initiatives have either taken root or convinced citizens that the citadels of official politics are open to them. Political communication seems to be in flux, stuck awkwardly between known ways that don't work and unknown ways that might.

While political communication scholars are under pressure to expand their field of study and employ more innovative methods of tracking the interflow between elite and grass-roots politics, some norms remain persistently relevant. In his many writing collaborations, but especially that with the late Michael Gurevitch, Blumler has set out clearly what democracies should expect from the media, including

- surveillance of sociopolitical developments
- identifying the most relevant issues
- providing a platform for debate across a diverse range of views
- holding officials to account for the way they exercise power
- providing incentives for citizens to learn, choose, and become involved in the political process
- resisting efforts of forces outside the media to subvert their independence.

To what extent do these normative requirements encapsulate the requirements of democratic media in the current era? What are the obstacles to realising them? What sort of initiatives could feasibly be taken to implement them? In short, *Can the Media Serve Democracy?*

In celebrating the huge contribution that Jay Blumler has made to the study of political communication, not only as a pioneering and imaginative researcher in a range of areas, a theorist of uses and gratifications, a deeply thoughtful and influential policy thinker, and a generous leader in the field of media and communication studies, it is upon his unflinching normative commitment to a culturally enlarging conception of media democracy that we focus in this volume. In a recent lecture given at the University of Ljubljana, Blumler suggested that democracy should seek to realize 'the ideal of collective self-determination', and for this to happen, the media should adhere to what he called 'four purposes of civic communication'. The first is 'to feed citizens' need for surveillance of those parts of the political environment that matter to them'. The second is 'to uphold the norm of meaningful choice over those issues and problems that may ultimately determine how we live with each other'. The third is 'inclusiveness: that all parts of society that are likely to be affected by or hold views upon alternative approaches to policies should be hearable on them'. Fourth, the media must 'provide navigable avenues of comprehending exchange between citizens and decision-takers, affording the former real opportunities to influence the latter and for the latter to know the former better'. The simplicity, practicality and radicalism of these principles capture well Blumler the man and the thinker.

Some of the world's leading political communication scholars were asked to write chapters (and agreed willingly as soon as they knew that the volume was in honour of Jay Blumler) addressing the title question of this book. In endeavouring to address this broad but thorny question, the contributors wrote from a variety of perspectives and methods of study, reflecting the rich diversity of scholarship across which Jay's work has been a formative influence. There is inevitable overlap in the sections of the book, but we have organized chapters according to four broad subject areas: (1) Media Systems and Comparative Research, (2) Journalism and the Public Interest, (3) Public Cultures and Mediated Publics, and (4) Changing Media, New Democratic Opportunities, with a final section. (5) The Past, Present and Future of Political Communication, reflecting back on Jay's career as a founding father of media studies. In addition to arranging the essays along thematic preoccupations, the structure of the collection allows us to explore questions at the heart of Jay's body of work: the importance of empirical communications research and comparative studies; a strong normative concern with the public interest and the quality of public discourse and democratic politics; and an interest in the possible implications academic research can have for policymaking. In what follows, we outline the chapters in turn, noting the particular contribution of each author while placing their insights in wider debates within media and communications research.

Contributions

Part I: Media Systems and Comparative Research

The chapters in Part I focus on the institutions of political communication and the potential benefits afforded through comparative work and a macro-level overview of political and media systems. It is the notion of a 'system' which **Paolo Mancini** unpicks in his chapter, addressing how the term 'media system' has been defined (if at all) and understood by media scholars. Mancini suggests that as media scholars we can learn some lessons from 'sister' sciences, such as political science, which have used this notion for a longer period of time, and that their experience may be useful in creating a more precise definition of 'system'. Indeed, Mancini points out that it is with the work of Jay Blumler and Michael Gurevitch that the word 'system' begins to assume a more precise scientific identity, progressively abandoning its 'indicative' meaning to one which presents a framework of characteristics (structures, procedures, actors) and so allows for precise differentiation in comparative research. In responding to criticisms of the 'system' approach, Mancini notes comprehensiveness as its very 'advantage' in comparative use. Citing an even earlier elucidation by Almond and Verba that 'the concept of a system is an ecological concept that underlines the interactions between the sphere of politics and its environment' (1966: p. 26), Mancini reminds us not only of the problematic, indistinct boundaries involved, but that recognitions of the intricacies involved in an 'ecological' concept are hardly new. The chapter concludes with a caution on the dangers of 'going comparative' without a clear understanding of theoretical frameworks, but also makes the case for research based on national cultures: 'despite the global cultural market, the undeniable tendency towards homogenisation and hybridisation and the rise of the world-wide web, each media system is still affected by the local culture, by the national language and by all those cultural symbols that still characterize cultural production'.

The challenges of comparing media systems are further addressed in our next two chapters, by **Frank Esser** and **Kees Brants**. Taking up Mancini's challenge, Esser argues that although comparative research has made more progress in some subject areas than in others, we are observing the gradual emergence of comparative communications as a recognized subdiscipline, comparable to *comparative politics* in political science. The chapter explores whether and how structural and semi-structural 'independent variables' suggested by Jay's and others' empirical work (political structure and culture, campaign professionalism, media structure and culture, and media professionalism) can help explain content-related 'dependent variables' like media depoliticization, media interventionism or media negativity in election news discourse. Esser stresses the democratic role of the media, especially during election periods, and expresses a strong commitment to investigating national news contexts and cultures through a more thorough and explicit conceptualization of key concepts. For Esser, an ultimate scholarly goal would be a comprehensive system-sensitive news theory – something that he argues is so far absent from the field of mass communication research.

In addition to commenting on the intellectual benefits (triggering creative imagination, spurring new modes of analysis) and the practical or pragmatic concerns (crucial availability of funding) of comparative research, Kees Brants also notes the continuing influence of Blumler and Gurevitch's (1995) framework for political communication in the design of models and classifications, here summarized as degree of state control; mass media partisanship; media-political integration; and the nature of the legitimating creed of media institutions. Brants considers five types of pitfalls, which appear to be only increasing in seriousness: methodological issues, especially where concepts might be understood differently; value judgements or normative assumptions; decisions on what to compare (media forms, units of analysis, tools); Anglo-American bias; and an inherent determinism or assumption of a one-directional trend. As suggested in Mancini's chapter, it is the Internet which presents a fundamental problem in comparing media systems. Where Mancini concludes that each media system is still strongly dependent on country traditions and language, Brants sees a greater challenge to the boundaries involved. For example, structures of governance, finance and ownership are not easily confined to national borders, the professionalism of journalism is challenged by citizen-journalists, and what we might count as Internet content becomes almost limitless.

One concept which seeks to explain fundamental changes in political communication, and beyond, is mediatization. **Winfried Schulz** poses two questions in his chapter. First, to what extent does the notion of mediatization interface with the inspiring ideas introduced by Jay Blumler? And second, what can mediatization proponents learn from his analyses of the modern publicity process? Taking Blumler and Dennis Kavanagh's seminal 1999 article, 'The Third Age of Political Communication', as a starting point, Schulz discusses three propositions developed in further studies: the presence of communication media as an impetus for social change, often alongside other '-izations' such as individualization and commercialization; the increasing social importance of media technologies as they evolve, linked to notions of media power; and finally, political reactions and adaptations to perceived increased media importance, with political actors utilizing media for their own strategic interests. Schulz questions whether mediatization provides a brand new approach, but it could present a potential perspective which has not yet been fully advanced, especially with its focus on various political actors and their anticipative and adaptive responses, rather than emphasizing the (negative) tendencies of political journalism. Systems approaches and theoretical concepts such as mediatization offer comprehensive means to compare the institutions, cultures and contexts of various countries, with the further possibility for mapping continuities and transformations in longitudinal studies. Ensuring that the instruments or tools selected for measurement and analysis provide the most illuminating and representative portrait for each country involved is only one of the challenges facing those who 'go comparative' in an era of what can feel like warp-speed developments in media technologies and the accompanying political responses. Mediatization stresses the central role of media in society, but exactly what form that media takes raises serious issues for political communication researchers, with a concurrent, and possibly contradictory, dispersal of media influence, in the sense of the traditional roles of elite press, public service broadcasting and political commentators acting as key intermediaries or gatekeepers.

Part II: Journalism, Democracy and the Public Interest

The chapters in Part II pick up another key aspect of Blumler's work, exploring the media's connection to the public interest and how this might be strengthened through appropriate policy and regulation. It is commonplace to say that media and especially journalistic media serve the public interest through the role they play in a democracy, but then how effectively they perform this role is disputed. To say that democracy is well served by media, we need media that hold governments and powerful economic groups to account, host meaningful public discussion across different perspectives, and provide citizens with independent and high-quality information. However, the evidence suggests that media are unlikely to achieve these things if left to their own devices in an unregulated market, something which has become more apparent in recent years as media have become increasingly marketized and so subject to economic forces. As Jay stressed in his work on public service broadcasting (Blumler, 1992) and in his more recent work on the Internet's potential to support a 'more deliberative democracy' (Coleman and Blumler, 2009), ensuring the media serve the public interest requires appropriate policy interventions. **Denis McQuail's** chapter re-examines the media's connection with the public interest and the democratic public sphere. McQuail surveys the shifts that have taken place in media and political communication since Jay's early research in the 1960s. Over this period, changes in media systems and government policy have meant that economic imperatives have tended to take priority over the media's contribution to democracy, with the result that 'the potential of new means and systems for enhanced communicativity is largely being left to chance and the market'. However, McQuail argues that the principles of the public interest and the public sphere, which shaped early media and political communication research, remain valid and important guides for future research and policy. He calls for new thinking on the public sphere that is informed by comparative media research and studies of the use of media across generations, and which explores the changing nature of key mediators and communicators. Following Jay's lead, such research should keep normative principles in mind while also being empirically rigorous and focused on what is practically achievable.

Taking up McQuail's challenge, **Stephen Cushion** and **Bob Franklin** examine the principle of public service media and its enduring importance in realizing the media's contribution to the public interest and democracy. In the face of technological change and the growing marketization of media, the principle of public service media has increasingly been put in question, becoming more 'vulnerable', as Jay warned in his own writing on public service broadcasting (Blumler, 1992). But the empirical evidence suggests that public service media is more, not less, important today. Citing studies of television news coverage, Cushion and Franklin argue that the news produced by public service broadcasters has maintained its high standards and is distinct from and more trusted by the public than its commercial counterparts. Meanwhile, the newspaper industry – where the principle of the free market prevails – is facing significant financial pressures, and the quality of the journalism is deteriorating as a result. Against the current move towards the marketization of media, Cushion and Franklin conclude that we should focus instead on extending the principle of public service into areas where the market prevails. 'Regulation of newspapers', they conclude, 'may be required as much as for broadcast media if the values of public service are to inform the production of news in the public interest alongside, but superior to the influence of the marketplace'.

Drawing on a wide range of empirical research, **David Weaver's** chapter takes stock of what we know about journalism today and reflects on its future. Survey research indicates that journalists remain committed to public service and producing news in the public interest. He also finds that journalism continues to play a powerful role in shaping public opinion and the political agenda. However, like Cushion and Franklin, Weaver points to the significant financial pressures affecting the newspaper industry in the United States and elsewhere, which means there are fewer journalists employed, and the professional autonomy of those who remain is increasingly curtailed. Weaver concludes by considering how the future of journalism can be ensured, arguing that 'whatever happens, it seems that high-quality journalism is too important to democratic forms of government to let it wither away'. While media and political communication researchers have rightly stressed its essential democratic role, Weaver concludes that research is now urgently needed on the economics of journalism in order to solve the increasingly pressing problem of how to make it financially sustainable.

In his chapter, **James Stanyer** examines the regulation of the press in the wake of the recent phone-hacking scandal in the UK, an event which led to the closure of a prominent weekly tabloid newspaper and the British prime minister's intiation of an inquiry into 'the culture, practices, and ethics of the press' (Leveson, 2012). Stanyer argues that the tabloid press in the UK, driven by economic objectives, often falls far short of ideal normative accounts of journalism's democratic role.

The claims these newspapers make to be serving the public interest are too often just a convenient smokescreen to justify ethically questionable practices and to resist media policy and regulation that is against their economic interests. Yet, however regrettable events like the phone-hacking scandal are, Stanyer finds some grounds for optimism. By putting the existing regulatory system in question, events like the phone-hacking scandal open up a valuable space for policy reflection and debate and the possibility to transform established ways of doing things. Despite the 'negative connotations of scandals', he concludes, they can also be 'important moments or critical junctures which can open political communication systems or subsystems to regulatory change'.

Moral and ethical concerns are also at the heart of the final chapter in Part II: here **David Morrison** refocuses attention from the questionable practices of the press, to the moral concerns which underpin our work as researchers. Morrison traces the development of empirical social research in Europe and North America throughout the 20th century, arguing that as quantification techniques came to predominate, such survey-based research lost sight of the moral aspects that had marked the work of the social research founders. Morrison concludes that while Blumler's work operates with a clear methodological frame for understanding the audience, it is his moral outlook and his regard for the individual as an expressive actor that locks his work 'into a humanistic tradition of social enquiry'.

Part III: Public Culture and Mediated Publics

In Part III, we move on to notions of public culture and public engagement, especially in relation to broadcasting. The role of television in public culture has been a central research interest in Blumler's academic life, joining Leeds University in 1963 as Granada Television Research Fellow. It is apt then that **John Corner's** chapter considers the aesthetic and formal qualities of a documentary film broadcast in 1964, *The Dream Machine*; the title directly refers to the emergent social identity of television. Corner pursues questions about television's character, on matters of cultural form and content, as well as on broader questions of the television economy and the institutions and structures which affect policy and practice. Corner ends the chapter by referring across to Blumler's paper of the same year, 'British Television: Outline of the Research Strategy' in which he raises a number of issues for the attention of empirical research: about the positioning of television in everyday life, about 'escapism' and what he calls the world which the 'entertainers, themselves, have created' (pp. 231–2). The tentative treatment of television values and the expressed reservations about 'light entertainment' pleasures presented in the documentary are the kinds of anxieties mirrored in academic accounts to this day, and confronted by Jay in his early call for 'attention upon the uses which ordinary people make of mass media' (1964: p. 224).

How media scholars perceive 'ordinary people' is a theme taken up by **Sonia Livingstone** in the next chapter. Livingstone revisits her earlier work on the intellectual and empirical complexities of the collective terms 'audience' and 'public', noting that Jay 'has long been a firm advocate of the audience as public'. Rather than the 'audience' becoming obsolete in the age of networked digital media, Livingstone takes issue with the term 'users' for its separation from the public sphere of action when considering motivations and mediation contexts. High ideals for publics have been misleadingly contrasted with the denigration of (television) audiences, Livingston argues, with underlying assumptions about popular culture and passivity perpetuated, and now stereotypically contrasted with the interactivity of online users and consumers. It is in political mobilisation and engagement that the most direct line is drawn between audiences and publics, even if such mediated citizenship tends to be dispersed in nature rather than as an identifiable crowd or mass. Drawing on Habermas, Livingstone suggests that it is in the everyday lifeworld that media and audiences sustain public culture; such participation can then shape the actions of the system world, as Jay's past work has also observed (Coleman and Blumler, 2009).

One example of a 'media event' (Dayan and Katz, 1992) designed to engage its audiences as publics is the televised presidential or leadership debate. Although, as **Elihu Katz** and **Manehem Blondheim** show in their chapter, Sweden can claim the first televised debates, it is the US presidential debates of 1960 which hold mythical status and serve as a model for subsequent debates. These contests still attract large audiences, including the first- ever prime ministerial debates in the UK in 2010, where around 60% of the population tuned in for a 'civics lesson'. The chapter cites a study of voters' responses authored by Jay which suggested that political 'substance' prevailed over the race or game aspects as a prime motivation for watching the UK debates. Reflecting on the 2012 US debates, Katz and Blondheim offer a number of concerns related to their democratic purpose: for example, whether the debates exaggerate the power of the president and encourage cynicism when the inevitable compromise follows election; how the staging of the events and role of the moderator enact different models for engagement, as well as symbolize certain democratic ideals. The increased capacity for observing and monitoring the tweets, shares and 'likes' of audiences (by political advisers, media commentators, and indeed communications scholars) certainly gives the impression of an ever more involved and responsive audience, but these new traces of audiences' affinities also 'wink back' to the uses and gratifications school, as Katz and Blondheim conclude.

Part IV: Changing Media, New Democratic Opportunities

While changes in the media environment pose challenges to the traditional democratic roles played by established media, as noted by a number of chapters in the Festschrift, they also present new democratic possibilities. Following Jay's lead, we need to approach the present with a critical eye in order to diagnose its normative shortcomings but without falling into an unduly pessimistic analysis that misses the democratic opportunities that may present themselves. The chapters in Part IV examine the changing nature of media and the contemporary public sphere and in particular the potential it may offer for more decentralized, inclusive, and democratic forms of media and communication. In his chapter, **Lance Bennett** explores three broad and interrelated social changes in Western societies: the fragmentation of public life and the breakdown of existing institutions, a change in media system towards more personalized and distributed communication, and new forms of networked participation and political organization. Bennett argues that just as media systems are changing shape, so are citizenship and the public sphere. Younger age groups are moving away from traditional sources of information to less conventional ones and from established political organizations such as political parties toward single-issue and lifestyle-oriented social movements. Meanwhile, alongside the modernist public sphere, which was dominated by mass media organizations and political elites, Bennett argues that we are seeing the emergence of a 'networked public sphere' where 'many citizens are actively creating their own channels and methods to communicate directly with each other and to make that communication increasingly hard for both elites and the mass media to ignore or marginalize'. He concludes that 'a fourth era of personalized, technology-enabled communication is clearly emerging, and our challenge is to understand it'.

William Dutton's chapter also focuses on the contribution of the Internet to the public sphere outside the formal institutions of democratic politics. Dutton describes the emergence of what he terms the 'Fifth Estate', arguing that the Internet has facilitated new forms of political accountability and democratized communicative power. 'Individuals who are online can create and source information and network with others in ways that are not tied to local or formal institutions', Dutton argues, while 'networked individuals' can 'be armed with the information and social support to hold politicians and mainstream institutions more accountable'. However, as Dutton goes onto argue, the 'Fifth Estate' also faces significant challenges today and its future is uncertain. The free flow of content and information upon which it is based is in danger of being chocked off should 'regulations, online gatekeepers and other controls constrain or block the Internet's original conception as an open, end-to-end network allowing a free flow of content'. According to Dutton, new forms of self-regulation and self-governance are required in order to maintain the Fifth Estate.

In a similar vein to Bennett and Dutton, **Gianpietro Mazzoleni** explores the changing nature of the public sphere today. Mazzoleni describes the transformation of the public sphere as a shift from top-down mass-mediated communication towards what Castells (2009) calls 'mass self-communication', where communication is initiated by citizens but can still potentially reach large audiences through horizontal, many-to-many structures of communication. In relation to political discourse specifically, Mazzoleni argues that we are seeing the emergence of an 'enlarged digital polity', where political elites must increasingly engage with and respond to the citizens organized online. Optimistically, he argues that the new media environment may in these ways be providing the conditions with which the Habermasian ideal of the public sphere can be de-sublimated today. 'The escalation of the interactive digital media', he writes, 'is creating the conditions for the establishing of a genuine public sphere in the original, romantic, Habermasian sense, where all actors, on equal bases and with equal access to communication resources can diffuse their ideas, voice their claims, compete in advocating policy solutions, in a word shape the public/political agenda'.

Finally in this section, **Stephen Coleman** reflects more theoretically on what the concept of the public sphere means today and considers the implications of the recent affective turn in social and political thought for the way we theorize the public sphere. The public sphere is often an uninviting and elitist space, Coleman argues, which tends to exclude the public from participation through its commitment to sober, reasoned-governed discourse. 'Governed by an ethos of instrumental rationality that celebrates the analytical and eschews the pre-cognitive', Coleman argues, '"proper conduct" in the public sphere is increasingly at odds with quotidian sociability'. Yet, alongside the 'po-faced public sphere', he argues that a 'new publicness' is emerging, connected with new media practices, which assumes a more networked and distributed form and which is more inclusive and open to diverse modes of popular expression. 'The potential spaces of intersubjective discourse and recognition that have emerged in recent years', he argues, 'seem to be closer to the ground, lighter to the common touch, less culturally prescriptive and more open to the bricolage of everyday conversation'.

Part V: The Past, Present and Future of Political Communication

Our closing section brings our focus directly back to the career of Jay Blumler and how his immense contribution has helped to shape our understanding of the media's role in democratic societies. In a selective examination of Jay's early publications, **James Curran** first notes the debunking power of Blumler and McQuail's study of the 1964 British electorate. Published in 1968, the study defied the prevalent assertions on the seductive powers of television in order to explore the ways in which prior attitudes and beliefs played a significant part in how people make sense of media information. From this starting point, the chapter deftly covers the vast range of Jay's contributions, noting a critical openness to US and European research traditions, which engenders forward-thinking insights and the ability to adapt to the shifting balance of power between media and politicians. As Curran sums up: 'He was also a pioneer of comparative media research, an exponent of an influential, totalizing conception of the political communications system, an insightful, critical observer of changes in British media and politics, and an eloquent media reformist'. The final point in this chapter concerns Jay's 'irrepressible geniality' and encouragement of others. As editors of this collection based at the University of Leeds, and indeed along with all our contributors, we are fortunate to share in Jay's noted 'dynamic presence' and benefit from both his kindness and appetite for debate. In the final chapter, Jay kindly agreed to be interviewed by **Katy Parry** and **Giles Moss**, so that we could further explore some of the key themes raised in this collection with the great man himself. In his inimitable style, Jay outlines the central importance of communication, and especially journalistic organizations, for politics and for meaningful democratic participation. At the heart of Jay's work is the importance of values, and he summarizes here how these normative concerns operate at four levels: the civic level (role of voters/citizens); the level of media organizations (public service vs. commercial); the level of political journalism (pragmatic vs. sacerdotal status); and finally, at the level of communication research itself (critical vs. administrative). Asked if he could count himself as an optimist despite the well-known pressures on public interest journalism, Jay offers hope rather than optimism: 'that there are what might be called civic resources in the prevailing system which if built upon effectively and imaginatively, might give one grounds not for optimism but hope'. In asking how the media can serve democracy in this collection, such hopeful recognition of existing civic resources, and the call to build upon them in effective and imaginative ways, sounds like a great place to start.

Part I

Media Systems and Comparative Research

2
The Idea of 'Systems' in Media Studies: Criticisms, Risks, Advantages

Paolo Mancini

Three conceptions of media systems[1]

Criticisms against the use of the notion of 'systems' in media studies are common (Norris, 2009; Roudakova, 2011; Hardy, 2012). In this chapter, I discuss the use of the concept of systems and its criticisms. Despite its wide use, the term 'media system' has never been clearly defined by media scholars (Bastiansen, 2008). There are different reasons for this lack of a definition. Indeed, the term 'media system' is very often used today, but it arrived at the forefront of media scholarship only recently. I also examine the manner in which 'sister' sciences and, in particular, political science, have used and still use this notion. Finally, I propose justifications for the use of the systems concept in comparative political communication research.

In media studies, the notion of systems is primarily used in comparative research in political communication and in journalism studies. In these disciplines, there are three primary uses of the word 'system'. The first use can be defined as purely indicative. This use is the everyday use of the word; it simply indicates an object, the media, distinguishing it from other objects without adding any other attribute or specific meaning in terms of approaches and possible interpretations. In this sense, the word 'system' does not connote specific methods of study, interpretation and evaluation of the object that has been chosen. 'Media system' simply indicates the subject to be studied.

The second use of the term 'system' in media studies is its confrontational sense. This meaning of the word 'system' in political communication and media studies is the most frequently used and, undoubtedly, also the most criticized. 'System' is used when the media confront something else; it is used not only to distinguish (as in the previous case) but also to list (often not in an explicit manner) and order features of the media that are different from the features that characterize some other system. I also place in this category the 'comparative' use of the word 'system' through both space and time. According to the 'confrontational' meaning, the word 'system' indicates a framework of characteristics that constitute the 'media system' itself and that are different from the characteristics of some other system. In this sense, the 'confrontational' use does not simply indicate an object but also attempts to define and interpret a framework of character-istics that distinguish that 'specific' system from other systems. The use of the word 'system' is confrontational when media are observed in relation to politics or business; the use is confrontational when the media in one country are compared with media in another country, and so on.

The following is a vivid example of this use of the notion of system. In a recent report for the Reuters Institute for the Study of Journalism (2012), Rasmus Nielsen writes,

> The object of analysis is 'media system', shorthand for the aggregate of news media in a given country. Like political systems or national economies, media systems are not neatly delineated, without internal friction, or indeed fully contained. But one can still speak usefully of a French media system, in the way one can speak of a French political system or a French economy. (p. 9)

The third use of the word 'system' in media studies can be named 'func-tional', as it refers specifically to scholars' use of the term 'media system', according to differentiation theory. Here, 'system' assumes all of the theoretical and empirical connotations that derive from the application of functional systems theory to the universe of the mass media. Jeffrey Alexander wrote two very interesting papers on this topic, describing the birth of a system in charge of spreading 'universalistic information' (1981, p. 25). Niklas Luhmann (2000) has used the concept of the media system extensively in a purely differentiating manner. The 'functional' use of the word 'system' implies precise theoretical and interpretive connotations that appear to be missing from the other two uses.

For many years, the attention of media scholars has been devoted to the individual level rather than the aggregate level. Media studies have developed primarily (not exclusively) out of the interests placed on the 'effects' of the message. Primarily in the United States, media studies focused on this topic are conducted in response to the specific requests of large industries, governments and companies that sponsor such studies. The development of mass media was primarily linked to a major question that was addressed to social researchers: How powerful are the mass media with regard to their consequences both in the market of goods and for public opinion? How much do the mass media affect the attitudes and behaviours of consumers and citizens? The consequences of mass media activity (and the requests of research funders) were primarily related to the choices and behaviours of single individuals. For many years, there was no interest (or very little interest) at the aggregate level. This tendency was also a result of the strong influence that psychology, and particularly behaviourism (focusing primarily at the individual level), has had on the development of the field.

Comparative research was not the primary focus in the very early years of the media studies field. The initial development of this field was essentially related to research funds that based their interests in single countries and very rarely considered other social realities as well; there was no interest in comparing one system with another.

Despite attempts to internationalize research in sociology and mass communication through the creation of initial international data archives, the creation of international organizations of researchers and the launching of international research projects, 'the largest volume of research was generated nationally and the internationally comparative studies never became a matter of economic value for any of the institutes' (Scheuch, 1990, p. 22).

Indeed, during the infancy of media studies, the word 'system' was applied exclusively in what I defined as the 'indicative' sense; it did not imply a theoretical and interpretive framework, and it did not indicate a precise list of features that differentiate the system from something else. The word was used simply to indicate a subject, distinguishing it from other subjects.

As Bastiansen reports, in one of the first 'classic' texts of media studies that had a clear comparative (not empirical) approach, *Four Theories of the Press* (Siebert et al., 1956), the word 'system' is used several times, but only the 'indicative meaning' is used: 'several times in the course of their book, the authors use the concept of "system" as a designation for all mass media in a given society seen as a whole' (Bastiansen, 2008, p. 96). Additionally, in another classic text of mass communication that contains the word 'system' in its title, *Media Systems in Society*, by Joseph Turow (1992), no extensive definition of the term 'system' is provided; the word is used simply to indicate a subject; no clear boundaries for this subject are proposed.

It is with the work of Jay Blumler and Michael Gurevitch that the word 'system' begins to assume a more precise scientific identity, progressively abandoning its 'indicative' meaning. In several of their works, the two authors stress the need to introduce this concept in media studies. It is in their contribution to *Mass Communication and Society*, edited in 1975 by Curran, Gurevitch and Woollacott (later republished in Blumler and Gurevitch's *The Crisis of Public Communication*), that the two scholars debate in a more in-depth manner the possible introduction of the concept of 'system' in political communication studies. They stress the following advantages deriving from such an adoption: first, the notion of systems may allow for a more comprehensive view of the subject under analysis, linking together its various aspects; second, this more general view may avoid the risk of overemphasising or underestimating one element over the others; third, the notion of systems may be very useful in comparative analysis. In the view of Blumler and Gurevitch (1995), the following constitute the political communication system: political institutions in terms of their communication aspects, media institutions in terms of their political aspects, audience orientations towards political communication and communication-relevant aspects of political culture (p. 12). In their definition, they stress the framework of input-output relations that 'bind its constituent elements in a network of mutual dependence' (ibid., p. 23).

This definition marks the first time that media scholars have attempted to indicate with major precision what they mean by the word 'system' and the improvements that this notion introduces. The use that Blumler and Gurevitch suggest is the 'confrontational' use, as it indicates a set of qualifications that differentiate the media from other activities and structures. At the same time, this use is 'confrontational' because, as is well known, much of the work of the two scholars focuses on comparative research, in which the term 'system' is used to distinguish the media system of one country from that of another country, therefore including system specificities that operationalize such a distinction.

I must admit that in our *Comparing Media Systems* (here, too, the word 'system' appears in the title) as well, the notion of 'system' is not satisfactorily defined, and some confusion may arise between our use of 'system' and our use of 'model'. Often, we use the two words somewhat interchangeably, although there is no doubt that with the term 'model', we were referring to specific features, essentially the type and the level of professionalism of a mass media system that were different from those of some other media system (Hallin and Mancini, 2004a).

Before moving to a different topic, it may be useful to stress the similarities between the 'confrontational' and the 'functionalist' meaning of the concept of 'system' on one side and Bourdieu's concept of 'field' on the other. We all know that 'field theory' is highly diffused in sociology and affects many empirical studies. This theory has some influence in media studies as well, Erik Neveu and Rodney Benson being primary followers of this approach. In the introduction to their book *Bourdieu and the Journalistic Field* (2005), the two scholars write the following: 'Bourdieu's field theory follows from Weber and Durkheim in portraying modernity as a process of differentiation into semiautonomous and increasingly specialized spheres of action' (for example, fields of politics, economics, religion, cultural production) (p. 2). This definition is very close to that of Jeffrey Alexander and Luhmann when both scholars discuss journalism as a system. For Benson and Neveu, there exists a journalistic field that is part of the wider field of cultural production, with specific features, structures and procedures that distinguish this field from others. In accordance with Bourdieu, Benson and Neveu write that in its interactions with other fields, journalism is demonstrated to be essentially heteronomous – highly dependent on other fields – and not autonomous, as other fields are.

Political science and the idea of 'system'

As noted above, the existing definitions of 'system' in media studies are not completely satisfactory, although in recent years, various attempts at clarification have been made. Is the notion of 'system' better defined in political science? Indeed, there is no doubt that media scholars have essentially taken the idea of 'system' from the work of political scientists, who addressed this notion much earlier than media scholars. Sociologists, too, have been working extensively on the same concept, but as to political communications research, there is no doubt that the hybridization between political science and communication studies has been more frequent and more significant, at least with regard to political communications research.

Already in 1966, Almond and Powell, summarising previous studies, had written the following: 'the term political system has become increasingly common in the titles of texts and monographs in the field of comparative politics' (p. 16). For the two authors, the idea of the political system has replaced previous concepts such as state, nation and government that have not disappeared but, rather, are used to indicate more restricted fields. Later in this work, Almond and Powell explain how 'political system' should be defined: 'the concept of political system has acquired wide currency because it directs attention to the entire scope of political activities within a society, regardless of where in the society such activities may be located' (ibid., p. 17). The authors then carefully explain which components of the system emerge from the existing definitions. 'Legitimate physical coercion' (ibid.) is what characterizes most of the definitions of political system to which the two authors refer. From this characterization derives the notion that most of the time comparative research in the field of political science has implied the comparison of countries where different political systems take form and where 'legitimate physical coercion' is exercised.

For the two authors, the notion of 'system' is primarily related to the 'interdependency' of its components. Blumler and Gurevitch later apply this idea to the 'media system'; for example, they take from Almond and Verba the idea that systems are characterized by a framework of inputs and outputs, while recognising that the issue of the 'boundaries' of a system is a problematic one: where does a system begin and end? (ibid., p. 19).

At the end of their discussion on the notion of the system, Almond and Verba specify that 'the concept of system is an ecological concept that underlines the interactions between the sphere of politics and its environment' (ibid., p. 26). This specification is very useful, linking the idea of the system to the surrounding society, returning to the problem of its boundaries; in this regard, Almond and Verba specify that the boundaries of a system are 'fluctuant' (ibid., p. 21), as they depend on and are linked to the interactions that each system has with the other systems in the society, thus depending on the contingencies as well as on the specific point from which one examines the system and its interactions with other systems.

Although they do not directly refer to them, Blumler and Gurevitch rely heavily on Almond and Verba's hypothesis. In all of their works, the notion of 'system' offers the possibility of examining the research subjects, thus incorporating a large number of variables. This possibility is what Blumler and Gurevitch clearly write and what Almond and Verba assume when they mention 'the entire scope of political activities within a society'. In all of their hypotheses, the idea of 'system' is also essentially characterized by its framework of interdependence both within the system itself and outside of the system. Finally, both for these media scholars and for these political scientists, the idea of a system fosters comparative research.

Almond and Verba's thoughts in 1966 also derive from a point made by David Easton in 1953 in his *Political System*, in which he suggests the use of the notion of 'political system' 'to abstract from the whole social system some variables which seem to cohere more closely than others'

(1959, p. 97). These variables pertain to the world of politics, differentiating it from other social systems. In this sense, the political system is a sub-system (Easton uses this precise word) of the larger social system, characterized by 'close variables'. 'In the concrete world of reality not everything is significantly or closely related to what we call political life: certain kinds of activity are more prominently associated with it than others' (ibid.). The reference to the idea of a sub-system indicates the strong influence of functionalism and, particularly, Talcott Parsons's overall approach to the world of politics.

What do we learn from this debate in political science? A precise definition of 'system' that includes clear indications of borders appears to be nonexistent; at least, all scholars recognize that the determination of clear borders is not an easy task. In political science, a field in which this word has been in use for many years, a 'system' indicates a framework of structures, procedures and actors that differs from other wholes, but further precision appears to be absent. The notion of 'system' appears to be a useful tool, particularly when a 'system'is compared with another system or when it indicates a 'variable' interacting with other variables.

It is possible to find a richer meaning of the term 'system' if we simply shift closer to functionalism. In Jeffery Alexander and Niklas Luhmann's interpretive frameworks, the news media are inserted within a broader 'theory of the social system and a theory of social differentiation' (Alexander, 1981, p. 17). A system not only includes a whole set of characteristics that is different from other wholes but also implies a theory that places systems within a larger interpretation of how social structures evolve and work.

As noted above, Talcott Parsons's influence on these definitions is clear, although his interpretation of 'social system' is primarily focused on culture and symbols that, along with 'personality system' and 'cultural system' (1952, p. 6), determine 'instrumentally oriented interaction' (ibid., p. 70). For Parsons, modernity is linked to the continuing differentiation in sub-systems performing more specialized social functions. Alexander's interpretation of the 'media system' must be viewed in this light. Even if one does not want to 'buy' functionalism in toto – that is, even if one does not feel convinced by the more general implications that derive from social differentiation theory (unilinear evolution towards more complex social structures, modernity linked to social complexity, and so on) – there is no doubt that the idea that society may be divided into different systems that interact and affect one another constitutes a useful interpretive tool for communication research.

The criticisms

In opposition to the use of the notion of systems in media studies, and particularly in political communication studies, some major criticisms have been advanced (here, I am referring essentially to criticisms that have been raised against the use of the idea of system that we introduced in *Comparing Media Systems*). Natalia Roudakova (2011) stresses that the idea of 'system' is 'static', whereas the structures of societies are always changing. Therefore, she suggests that processes rather than systems be examined, which in her view allow for the combination of structure and agency and their interplay. Roudakova's criticism is seated within her anthropological approach, pushing the researcher's attention towards different social features using different methodological tools. For her, the best way to combine agency and structure is not through the use of the notion of system but, rather, through the use of a study aimed towards observing how societies change.

Pippa Norris' criticism is well advanced and, in some ways, more radical. What are the boundaries of the concept of 'media system'? What does this concept include and what does it exclude? Is the notion of 'system' able to define and isolate a framework of different entities characterized by a sufficient level of homogeneity? How should tabloids be considered in light of the elite press? Are they part of a unique system? Do they involve the same type of professionalism? What about the different structures, procedures and routines of the television, on one hand, and those of the print press, on the other hand? Additionally, to follow her more closely, are bloggers part of the media system? In addition, to reiterate, 'political parallelism' (that in *Comparing Media Systems* represents one of the distinguishing features among different media systems) is part of the media system or part of a 'system of political communication' that, according to Norris, is a 'very different animal' (2009, p. 328). She goes on to stress that the notion itself of mass communication is currently dissolving in response to the increasing importance of interpersonal relations through the web. Thus, when we speak of a media system, shall we also include the framework of these individual relations? These are very important points that deserve discussion.

Norris (2009), along with Hardy (2012), raises another problematic point regarding the relation between system and country. Most of the time, primarily in comparative research, the idea of 'system' refers to the media in one specific country, but is this equation always valid and does it still work in the age of globalization, satellites and digitalization? Is it possible to talk about an Italian media system when one of its major competitors, Sky, is owned by a well-known Australian tycoon? Additionally, what about the reality TV show *Big Brother*? Is it a production that characterizes the Italian media system while it is invented by a Dutch company?

Possible answers

Despite these criticisms, I still believe that the notion of 'system' can be a valid instrument for a number of reasons, which I will discuss in the following pages. First, I observe that in other scientific fields, the concept of system does not appear to be particularly well defined – leaving space for different interpretations and enlargements of various variables and elements – and it appears to involve different levels of analysis.

Additionally, in accordance with the suggestions of Blumler and Gurevitch, it appears that the first advantage of the 'system notion' is its comparative use. Indeed, the idea of systems may provide a comprehensive view of how the media work in a country in comparison with some other country. The very 'advantage' of the systems notion in its comparative use is its comprehensiveness: it may provide a very general view of how the entire field of the media is organized and works within a country in comparison with some other realities without the risk of the inclination to 'under- or over-emphasize any single element of the political communication system', as suggested by Blumler and Gurevitch (1995, p. 12). Indeed, scholars are often inclined to assign exaggerated importance to the single variable or element on which they are working (journalists' education, professional routines, journalists' self-perception, and so on), assuming that this is the variable that primarily determines the differences from other realities. The notion of systems may allow for the avoidance of this risk, as it is inclusive and therefore able to provide a broader view of similarities and differences.

Indeed, with the adoption of a 'system approach', it will be possible to stress how different systems work in society, how they interact with each other, which of these systems is more capable of affecting the others and their level of autonomy/heteronomy using Bourdieu' suggestions. In other words, the notion of system may place the news media within a broader interpretive framework, thus avoiding the risk of abstracting the media from the surrounding context and assuming that one single media variable is dominant in relation to others. Indeed, one of the primary problems of media studies is that in many cases, they are self-referential, as scholars are not able to place the news media in relation to other elements of society; media are abstracted from the surrounding context, and the possibility of explaining their action and structure in relation to the most broad context, its structure and culture, is limited.

The problem of what to include and what to exclude is still unresolved. Is political parallelism part of the media system, as Norris asks? This supposition is of course correct, representing a perfect example of what Almond and Verba define as 'fluctuant boundaries': if the focus of the investigation is on the interaction between media and politics, political parallelism must be considered part of the media system. Indeed, political parallelism is the dimension that both explains many features of news media and, at the same time, depends on specific features of the news media. When using the notion of systems, we are supposed to view society as a whole of systems, and therefore, the area of their interactions is an essential part of our observation. Political parallelism is a cause and a consequence of specific interactions between systems in a society; it is located at the border between different systems. At the same time, political parallelism explains specific features of one specific media system itself and other interacting systems: the type and the level of organized political pluralism, the strength and the diffusion of political parties, the degree to which they are rooted in society and other features.

What about the different components of a media system? How is it possible to treat the print press and television in the same manner? How should tabloids and the elite press be considered together as, again, Pippa Norris stresses? Undoubtedly, a risk of overgeneralization exists when the concept of 'system' is used, and specificities may be lost, but we must assume the possibility of a more general level of analysis within which it is appropriate to ask general questions such as 'What about the news media in Italy?' and 'What are the main characteristics of news media in Italy?'These questions are perfectly legitimate and deserve scientific answers. These general questions imply the observation of both television and the print press. Are these outlets different? Of course they are. Do they respond to different (and often competing) logics? Of course they do. In addition, they nevertheless share some commonalities that primarily emerge when comparisons are made between the Italian media system and the British system, for instance. Both Italian television and the Italian print press are much more partisan than their British counterparts, despite the differences between the print press and television. Journalists moving from the print press to television, and vice versa, bring with them attitudes and habits, which push them to be professional journalists and political actors simultaneously. In this manner, the news outlet they enter is permeated by a framework of procedures, attitudes and beliefs that also derive from the news outlet from which the reporter originates. In other words, there is a general cultural habit and a framework of more general social expectations (also on the part of political actors) that is common to television and print press.

Are all of these ideas overly general and not empirically verifiable? Many of these interpretations must be empirically tested, but that can be accomplished. At the same time, one can admit that the explanations that derive from the application of the notion of system are more comprehensive than explanations deriving from the observation of single variables. The comprehensiveness of this approach allows the researcher to place the news media 'in context' without abstracting them from the surrounding society.

Concluding remarks

It is possible to draw some conclusions from this discussion. First, it is not difficult to admit that the idea of 'system' remains vague and difficult to precisely and narrowly define. Nevertheless, in my view, this notion has important cognitive advantages that may facilitate a better understanding of the place of mass media in society.

We can learn some lessons from sister sciences that have used this notion for a longer period of time. Their experiences may be useful in creating a more precise definition of 'system'. Indeed, there is no doubt that media studies have only recently begun to use the notion of system extending beyond what I have defined as the 'indicative use'. Media studies must better reflect the instruments they adopt, primarily in comparative research. Otherwise, there is a risk of what David Swanson once referred to as a 'pre-theoretical strategy' with regard to comparative research (1992). He did not view this type of strategy as a problem for comparative research; in my view, instead, the 'pre-theoretical strategy' thoroughly defines the frequent choice of media scholars to 'go comparative' without a clear understanding and clear definitions of the instruments they are applying and the theoretical frameworks within which to place their results. Such a process may generate confusion and misunderstanding.

The last point I want to discuss regards the overlap of media systems and countries. Is it still possible to assume identification in today's globalized world? I believe it is; despite the global cultural market, the undeniable tendency towards homogenization and hybridization and the rise of the World Wide Web, each media system is still affected by the local culture, by the national language, and by all those cultural symbols that still characterize cultural production. Indeed, there is no doubt that, as Bourdieu states, the media system is part of the more general field of cultural production, which is still strongly dependent on country traditions, history, language and symbolic dimensions. These dimensions still work in a globalized world; most of the time, they undergo a process of hybridization, but I believe that national cultures still matter even though the influence on them is becoming more and more relevant.

Note

1. I presented earlier versions of this paper at the ECPR Conference 'Advancing Comparative Political Communication Research', Antwerp, April 2012 and at the 4th ECREA Conference, Istanbul, October 2012.

3
The Fine Art of Comparing Media Systems: Opportunities, Pitfalls and Challenges

Kees Brants

It must have been sometime in the 1990s. The Hans Bredow Institut, a very respectable and independent research organization set up by the German public broadcaster NWDR and the University of Hamburg, was convening a roundtable discussion about media policy in Europe. Or it might well have been about the state and future of media systems or public service broadcasting in the EU member states. Senior moments these days erase the clarity and exactness of memories; they tend to fade into a blurred picture of the past. I am also not sure how many people participated, but I do know that it was a group of learned scholars, all experts from different countries who had published extensively about the topic under discussion. I was replacing my then Amsterdam colleague Denis McQuail.

The meeting was sponsored by the Bertelsmann Stiftung, a foundation which prides itself on serving the public good by identifying social problems and challenges and developing solutions. All around the table were well aware of that – and, of course, that the foundation's 'mother' is a global media conglomerate. Two of the foundation's more prominent representatives sat in at the meeting. They listened quietly, just off the roundtable, evidently (or at least we assumed so) in hopeful expectation of learning something from such a diverse bunch of experts. Generally, there was synergy in the air: the sum of the individual knowledge expressed would be way more than the total of each separate contribution.

The two representatives must have been deeply disappointed – and I will be the first to admit guilt. Certainly, we enthusiastically talked about the state of broadcasting in our own countries, about commercialization, I'm sure, the anxiety of public organizations, and the failure of our governments to take their plight seriously. Almost self-evidently, all of us started from the perspective of our own country, taking it as the frame of reference, the nodal point of reality – but also staying there and never taking the blinkers off. Since we drew from the cognitive reservoir of our own work (and the clever ideas we had developed over time), we expected that the rich colours of a landscape painting would emerge, clear for everyone to see and make sense of.

The discussion, however, was chaotic and racy, without much listening to each other, jumping from one topic to the next, each of us very much looking inward. It took more than an hour of anxious discussion before it began to dawn on us. Although the Bertelsmänner did not blink, the air of expectation had turned to one of desperation. When all of us increasingly began to feel a sense of embarrassment, at least towards our sponsors, the chairman of the session (who in vain had done his best to bring some order and logic to the discussion) handed over to Professor Jay Blumler. He had been sitting at the table, listening and, though it was very unusual for him, never really participating in the exchange. His role and position were obviously different. The chair asked him to make some sense of the meeting – although he used a more euphemistic vocabulary – requesting a summary of the points raised, their cumulative value and comparative importance, and some conclusions about the future of EU media and policy.

Blumler, in spite of his seniority, never seems to suffer much from senior moments. His presentation was a masterpiece of clarity: systematic and intelligent, eloquent and significant. Where we never stepped out of our frame of reference, our common sense, he crossed borders, drew lines, compared, pointed to similarities and differences, indexed, magnified, signified. He brought light where there was darkness or mist, and in his familiar enumerating style, came up with five conclusions which sounded as logical as they were original. I cannot remember them, but everything he said brought the synergy we had hoped for but never achieved ourselves. Where until then we had felt ashamed towards the Bertelsmann people, we now began to feel proud and to shine. Had we said all that? Had we really contributed so intelligently and so beautifully to what now emerged as almost a Rembrandt painting, but until then had looked more like a Jackson Pollock?

His presentation brought memories of the first European Parliamentary elections in 1979, when he had chaired an international research group looking at political communication in the participating countries. It was the first attempt of a truly comparative approach in this field, and its success was mainly due to him (Blumler, 1983a). He lifted the research above traditional country studies and gave it an across-the-board comparative edge, from which many scholars in this field have subsequently benefitted. He made clear what the relevance of this often complicated exercise is – the opportunities and the attractions of doing it, as well as the problems one faces. In this contribution, I will try to follow in his footsteps, not only to reiterate the beauty and the pitfalls of comparative media system research, but also to look at new challenges that it faces.

Go compare?

There is nothing wrong with single-country studies of media systems. Most research is of individual nation states, and it has often provided good descriptive insight into and understanding of the workings, the organizational structure, the institutions and the details of national (regional, local) media systems. Single-country studies generally ensure a high validity and the opportunity to look more in depth than is usually possible in cross-national studies. They can also overcome the heterogeneity of cases. The problem is that such studies often remain at a very descriptive level and run the risk of ignoring the fallacy of idiosyncrasy. And where systematics and key elements are introduced in the description, they cry out for comparison.

There are both more banal and more relevant reasons to compare countries or systems. In the first category falls the simple fact that comparing is fun to do. It usually allows for travel, meeting colleagues, and discussing and being surprised about similarities and differences in national systems. That often leads to insight and new questions, and it furthers and satisfies academic curiosity into what one took for granted and what for deviant. That realization is the beginning of true comparative research, as it triggers the creative imagination of researchers, opens hidden conceptual doors, and spurs improvisation of new modes of analysis (Blumler and Gurevitch, 1995, p. 78).

A more forceful reason for comparison is funding. The best sources and organizations for research funding usually demand the participation of different countries. The EU used to ask for a north-south representation in proposals, and later, with the extension towards the east, also for old as well as new democracies. Comparison here is the result of necessity – not always the best motive. A lot of practical media system research is also done for policy reasons: look elsewhere for possible best-practice models that could be applied to solve institutional, financial, structural problems in your own country. The drive to come up with policy solutions may, however, blind both the cherry-picking requesting party and the researcher to cultural differences.

But there are more relevant reasons for comparative research than mere curiosity, necessity and fun. First, it may sound paradoxical, but by confronting characteristic features and practices with those in other countries, we learn about our own. 'To compare with what we see as strange', my wife, who is English, keeps reminding me, 'serves to elucidate the familiar by highlighting the contours otherwise obscured by self-evidence'. As such, it can serve as 'an effective antidote to unwitting parochialism' (ibid, p. 76). Second, comparative research allows us to broaden our contextual horizons, to learn about cross-national similarities and differences, to test hypotheses about the interrelationships between phenomena, and to make causal inferences and broader generalizations. By avoiding naïve universalism – that would lead us to presume that national findings are applicable everywhere, where one or two cases might well reflect exceptions – we can reduce national idiosyncrasies in the search for broader regularities (ibid., p. 75; Norris, 2009).

Probably the best-known classification of media systems is Siebert, Petersen and Schramm's (1956) *Four Theories of the Press*, which, however, is so tarred by the brush of the Cold War, that it has little comparative value to date. Twenty-five years later, with the same publisher, five scholars who represent a variety of countries and who have long been involved in the normative debate about roles and functions of media, edited a less time-restricted study of journalism's role in democratic societies. The focus here is, however, more on professional roles than on cross-national media systems (Christians et al., 2009).

Almost paradigmatic in comparative communication studies are Hallin and Mancini's (2004a) *Three Models of Media and Politics*. In most PhD-proposals these days, the models legitimize (but do not necessarily substantiate) the choice of countries. Hallin and Mancini classified media systems in Western Europe and North America along four dimensions: the development of media markets (particularly the mass circulation press); political parallelism (between media and political parties); the developments of journalistic professionalism; and the degree and nature of state intervention in the media system. The two authors had been much inspired by similar dimensions that Blumler and Gurevitch (1995; originally 1975) distinguished in their comparative framework for political communication: the degree of state control; of mass media partisanship; of media-political elite integration; and the nature of the legitimating creed of media institutions.

The attraction of all these models is that they allow for classification and comparison, and for making sense of a variety of relevant elements, similarities and differences. The problem, however, usually lies in the lack of agreement over the relevancy and applicability of each dimension and the omission of others. And there is more, because the beauty of comparison has its flipside too.

Thresholds and pitfalls

Five types of problematic issues in comparative research need to be recognized. Some are not new, but these seem to increase in *problematique* and seriousness instead of fading away and being solved.

Methodological issues. Where comparative analysis sensitizes us to variation and similarity, as Hallin and Mancini (2004a, 2) have reminded us, several methodological problems or challenges arise from its exercise. Firstly, cross-national research teams are often marred by language problems regarding the meaning and translation of concepts, questions and coding. The team researching the 1979 European Parliamentary elections spent most of its time (dis)agreeing on the wordings of the survey questionnaire. The Eurobarometer survey asks in single questions whether the inhabitants of the different EU-countries trust politics, the media, and other socio-political institutions. As if there is cross-cultural consensus on what we mean by trust or, for that matter, politics or 'the' media.

Secondly, how can we be sure that what we perceive as different is not a misreading of the situation based on concepts with which we are familiar but that might have a different meaning (Norris, 2009)? Often 'functional equivalents' are introduced when researching and comparing for example regulatory media institutions of accountability or complaint that do and sometimes do not exist in the countries under study. These bodies usually do not have the same name and may have more or less different compositions, appointment procedures, authority, power and influence. Can we then agree on what we mean when we say that they share the same function and where equivalence ends and difference begins?

Thirdly, the incommensurability of notionally identical measures (for example, data without national cultural context about programme formats like comedy, infotainment) and the usually small number of cases (a few countries) may well create problems (Blumler and Gurevitch, 1995, 81). What do we know when we compare press freedom in countries with considerable differences in political and legal culture? What have we learned when we compare newspaper subsidies in countries that do and do not have a tabloid press, or film subsidies in countries with no or a substantial film industry?

Value judgments. Norms and values create a double problem for comparative observations. First, much research in systems analysis has implicit value judgments about other systems, based on prejudiced assumptions as to which one is best. Researchers tend to take their own system or country as standard, benchmark, normal, and judge the others (often in a mixture of surprise and disgust) according to where they are similar and how much they deviate. Second, dimensions of media systems usually have a normative origin. Political parallelism is bad, especially when it reeks of propaganda. Professionalism is good, especially where it strengthens independence. State interference is bad, except when it is to support newspapers or to restrict commercialization. Public broadcasting is good and should be saved by state intervention or guardianship. Americanization is a threat to European values (unless we call it modernization), but we are not sure or do not agree what exactly the phenomenon is.

No social scientific research is value free, but it might be good to look for more neutral dimensions in systems analysis. In our teaching to foreign students, Denis McQuail and I used a different, less normative set of dimensions than Hallin and Mancini or Blumler and Gurevitch. Its function was to allow for comparison of both public and private broadcasting systems and of cross-national differences and similarities. We looked at: (1) market structure (monopoly, oligopoly, competition) and ownership (private, public); (2) source of financing or income (license fee or taxation, subscription, advertising, mixed revenue); (3) mission (cultural-pedagogic logic versus selling eyeballs and maximizing profit); (4) accountability (to the public, politics, shareholders, and how independent); (5) politicization (as the level of prescribed neutrality, balance and independence) and political parallelism (structural linkage to political parties or other political institutions); (6) diversity of programme genres and content (ratio of information, education, culture and entertainment); (7) address of audience (as citizen, consumer, client, customer); (8) form and level of regulation/governance (state versus self-regulation, what is regulated, how weak or strong). These dimensions worked didactically, as they were key in comparing broadcasting systems and were less value laden. But it did not solve the problem of specific cultural context.

Comparing what? Are the units of analysis, the system dimensions and the conceptual labels the right ones? Much discussion about Hallin and

Mancini's three models circled around the problem that often colleagues were unhappy with what country was placed where. Either theirs was nowhere to be found or they did not recognize it: the UK, Ireland and Canada lumped together with the USA; considerable differences in professionalization and parallelism, but still *bien étonnées de se trouver ensemble*. The overriding issue, however, is whether the four dimensions proposed are indeed the critical ones clarifying and explaining major contrasts among contemporary media systems. Where is media content (except in political parallelism), why focus on the press and where broadcasting is taken into account, only with regard to state intervention? Why are new information and communication technologies missing, whereas the internet might well have an effect on the form and relevance of professionalization and put into question the dimension of parallelism and state intervention?

In the tools analysing media systems we should distinguish between law in books and law in action. When I compared the democratic level of media systems in Ukraine, Russia, Germany and the Netherlands, the surprising result was that they scored in that order, with the two East-European countries right at the top (Brants and Krasnoboka, 2001). But my Ukrainian co-author reminded me, almost disdainfully, that by looking at media laws and legal regimes, we had missed the reality of law in action. In the former Soviet republics' regulation can take the form of covert policing: threatening and killing journalists who do not report 'properly', closing down the printing press for so-called failure to pay taxes. None of these regulatory 'measures' could be found in their media laws, but it rubbed our noses in the limits of our comparative methodology.

Moreover, comparison is often done on the basis of juxtaposition. Many books on media, journalism, policy consist of single-country studies not systematically based on analytical criteria or theoretically argued concepts. Instead, the books end with a comparative chapter, in which the editor draws lines from the separate contributions, on the basis of what they now deem relevant or striking, not on what in advance has been laid out conceptually.

(Anglo-)American bias. Most research in the field of communication originates from the USA – with the UK probably coming in second – and the majority of articles are published in the English language. In comparative research those two countries, their media systems and organizations are often the benchmark against which other countries are assessed. That raises a number of issues. Firstly, English has become the *lingua franca,* a language that most non-Anglo-American researchers

think they master, but when push comes to shove in discussing concepts, questionnaires and findings, they often don't. Considerations are hazed in a linguistic and conceptual fog around fuzzy, but in comparative media systems so central, phenomena as professionalism, political parallelism, public sphere. The latter for instance, comes from the German *Oeffentlichkeit*, but contains only one aspect – the social 'space' between the state and civil society where public opinion is formed – of the much more polysemic German concept (Kleinsteuber, 2001).

Secondly, English is the language of specific liberal democracies with majoritarian political systems, an adversary political culture, specific party and electoral systems, and common law (where in most continental European countries we find the untranslatable but quite different notion of *Rechtsstaat*). To make a sweeping generalization, for the sake of argument but not completely devoid of reality, much European research in the area of political communication is flawed by the US example. Their concepts and research questions are copied and the outcomes compared. The assumption often is that the countries in the other models bluntly and blindly copy the format, genres, negative tone and focus on scandal apparently paramount in the USA. European researchers are quite often surprised to find little or no proof of that.

Thirdly, with language come institutional background and specific media and journalism cultures. These ideas, values, expectations, attitudes, beliefs create a specific mind set towards institutions and legal arrangements that are shared with, or in opposition to, decision makers and publics. The liberal model Hallin and Mancini describe for the US and UK often recognizes mistrust of the state, so different from the relative benevolence one often expects of the state in democratic-corporatist countries of continental northern Europe. The lack of trust is also not the same as the more populist anti-establishment cynicism in many Mediterranean countries of the polarized pluralist model. Not to take such cultural differences into account, when defining and making sense of the relevant dimensions, runs the risk of comparing (and explaining) apples and oranges.

Inherent determinism. Much comparative research tends towards assuming a specific and one-directional trend or development, an assumption which, by the way, not only necessitates comparative but also longitudinal research. Hallin and Mancini (2004a) first introduce three separate media systems, the characteristics of which they then extensively and historically describe. But they are also trying to find out whether there is a trend, a process of globalization or modernization or americanization (Hallin and Mancini 2004b). That question, one way or the other, influences what they see in, and find through, their magnifying glass. Not that they ignore certain data and amplify others, but that they find convergence does not surprise the reader, nor that the direction of that trend is towards the North Atlantic or Liberal Model. Such developmental determinism is not uncommon. The three *ages* that Blumler and Kavanagh (1999) distinguish in the process of political communication in many democracies over the post-war period, are consecutive phases: one following from and developing out of the other. The same goes for the three *logics* that Philip van Praag and I distinguish when longitudinally describing electoral communication in the Netherlands. First there was a closed partisan logic, followed by an open public logic, to end in a commercialized media logic (Brants and van Praag, 2006). It is as if these changes, developments and convergences are irreversible and unavoidable. Media systems and countries follow suit or are forced to do so.

In comparative terms – and I may exaggerate for the sake of argument – the syllogism goes like this: in some countries some media are not as far in their route along a set path as others, but one way or the other and at one time or the other they will have to give in and go along. That is, however, an empirical question which may well lead to quite a different outcome, as the discussion about advertising-free public broadcasting in France has made clear.

Beyond media systems?

Analysing media systems is to look at all the relevant dimensions along which different media in different countries can be described, analysed, made sense of, compared and grouped. That allows for inferences about the how and why of similarities and differences. In doing so, one may encounter, as we have seen, many pitfalls and considerable problems. Moreover, as McQuail (1994, p. 133) has reminded us, 'the media do not constitute any single "system", with a single purpose or philosophy, but are composed of many separate, overlapping, often inconsistent elements, with appropriate differences of normative expectation and actual regulation'. But at least researchers agreed that they confined their research to (comparing) individual nation states. They looked at the financial structure, the regulatory bodies and practices, and the content of different media in different countries, hoping to speak the same conceptual language. That was already difficult enough.

Hallin and Mancini have argued that differences among media systems in general have diminished to a point of convergence where it is reasonable to ask 'whether a single, global media model is displacing the national variation of the past' (2004a, p. 251). That would make system comparisons a superfluous exercise. Others still see significant differences with regard to, for instance, the level of advertising dependency and audience fragmentation (Arbaoui, 2014) and, I would add, in mission statement, political parallelism and accountability. The rise of the internet, however, may have introduced a more fundamental problem in comparing media systems: that of boundary. Just follow the dimensions.

- The ownership structure of different applications of the internet may be national – the market structure is clearly global – with an interesting exception that may be relevant for comparison: national levels of adoption and reach. These may not only affect the market structure, but also the comparative relevance of different levels and kinds of usage.
- The source of finance is ambiguous, with many applications of the internet still struggling to find a proper business model. Attracting advertisers seems to be the main aim, with subscription a possible option and license fee or taxation not.
- Journalistic professionalism is a problematic comparative dimension. The citizen-journalist and the content-generating user are by definition non-professional. Within the normative model, however, professionalism is a *conditio sine qua non* for reliability and a driver of convergence.
- The internet as such has no single mission; different applications may. It can be educational, cultural, deliberative, to extend the public sphere, to make money, to entertain, and as such they are comparable to broadcasting and the press. The user may have a different perspective.
- Although accountability of the more commercial applications of the internet is usually to shareholders, users may well have a more demanding position than with traditional media. Not only can they boycott the content, they may much more actively engage in discussion and critique and as such affect content.
- Politicization – as prescribed balanced information – is generally absent, although in its totality the internet may present a relatively balanced picture. Political parallelism (interlocking directorships) does exist where websites or social media are owned or organized by specific (party) political interests. But that is more comparable to political advertising.

- Content is a complicated dimension with the internet, since applications seem limitless. As such there is diversity – from porn to Wikipedia, from debate to chat, from games to the offline online – but comparing the internet with traditional media on ratio of information, education, culture and entertainment is a sheer impossibility.
- The way the audience is addressed is equally problematic. It will differ per site: in social media users are friends and colleagues, in other applications they can be addressed as consumer, co-producer, client, object of hate/lust/love, and so on. Applying this dimension will differ by application.
- Governance of the internet is a contentious issue. There are boundary problems: is it a medium or do we have media, and offline media go online. The distinction between the private and the public, between consumer and producer is blurred. New issues (online stalking, anonymous threats and insults, terrorism) make comparison with old media problematic.

The internet is a global phenomenon that challenges the relevancy of media system dimensions. It will make it difficult to just add internet to the comparison of press and broadcasting and maybe to compare media systems altogether, since more and more offline media go online (as well). The picture that emerges is that some of the dimensions go beyond nation state boundaries, others open up new avenues for looking at old and new media, others may sound out of date and out of touch. In an already pitfall-filled environment, simply adding internet to the other media, may well turn out to be adding insult to injury.

4
Comparative Political Communication Research: The Undiminished Relevance of the Beginnings

Frank Esser

Jay Blumler deserves credit for introducing the comparative approach to the communication discipline. He and his long-time colleague, Michael Gurevitch, described comparative communication research as 'an extending frontier of the field that deserves yet more intensive cultivation' (Blumler and Gurevitch, 1995, p. 73). Their early pleadings have borne fruit, and the comparative approach has now extended to many subfields of the communication discipline, as the recent publication of the ICA *Handbook of Comparative Research* demonstrates (Esser and Hanitzsch, 2012a). Originally labelled as being in its 'infancy' (Blumler and Gurevitch, 1975), the state of comparative analysis has now reached 'late adolescence' (Gurevitch and Blumler, 2004). Although it has not yet attained mature adulthood (Mancini and Hallin, 2012), one may agree with Hardy's assessment that comparative communication research has advanced significantly, and is producing 'a common body of knowledge, theories and concepts' (2012, p. 202). Uninformed comparison by convenience is becoming less and less defendable. Although comparative research has made more progress in some subject areas than in others (see Esser and Hanitzsch, 2012a), we are observing the gradual emergence of comparative communications as a recognized subdiscipline, comparable to comparative politics in political science. In Blumler's words, we see 'for the first time in the evolution of comparative communication research ... a more or less coherent collective awareness of what the comparative venture is or can be about', as well as of the 'challenges that must be faced for further progress to be achieved' (2012, p. xii).

Clear indications of the maturation process are the growing number and range of countries analyzed, books and articles published, and variables used in increasingly sophisticated research designs.

The rationale of comparative enquiry

One of the high points of Jay Blumler's career was his term as president of the International Communication Association in 1989. In that year, he got to choose the theme of the annual ICA conference which took place in San Francisco at the time. He chose 'Comparatively Speaking...', and this made him the first and only president to devote an ICA conference to comparative research. In a book that later summarized some of the best papers of that conference, he and his colleagues defined a study as comparative 'when the comparisons are made across two or more geographically or historically (spatially or temporally) defined systems'; situated within these systems are 'the phenomena of scholarly interest which are embedded in a set of interrelations that are relatively coherent, patterned, comprehensive, distinct, and bounded' (Blumler et al., 1992, p. 7).

A recent synthesis by Esser and Hanitzsch (2012b) concluded that comparative communication research involves comparisons between a minimum of two macro-level cases (systems, cultures, markets, or their sub-elements), with respect to at least one object of investigation relevant to the field of communication. Comparative research differs from non-comparative work in that it attempts to reach conclusions beyond single cases and explains differences and similarities between objects of analysis against the backdrop of their contextual conditions. It is essential that the objects of analysis are compared on the basis of a common theoretical framework, and also that this is done by drawing on equivalent conceptualizations and methods. It should also be pointed out that spatial (cross-territorial) comparisons ought to be supplemented wherever possible by a longitudinal (cross-temporal) dimension in order to account for the fact that systems and cultures are not frozen in time, but constantly changing under the influence of transformation processes like Americanisation, Europeanization, globalisation, modernisation, or commercialisation. Despite these constant changes, the comparative scholar has no choice but to define the respective boundaries of his cases. Still, he or she can do so in a variety of ways based on structural, cultural, political, territorial or temporal qualities. The contrasting cases in comparative analysis – be they world regions, countries, subnational regions, social milieux, language areas, or cultural thickenings – are assumed to contain characteristic factors of influence (*conditions*) that help to explain differences and similarities in the objects of analysis (*outcomes*) embedded in the different cases.

This last aspect is crucial. Comparative research guides our attention to the explanatory relevance of the contextual environment for communication outcomes. It aims to understand how the systemic context shapes communication phenomena differently in different settings (Blumler et al., 1992). The research is based on the assumption that different parameters of political and media systems differentially promote or constrain communication roles and behaviours of organizations or actors within those systems (Gurevitch and Blumler, 1990b). Thus, comparativists use factors at the macro-societal level as explanatory variables for differences found in lower-level communication phenomena embedded within the societies (Blumler et al., 1992). This explanatory approach aims to overcome more pedestrian comparisons of convenience that 'use other countries merely as places to situate the same investigation that one would have conducted at home' (Gurevitch and Blumler, 2004, p. 327). The recognition of the (causal) significance of contextual conditions is what makes comparative research exceptionally valuable. In the words of Mancini and Hallin, 'theorizing the role of context is precisely what comparative analysis is about' (2012, p. 515). This explanatory logic can be distinguished from mere descriptive comparison that is considered less mature (Gurevitch and Blumler, 2004).

The link to democracy

Blumler's own empirical research was often related to the domain of news, as can be seen from his seven country study of the 1979 EU parliamentary election (1983a) or the pair-wise comparison of campaign communication in the United States and UK (Semetko et al., 1991). Comparative analyses of election news coverage exhibit important information about how the mass media fulfil their political role in divergent national settings. Democratic theory expects the mass media to serve several roles (Gurevitch and Blumler, 1990b; Graber, 2003): informing voters about the candidates and their ideas; reflecting a wide array of diverse political standpoints and perspectives; interpreting actions of candidates and their opponents; controlling those in power; and mobilizing voters politically.

With respect to their informative role, the mass media have an important conveyor belt function for candidates and their parties. Yet some national settings offer more favourable opportunity structures for political messages being relayed to the public in a comprehensive and neutral way than others; some national settings foster a more partisan, depoliticized or personalized campaigning and reporting culture. With respect to the democratic role of inclusion, the mass media are expected to function as a pluralist forum for public debate in which the diversity of political arguments and standpoints is adequately reflected. Regarding their interpretative role, many democratic news systems have experienced a cultural shift from the media acting as passive informant to active shaper of public opinion, with some organizations pursuing an interventionist role and posing as being a better public representative than elected politicians. While interpretation and analysis can provide important background for audiences and facilitate deeper understanding of the issues (if driven by goals of social accountability and public service), an overly interventionist role can become a source of conflict between political actors and media actors, especially if aimed at 'confrontainment' or 'politainment' (driven by commercial interests). This borders on another political role discussed in democratic theory, namely the watchdog or control function of the media. Here the media are supposed to guard citizens against undue infringements of their rights by the apparatus of the state, and uncover abuse of power as well as unfitness for public office. Yet an excessive abuse of the control function by the media may be equally dysfunctional.

Against this background, some features of election news coverage have raised particular interest among comparativists, like media depoliticization (with policy coverage being marginalised, sensationalised, or strategy-framed), personalisation (with stories being leader-centred instead of institution-centred), interventionism (with interpretive style being used to enhance journalistic voice and diminish political voice) or negativity (characterized by negative topics and tonality, and confrontation and conflict). The pervasiveness of such reporting patterns in election news is dependent on the transnational spread of a certain kind of 'news logic', linked to increasing mediatisation of politics (Mazzoleni and Schulz, 1999). Evidence of such a spread was first discovered in Swanson and Mancini's (1996a) analysis of 11 countries, which noted, 'The independent voice of mass media in politics reflects the development and spread of an ideology of journalism as a profession in its own right with an autonomous role to play in the political process' (Swanson and Mancini, 1996b, p. 251). The comparative study of election news coverage is interested in describing and explaining transnational similarities and nation-specific differences in 'news logic', classifying national reporting styles according to relevant dimensions, and assessing news performance according to democratic norms.

An early framework

Comparative research aims to understand how characteristic factors of the macro-contextual environment shape communication processes differently in different campaign settings (Blumler and Gurevitch, 1995, p. 74). To understand the relationship between the macro-contextual environment and political communication processes better, Blumler and Gurevitch (1995, pp. 5, 12, 32, 42, 100, 182, 204) developed the idea of a 'political communication system' as a kind of root concept. It is worth examining the development of this idea, and to evaluate its heuristic value for researchers today.

The original idea emerged in the context of the bi-national study by Semetko, Blumler, Gurevitch, Weaver, and Barkin (Semetko et al., 1991) that compared campaign news coverage of the 1984 US presidential election with the 1983 British general election. The phenomenon to be explained was journalistic practices (examined by way of newsroom observations at the NBC and the BBC) and news coverage (by way of content analyses of print and broadcast media). Election news coverage was described as 'the *joint product* of an interactive process involving political communicators and media professionals' (Semetko et al., 1991, p. 3; emphasis in the original). The expectation was that in the United States journalists would have the upper hand in this process, and in Great Britain, the politicians. In particular, US journalists were expected to be more 'interventionist' in their news approach and use more 'discretionary power' in shaping the campaign agenda in their own terms, instead of just amplifying the agenda of the candidates and their parties.

Adopting a *Most Similar Systems* logic, the authors theorized that despite many similarities, 'the British and the American political communication systems exhibit different characteristics both in the structure and the culture of the political systems ... and in the structure and the professional culture of their respective media systems' (Semetko et al. 1991, p. 9).

But what were these structural and cultural factors that would need to be examined in order to explain cross-national differences in election news? This brought the authors back to an earlier framework by Blumler and Gurevitch (1975), which tried to answer the question: 'How does the articulation of a country's mass media institutions to its political institutions affect the processing of political communication contents'

(p. 167). Taking this as a starting point, Semetko et al. (1991) developed a new framework that identified several structural and cultural factors that enhance or inhibit journalistic intervention into the agenda formation process. This framework from 1991 was put to the test of time when Blumler and Gurevitch (2001) revisited it ten years later for a follow-up comparison of US and British elections. The following dimensions of their framework were found to be most influential for patterns in election news (see Semetko et al., 1991; Blumler and Gurevitch, 2001):

• Political structure: Party systems with weak linkages to societal cleavages will show higher levels of electoral volatility. This heightens the need for tightly controlled and professionally steered campaigns which, in turn, will provoke an interventionist counter-impulse by journalists if they feel threatened in their reporting options (Semetko et al., 1991, p. 178; Blumler and Gurevitch, 2001, p. 399).

• Political culture: Societies with low levels of public respect for politicians and their actions are likely to create a climate in which journalists feel legitimized to use their own discretion to set the campaign agenda and to prioritize news values over political values in their election coverage (Semetko et al., 1991, pp. 5, 178; Blumler and Gurevitch, 2001, pp. 387, 397).

• Campaign professionalism: The more election campaigns are 'stage-managed,' candidates 'packaged' and messages 'controlled' by handlers, the more this encourages a counter-tendency by journalists to resist the spin and exercise greater discretionary power in their coverage – for example by framing campaigns in more cynical terms (Semetko et al., 1991, pp. 6, 178; Blumler and Gurevitch, 2001, pp. 386, 397).

• Media structure: The more competitive and audience-driven a media market, the more inclined journalists are to exercise discretionary power and cover politics in ways that may be good for ratings but not necessarily for democratic discourse (Semetko et al., 1991, pp. 8, 178; Blumler and Gurevitch, 2001, p. 391). With regard to ownership, public service channels are expected to exercise less discretionary power in their election news coverage than commercial channels (Semetko et al., 1991, pp. 13, 178, 182; Blumler and Gurevitch, 2001).

• Media culture: In a 'pragmatic news culture', where the media's discretionary power is greater, candidates' statements are likely to be used to a lesser extent or only as raw material in the construction of the reporter's own story. In a 'sacerdotal news culture', however, political statements and activities are considered intrinsically important and deserving of being reported authentically and extensively (Semetko et al., 1991, pp. 6, 178; Blumler and Gurevitch, 2001, pp. 386, 397).

• Media professionalism: The more journalists assign themselves activist role perceptions like 'interpreter' or 'adversary,' the more likely their coverage of political actors and political agendas is shaped by interventionist characteristics. The opposite is true for passive media roles like 'informant' or 'transmitter'. On a related note, it emerged that the stricter the norms of balance and objectivity are upheld at a news organization, the more evenly spread the coverage for each candidate will be in terms of volume, perspectives and topics (Semetko et al., 1991, p. 179).

Its further development

The number of studies comparing the media's coverage of national elections in the aftermath of Semetko et al.'s classic *The Formation of Campaign Agendas* (1991) has remained rather small. The continued significance of this milestone study can be explained by its elaborated design and by the fact that it served as a foundation for a generalisable theoretical framework that still is of heuristic value.

For instance, a study I did (Esser, 2008) that compared election news coverage in four countries took up this original framework and adapted it to 'sound bite news'. This study focuses on 'dimensions of political news cultures' in France, Germany, Great Britain and the United States. It confirmed earlier evidence of a more interventionist American approach and a less interventionist French approach. The degree of interventionism was operationalised as the extent to which journalists grant politicians opportunities in TV news programmes to present themselves in their own words (that is, in their own sound bites). The study found that, over two election cycles, candidate sound bites in campaign news stories were consistently shorter in the United States than in Europe. At the same time that US journalists were found to compress candidates' on-air statements the most, it emerged that US candidates fought by far the most tightly scripted campaigns. This correlation indicates that the more politicians try to control news coverage, the more journalists resist covering them in the way the politicians would wish, instead reporting something different that gives expression to the journalistic voice (Zaller, 2001). The relationship between assertive news management style and assertive journalistic response (media intervention) was found to constitute an important dimension of political news cultures. The French news culture appeared as the least independent-minded. French election stories displayed a more passive, yielding reporting style, more structured by political logic (and the candidates' policy messages) than by interventionist media logic (which would, at times, be less willing to recycle those messages).

In addition to the impact from structural and semi-structural factors, the study also found evidence of an emerging 'transnational news logic' (Esser, 2008, p. 422) that trumps many of the differences across countries. A similar finding was made in another multi-country comparison of election news by Plasser, Pallaver, and Lengauer (2009). It content-analyzed TV news coverage of national election campaigns in Austria, Germany, Italy and the United States and found a strikingly similar proliferation of reporting patterns like depoliticisation, personalisation, game-orientation and negativity. Even when this primary country sample was expanded by a secondary sample of countries from Asia, South America and Africa, the findings indicated 'a common ground for a transnational operational logic of political television journalism that is primarily driven by a pragmatic, news-value oriented approach' (Plasser and Lengauer, 2008, p. 261). These studies confirm an earlier assessment by Blumler (1990, p. 111) that divergent institutional conditions of political communications serve as little more than brakes – the force of some of which are obviously weakening – on the accelerating power of a transnational news logic.

The number of comparative analyses of election news has increased somewhat since de Vreese (2003) stated that 'evidence from cross-national comparisons of national elections is virtually non-existent' (p. 238). Some of the theoretically important independent variables identified by Semetko et al.'s (1991) framework still seem to have an impact on how today's media cover national elections. On the other hand it is noteworthy how inconsistent some of the findings seem to be. Major reasons for this are the limited number of studies; that most studies only cover two countries and one election per country; and that the variables and operationalisations of the concepts that have been used differ. Taken together, this inhibits the cumulativity and the comparability of the results, while the limited number of comparative studies in itself makes it difficult to establish firm conclusions about the factors shaping election news. The question then is how future research should best proceed to alleviate these shortcomings.

Outlook

Any progress will depend on updating and expanding the original heuristic. The main question remains whether and how structural and semi-structural 'independent variables' in the various national settings can help explain content-related 'dependent variables' like media depoliticization, media interventionism or media negativity in election news discourse. If we take the initial framework by Blumler and Gurevitch (1975; 2001) and Semetko et al. (1991) as a starting point, the main independent variables are related to political structure, political culture, campaign professionalism, media structure, media culture and media professionalism. From these factors emerge powerful influences that shape the news in characteristic ways. These influences are the degree of media competitiveness and commercialism; the characterization of the political and media cultures by a pragmatic as opposed to a sacerdotal approach to politics; the extent to which media cultures and journalistic norms and values stress intervention, power distance and market orientation; the strength of political parties; and the degree of campaign and news management professionalism. The two important questions are whether these influences prove to remain relevant in future research and how they can be incorporated into a broader theory of international news.

To examine democratic news performance, a broader list of dependent variables than just media depoliticization, interventionism, personalization and negativity should be studied. Other potential variables are diversity and partisanship. In fact, one of the main challenges for future research is to work towards a standard set of key dependent variables, concepts and operationalisations. Only through a more thorough and explicit conceptualisation of key notions will it be possible to increase the comparability of findings and cumulativity of scholarship (Esser et al., 2012).

The more we know about the relationship between national contexts and newsmaking, the better we can explain similarities and differences in election coverage across societies. Ultimately, we will be able to draft a comprehensive system-sensitive news theory – something that is so far completely absent from the field of mass communication research.

Note

This essay draws on my contributions to chapters 1 and 19 of the *Handbook of Comparative Communication Research* (Esser and Hanitzsch, 2012a).

5
Mediatization of the Modern Publicity Process

Winfried Schulz

Political communication research during its history of more than 100 years has been highly fixated on mass media influences on politics.[1] More specifically, the dominant paradigm has centred on: (1) causal explanations of media-politics relationships; (2) micro-level phenomena; (3) isolated media and personality variables; and (4) single-country studies (Blumler, forthcoming). Jay Blumler has been passionately committed to exposing these deficits and to call for broadening the research perspective. With his own research activities, he has inspired many colleagues to pursue new directions, in particular to look at political communication in a systems perspective and to design cross-national comparative research.

Among the many stimulating ideas Blumler has proposed, three stand out as particularly influential: (1) The notion of the 'modern publicity process'; (2) the concept of the 'political communication system'; and (3) the idea that we have now arrived at the 'third age of political communication'. All three ideas focus on fundamental changes of political communication during recent decades. This is what the concept of 'mediatization', which has recently been gaining much popularity, also claims to explain. An increasing number of scholars have adopted the concept for analysing transformations of communication not only in the political realm, but also in the judiciary (Peleg and Bogoch, 2012), science (Peters et al., 2008), religion (Hjarvard, 2008a), sports (Nelson, 2010), and tourism (Jansson, 2002), and in society as a whole (Hjarvard, 2008b; Mazzoleni, 2008).

This raises two questions: First, to what extent does the notion of mediatization interface with the inspiring ideas introduced by Blumler? And second, what can mediatization exegetes learn from Blumler's analyses of the modern publicity process?

In their seminal article, 'The Third Age of Political Communication', Blumler and Kavanagh (1999) explicitly refer to mediatization as one of the exogenous changes to which 'political communication has been responsive (though also contributory)'. Mediatization implies 'the media moving toward the center of the social process', which 'promotes the concept and practices of a "media-constructed public sphere"' and elevates the role of communication experts charged with 'tooling up' diverse institutions for 'sophisticated public relations' (p. 211).

Several attempts at explicating the notion of mediatization refer to the aspects that Blumler and Kavanagh identify. The common denominator of most studies may be briefly summarized in three general propositions:

1. The sheer presence of communication media in society is a major impetus of social change, affecting individuals, diverse organizations, and social systems as a whole.
2. Due to the evolution of the media, their social importance has been growing continuously.
3. Consequences of the importance of the media are specific reactions in all areas of society which are contributing to social change.

The following reflections on these theses will concentrate on modern publicity processes in the political communication systems of our 'third age' of political communication.

The fact that mass media exist in society

In a groundbreaking article, Lazarsfeld and Merton (1948) argue that searching out the effect of mass media upon society addresses an ill-defined problem. They propose to distinguish different facets of the problem of which one should focus on the question: 'What role can be assigned to the mass media by virtue of the fact that they exist?'[2] Lazarsfeld and Merton illustrate this perspective by comparing the impact of the automobile and the radio, both new media at the time. The analogy seems to be justified if both the automobile and the radio are considered as techniques in a very general sense: both provide functions and services that 'emancipate from the constraints of organic life' (Sombart, 1927). Looked at in this way, techniques help people to expand their range of activities and to reduce – or even liberate them from – constrictions of time. They provide technical substitutes for organic functions such as locomotion and communication; they amalgamate with various activities of social life and demand from those who take advantage of a particular technology to accommodate their activities, their daily routines, as well as their social environment, to the operational modes of a particular technology such as the automobile or communication media (Schulz, 2004).

Major consequences of motorization in advanced societies could have been observed already in the 1940s, and they have been increasing since and continue to grow. The same applies to the impact of broadcasting and other communication media.[3] For example, the media business – like the automotive industry – has become an important economic sector in many developed countries, creating jobs, and ensuring private incomes and state revenues. Both cases represent a technology-driven development with continuous innovations resulting in improved performances and expanded uses. In both cases, the technology development brought many advantages, but also problematic consequences like a progressive consumption of scarce resources, harmful environmental emissions, and an increased dependence of individuals and whole societies on technology.

However, the analogy proposed by Lazarsfeld and Merton has its limits. A common characteristic of automobiles and communication media is that both serve to connect point A with point B. But an essential difference lies in the fact that the automotive transfer normally leaves goods and persons unaffected whereas the transfer of messages always affects both their shape and meaning. Messages have to be encoded and decoded, which implies physical and informational transformations. In addition, messages have to be shaped according to media-specific coding rules and presentation formats. Political messages in particular are framed by professional routines and conventions as well as by norms of the organizational and cultural contexts of message production.

The English-language term 'mediation' implies most of these aspects, but is at the same time burdened with several additional meanings and connotations (see, for example, McQuail, 2010, pp. 82–85). 'Media logic', a concept introduced by Altheide and Snow (1979), seems to be, at first glance, a useful alternative.[4] Altheide and Snow illustrate what they mean by media logic with references to the 'grammar' of entertainment television and to the professional conventions of news journalism. They use the terms 'logic', 'format', 'grammar' and 'style' mostly as synonyms. Mediating reality according to a specific media logic implies far-reaching societal consequences since it suggests a certain world view: 'In short, people may adopt a media logic as the interpretative framework through which definitions of reality are developed and problems solved' (Altheide and Snow, 1979, p. 44).

'Mediatization' may also be regarded as a conceptual alternative to mediation. Kent Asp (1990) was among the first to introduce this term (originally 'medialization') as 'a conscious effort on my part to coin a buzz word' in order to direct attention to a certain capacity of the mass media: 'They exert a force by virtue of their sheer existence.'[5] The 'crude neologism' – as Sonia Livingstone (2009) has called mediatization – points with its 'ization' ending to transformations, in particular to changes interrelated with media evolution and on par with processes of modernisation, individualisation and secularisation (Blumler and Kavanagh, 1999). Similarly, Krotz (2007) compares mediatization with change processes such as globalisation, individualization and commercialisation (which he qualifies as 'meta processes').

Growing importance of communication media

Several models have been suggested to structure the consequences of media evolution in a historical perspective. The 'three-ages model' proposed by Blumler and Kavanagh (1999) is the most prominent example. Concentrating on the time after World War II, the authors characterize the first two decades as 'party-dominated' due to the subordination of political communication to political parties and other political institutions. When television became the dominant medium of political communication in the 1960s, a new era began. A significant feature of this era (at least in Europe) was that the limited number of TV channels restricted audience selectivity. The situation changed fundamentally due to the immense proliferation of communication channels in recent times. The authors give no precise date for the dawning of this phase; they rather see a fluent transition into the 'third age' of which 'media abundance, ubiquity, reach, and celerity' is the most significant characteristic (p. 213).

Other authors who look further back into history identify Gutenberg's invention of mechanical printing as the initial spark for major changes (for example, Thompson, 1995). In a shorter perspective, the historians Bösch and Frei (2006) hold that the evolution of the press into a mass medium in the late 19th century was the beginning of mediatization. They contend that since then, in cycles of about 30 years, fundamental changes of the media system led to impulses of political mobilization and to societal changes. In contrast, for Hjarvard (2008b) only the 1920s mark the beginning of major transformations when the radio became a mass medium and the printing press emancipated as a 'cultural institution'. Until then, the press was merely an instrument of other institutions like the political parties. Another proposal by Asp and Esaiasson (1996) focuses on the introduction of commercial broadcasting around 1990 as the critical event that triggered mediatization.

Independently of their time perspective, most authors regard the growing power of the media as a key feature of the development. For example, Blumler and Kavanagh (1999, p. 209) emphasize that 'power relations among key message providers and receivers are being rearranged', and Kepplinger (2007, p. 13) holds that the media evolution 'has changed the balance of power between politicians and political institutions on one side and journalists on the other'. In their analyses of political communication systems, Gurevitch and Blumler (1977; 1990b) specify the notion of media power and lay grounds for explaining the growing importance of the media. Considering that certain expectations of media performance are vital for democratic systems, they present a catalogue of eight 'functions and services for the political system'. This catalogue may be interpreted in two ways. First, it covers expectations of media performance according to democratic requirements as well as audience demands. Second, it also substantiates the political significance of the media and their growing importance – or growing media power, as some prefer to say. Media performances are an essential contribution to the functioning of democratic societies. The continuous extension and strengthening of these functions and services in the course of its development has led to the media's growing importance in the 'third age' of political communication.

The following list of media functions and services is based on the catalogue presented by Gurevitch and Blumler (1990b). It has been somewhat rephrased and rearranged to show that the normative requirements at least to some degree correspond with theoretical assumptions and empirical findings of communication research.[6]

- *Mediating reality:* The media are expected to present a picture of reality which corresponds to the true nature of the reported events. This is especially a service required from mass media committed to the norms and ethics of traditional political journalism. In the course of their evolution, the mass media continuously widened their window to the world. Internet-based content has in recent times considerably extended this service.
- *Setting the public agenda:* In an open society where a great number of political groups and interests compete for public attention, it is the media's legitimate task to draw attention to the most relevant issues and most pressing problems. The mass media, through selecting

and emphasizing certain issues, contribute to setting the agenda of a political system. Internet-based outlets and social media may reinforce or modify this capacity.

• *Defining the relevance of actors:* In publicizing events and issues, the media play a key role in defining the relevance of political actors – even create celebrities – and thus contribute to legitimating their elite status and political power. Power holders may further benefit from the public visibility provided by websites and social media. The Internet also has the potential to promote social movements, protesters – even terrorists – and sometimes also confers status or prominence to ordinary citizens.

• *Providing a political platform:* The media's capacity to provide a public forum for disputing contentious issues is a service all types of individual and collective political actors rely on. This is particularly important during election campaigns when the political parties and candidates compete for public attention and when the voters want to find out whom they should vote for.

• *Indicating public opinion:* A key political function of the media is to aggregate the various interests in society and to represent major currents of political deliberation. Hence, the media public is seen as reflecting political preferences of the people and the prevailing climate of opinion.

• *Acting as watchdogs:* The media are expected to scrutinize power holders and, by investigative reporting, expose power abuses, corruptions and scandals. The Internet's capacity to denounce misbehaviour and to leak information that power holders would rather keep secret has made this increasingly effective.

• *Advocating citizen interests:* Traditionally, the mass media have been expected to voice the citizens' political demands and to support institutionalized forms of political participation such as voting, petitioning or striking. In recent times, this function has been largely transformed – and strongly increased – since the citizens themselves can publicize their demands and organize their political will using new media.

Apparently, the evolution of the media has strengthened and expanded their political functions and services. It seems that this process is continuously sustained and advanced by two conditions. First, expectations of the media's functions and services stimulate technological, economic and political efforts and thus further the importance of the media. Second, the expectations are to some degree self-fulfilling as citizens and political actors take media functions and services into account and behave accordingly.

Political reactions to increased media importance

Reactions to the existence of the media and their growing importance typically follow a pattern for which Kurt and Gladys Lang (1953) coined the term 'reciprocity effect' (Mazzoleni and Schulz, 1999; Kepplinger, 2007). In his analysis of the modern publicity process, Blumler specifies a number of such reactions to the growing importance of the media:

- Political actors are devoting more thought, energy and resources to media strategies and tactics,
- a more media-centric model of pressure group activity has been emerging,
- policy decisions are influenced by how they will play in media-filtered mass perceptions,
- political actors prefer personalization strategies over deliberating issues and policies,
- interactions among politicians and the media are increasingly governed by conflicts and negativity.

(1990, pp. 104–109)

Most of such reactions fall into two types: (1) Political actors anticipate the existence and the importance of the media and adapt to media functions and services, and (2) political actors take advantage of media functions and services and often utilize the media for their own purposes and strategic interests. All sorts of political actors show these reactions, most notably political organizations such as political parties, parliaments, interest groups, government agencies, nation states and international bodies. But citizens, political protagonists and other individual actors also react in one or both of these ways to communication media.

Both types of reactions may be illustrated with reference to each of the abovementioned functions and services. This can be seen most impressively – and has been most widely researched – in the context of election campaigns. For example, political parties usually anticipate the necessity to fight back on offenses, accusations or defamations from opponents by setting up a special website and a task force for instant rebuttals. An obvious function of this strategy is to correct the mediated reality of the campaign. Another striking feature of modern campaigning is 'spin doctoring' the campaign issues in order to get control over the media agenda. This requires investments of the parties in commissioning opinion surveys and monitoring the mass media, the blogosphere and various Internet-based social media. The parties not only want to see how they succeed with their own issue agenda, but also how to adjust their agenda if the public issue attention is changing. Moreover, since personalization strategies may foster electoral success, candidates – particularly those for top offices – strive to maximize their media attention and to accommodate their campaign appearances to the mass media's news values as well as to criteria that facilitate favourable resonance on the Internet.

Allocating major parts of their campaign budget to advertising, particularly to television ads, indicates how parties and candidates take advantage of the media's platform function. Also, staging 'pseudo-events' to get attention by mass media and on the Internet serves this purpose. These strategies correspond with the electorates' communication behaviour. Most voters rely on the media – particularly on television and increasingly on the Internet – as their most important sources of campaign information, and they may also respond to the media's presentation of the prevailing opinion climate. Depending on the media's framing of the race among parties and candidates, some voters adapt their electoral decisions by following the bandwagon; others are supporting the underdog. Moreover, attentive citizens take advantage of the capacities of digital media and post videos of candidates' blunders and gaffes on YouTube. The sometimes enormous publicity of candidates' misbehaviours multiplied by viral videos may interfere with the parties' campaign strategies. Like parties and candidates, the voters are increasingly exploiting the media for their political interests, partly by supporting parties and candidates, partly by counteracting their campaigns, for example through satirizing posters and television ads, creating attack websites, or spreading campaign-related spoof. All in all, the parties' and voters' reactions to media developments have been fundamentally changing the strategies and styles of election campaigning.

Improving mediatization studies

The idea of mediatization hardly represents a brand new approach. And it is definitely not a special theory, as some authors suggest (for example, Hjarvard, 2008a). Rather, mediatization is a research perspective focusing on political changes (and changes in other social realms) due to the existence of communication media and their growing importance in modern societies. In promoting this perspective, the concept goes beyond a causal explanation of the media's role in society (although there is some overlap with the notion of media effects). A characteristic feature of the mediatization perspective is that it regards political actors – including citizens, protagonists and organizations – not as objects of media influence or manipulation. Rather, the focus is on the actors' anticipative and adaptive responses, on how they take advantage of media functions and services and capitalize on media performances.

However, so far research has not been tapping the full potential of the mediatization perspective. Especially lacking are studies looking beyond short episodes of the third age of political communication. Rare instances of longitudinal studies are the analyses of the mediatization of parliamentary activities in Denmark by (Elmelund-Praestekaer, 2011) and in Germany (Kepplinger, 2002). Although there are already a few cross-national studies, it would be desirable to have more comparative mediatization research as an 'antidote to naïve universalism' (Gurevitch and Blumler, 1990a). A recent study by Schillemans (2012) comparing the mediatization of public service organizations in Australia, the Netherlands and the United Kingdom is a remarkable example. Van Noije, Kleinneijenhuis and Oegema (van Noije et al., 2008), in examining agenda reciprocities of the parliaments and the media in the United Kingdom and the Netherlands, combine the longitudinal and the cross-national comparative approaches. Their research demonstrates that a highly promising improvement results from taking a systems perspective. Since communication media and political actors are related by mutual expectations and dependencies, one would expect that both sides would show anticipative and adaptive reactions. This would imply a need not only to look at how politicians respond to media functions but also at the repercussions of media-induced political reactions on media performances. Often criticized tendencies of political journalism such as an increasingly interpretative reporting, shrinking sound bites of television coverage, and a growing negativity of political content may appear in a somewhat different light when interpreted in a mediatization frame, that is, as adaptations to media-induced political changes.

Notes

1. Doris Graber's definition of political communication is symptomatic of this orientation: 'What is "political" communication? It is the construction, sending, receiving, and processing of messages that are likely to have a significant impact on politics.' (1993, p. 305)
2. The other two facets Lazarsfeld and Merton mention are the effects of particular media contents and effects of the particular structure of ownership and operation of the mass media.

3. Although Lazarsfeld and Merton argue that the invention of the automobile has had a significantly greater effect upon society than the invention and development of mass media, they nevertheless, by specifying 'social functions of the mass media', give reasons for rather strong media effects.
4. However, there are also doubts whether media logic is really a useful alternative (see, for example, Lundby, 2009).
5. The phrase seems to echo Lazarsfeld and Merton, though without explicitly referring to their article from the 1940s.
6. The lack of space prevents documenting this here by relevant studies.

Part II

Journalism, Democracy and the Public Interest

6
Public Service Broadcasting: Markets and 'Vulnerable Values' in Broadcast and Print Journalism

Stephen Cushion and Bob Franklin

Broadcasting began life in competition with newspapers, first with radio in the 1920s and then again with television in the late 1940s/early 1950s. Its ability to reach mass audiences, however, prompted the state to make broadcasting comply with certain licence conditions deemed inappropriate for newspapers, where a free market was judged a precondition for an independent press. These regulatory obligations have long since been designated 'public service values' and acknowledged as profound influences on the past, present and future of the UK's broadcast ecology and wider media culture. According to Blumler (1992a), however, the values of public service broadcasting have become increasingly 'vulnerable' in the face of market forces and commercial competition.

Consequently, our contribution in this short chapter deals with a very big subject. The introduction offers a definition of public service, examines its significance and relevance in the UK setting, and argues for its value as an essential ingredient in *any* democratic polity and society. The subsequent sections unravel that conversation in the context of broadcast and newspaper journalism and suggest that for news media to remain a formative constituent in democratic life, the market will require some form of regulation to prevent excessive commercial influence on news output.

Public service broadcasting and public service journalism

John Reith, the first director general of the BBC, was convinced that broadcasting must be organized as a public service, remote from market forces and the search for profitability, which he believed would inexorably compromise programming decisions. His terse formulation that BBC programming should aim to 'inform, educate and entertain' captured the essence of public service broadcasting and marked its aetiology. Entertainment was unequivocally relegated to third place in the Reithian trilogy. 'To have exploited so great a scientific invention [as radio] for the purpose and pursuit of entertainment alone', he claimed, would have constituted nothing less than 'a prostitution of its powers and an insult to the character and intelligence of the people' (Reith, 1925, p. 17).

Subsequently, public service broadcasting or public service journalism has become an essentially contested concept, difficult to identify with any agreed precision, 'although it is undoubtedly seen as a good thing' (Barnett and Docherty, 1991, p. 23). Across the century post-Reith, the character of public service values has shifted, reflecting developments in media technologies, changing statutory requirements for media, the fluid ideological commitments of parties and governments, as well as journalists' changing professional practice. But it has always (1) offered a mechanism for funding the delivery of news and other programming, (2) guaranteed journalistic autonomy and independence from powerful economic and political interests, (3) provided a regulatory mechanism for journalistic content and thereby (4) established a professional benchmark for the quality and range of programme content and (5) delivered programming – especially news and current affairs – which served the public interest, and all this for radio, television and the printed press (Franklin, 2001, pp. 1–11). But in 1985, the Peacock Committee – the 'curtain raiser' for a period characterized by 'radically revisionist commercialism' (Blumler cited in Franklin, 2005a, p. 19) – launched an ideological critique of public service values by media executives and practitioners, as well as academics (Murdoch, R., 1989; Elstein, 1991; Ball, 2003) which has sustained to the present day (Murdoch, J., 2009); Eyre declared public service simply, 'a gonner' [sic] (Eyre, 1999). But public service values have also enjoyed stout advocacy with Cushion (2012), for example, illustrating their centrality to democratic cultures.

Vulnerable values, enduring influence: changing news agendas and public trust in public service and market-driven broadcast journalism

To paraphrase the title of Blumler's edited book (1992a), the values of public service broadcasting appeared considerably more vulnerable as the

21st century approached. Even though multichannel television was still in its relative infancy at this point, Blumler (1992b, pp. 14–15) believed it created difficulties for public service broadcasters: 'The impact of new communication technologies (notably cable and satellite), offering both a vastly expanded channel capacity and a simultaneous transmission of programmes and advertising from external sources...was inherently destabilizing'. A few years later, in a co-authored article with Dennis Kavanagh, he asked ominously whether public service broadcasting could 'withstand the full ravages of competition over the longer term' (Blumler and Kavanagh, 1999, p. 219).

More than 20 years on, this section explores whether the values of public broadcasting have, as Blumler suggested, proved vulnerable to compromise in a more market-driven landscape, as we assess the impact of commercial competition on television news. In doing so, we draw on a number of recent empirical studies comparing the nature of coverage on public and commercially driven outlets and explore the public perception of news delivered by different broadcasters.

Barnett et al.'s (2012) longitudinal study of UK national television news from 1975–2009 systematically examined the changing nature of news agendas on public and commercial television news, asking whether tabloid (crime, human interest, royalty, celebrity, sport, and so on) news had increased or not (see Table 6.1).

Table 6.1 reveals that while all UK television channels enhanced their reporting of tabloid stories, the BBC – a wholesale public service

Table 6.1 Tabloid news on UK television news nightly bulletins from 1975–2009 (Expressed as %)

	1975	1980	1985	1990	1995	1999	2004	2009	Difference over time
BBC 6 pm	18.4%	18.8%	25.9%	6.5%	17%	28.9%	20.1%	23.2%	+4.8%
ITV early evening	15.4%	22.6%	32.2%	18.7%	29.5%	33%	32.9%	34.4%	+19%
BBC 9 pm/ 10 pm	16.2%	17.1%	22.6%	4.9%	13.2%	13.3%	14.3%	19.2%	+3%
ITV late evening	14.8%	18.9%	24.9%	10.9%	26.1%	42.1%	33.1%	34.1%	+19.3%
Channel 4 7 pm	/	/	11.1%	5.1%	4.8%	10.6%	16.9%	18.8%	+7.7%
Channel 5	/	/	/	/	/	45.6%	22.9%	51.2%	+5.6%

Source: Barnett et al., 2012.

broadcaster – increased its coverage the least (between 3% and 4.8%). BBC bulletins, moreover, had the most broadsheet agenda, with more serious issues reported such as politics, social affairs and business stories (see Barnett et al., 2012). By contrast, ITV, a commercial public service broadcaster, increased its tabloid agenda by approximately a fifth over 34 years. But perhaps most strikingly, Channel 5 – a commercial broadcaster launched in 1996 with minimal public service broadcasting obligations – dedicated over half its agenda to tabloid news in 2009. A similar distinction between public and market-driven media was evident in campaign reporting of the 2010 general election. While over half of Channel 5 and Sky News coverage contained no reference to any policies, the BBC had the greatest amount of election news, either entirely or significantly about policy issues (Deacon and Wring, 2010, cited in Cushion, 2012). Overall, then, although BBC bulletins have succumbed somewhat to tabloid news values, they appear, to answer Blumler's concern, to have withstood the ravages of commercialism. At the same time, it can be observed that UK news compares favourably with the United States, where a fully fledged market-driven system has been in operation since broadcasting began. In the 1980s and 1990s, it is argued, enhanced deregulation had resulted in the hyper-commercializing of US television news agendas (McChesney, 2000). By contrast, because commercial public service broadcasters continue to operate with public service broadcasting requirements in the UK, most of them continue to report a relatively high degree of broadsheet and foreign news stories, engage with election policy stories and routinely report ongoing political events (Barnett et al., 2012; Cushion, 2012; Cushion and Thomas, 2013). But this perhaps reflects more than formal regulation since Sky News, a commercial 24-hour news channel with no PSB commitments, has resisted the temptation to take its agenda downmarket or attempt to challenge its licence requirements to be impartial. This is in spite of pressure from Sky's owner, Rupert Murdoch, who is on record stating that he wants Sky News to become more like the United States' partisan channel, Fox News, but this has not happened, as 'nobody at Sky listens to me [Murdoch]' (cited in Gibson, 2007). Drawing on a longitudinal comparative study of Sky News and the BBC News Channel, little evidence was uncovered to suggest Sky was emulating the partisan antics of Fox or more recently MSNBC (Cushion and Lewis, 2009). Moreover, as Murdoch's frustration lays bare, the reluctance by Sky's editorial staff to undermine any of its impartiality credentials could be a product of the deeply ingrained culture of independence and integrity long established in UK broadcast journalism. The BBC, in particular, has long maintained a commitment towards these values and its rapport with audiences is built on trust and confidence. In other words, the standards of commercial broadcasters could be indirectly policed by the underlying presence of PSB broadcast journalism in the UK, irrespective of whether these values continue to be 'vulnerable' in the multichannel, multimedia age.

Indeed, the figurehead for PSB in the UK and elsewhere – the BBC – has undergone significant challenges to its independence over the last 90 years or so. From the reporting of the 1926 General Strike and the Suez Canal, to coverage of the IRA and the war in Iraq, its commercial competitors – most notably in the tabloid press – have been quick to undermine the BBC's credibility and lack of 'value' for licence fee payers. But even when the BBC was under enormous pressure after a BBC journalist suggested the government had sexed up the case for the 2003 Iraq war, the broadcaster continued to be the most trusted news information source (Gunter, 2005).

According to the BBC's long-standing world affairs correspondent, John Simpson, the most recent BBC controversy – beginning in 2012 and involving Jimmy Savile, a now deceased former children's presenter facing hundreds of allegations of paedophilia stretching back decades – 'is the worst crisis' to face the public service broadcaster over the last 50 years (cited in Sabbagh, 2012). Its handling of the affair caused widespread criticism and led to the director general's resignation. But even when the broadcaster was at its lowest ebb in the controversy, a representative poll of the British public suggested the BBC remained valued above rival broadcasters (cited in *The Guardian*, 2012b). So, for example, BBC journalism (39%) was far more trusted than all its commercial broadcast competitors, ITV (13%), Sky (10%) and Channel 4 (5%), and was by a considerable margin the most likely to be considered a 'national treasure' (44% compared to ITV's 14%). These figures contrast favourably with tabloid newspapers such as the *Mirror* (1%), *The Express* and *The Sun* (both 2%) which are trusted far less. Likewise, in the United States, where the public broadcaster operates with significantly less funding than the BBC and is watched by far fewer viewers (typically a 2–3% share of the audience), PBS remains significantly more trusted than network or cable television news (PBS.org, 2012). For all the crises and controversies PSBs have experienced, they appear to enjoy a higher level of support and confidence in their newsgathering than wholesale commercial broadcasters.

Overall, the evidence presented in this chapter suggests that while the values of PSB continue to be threatened by commercial competition, the main public broadcaster – the BBC – remains editorially distinctive from its more market-driven rivals and continues to operate as the most trusted source of information. The vulnerable public service values that concerned Blumler at the end of the 20th century have thus arguably not deteriorated to the degree initially predicted. However, this might not be a view Blumler shares wholesale. In a recent co-authored essay with Stephen Coleman, he observes over the previous decade a 'gradual dilution of the civic mission of … the BBC, which has adopted many of the news-reporting techniques of its commercial rivals' (Blumler and Coleman, 2010, p. 145). This was, they write further, 'not necessarily … a planned policy by the BBC, but a cumulative effect of absorption in a chase for ratings and diminution of resources devoted to serious political analysis' (Blumler and Coleman, 2010, p. 145). The BBC, in these respects, has cut its newsgathering resources over the last decade or so (Deans, 2012) and has changed its news programming to appeal to wider audiences, such as more effectively engaging with viewers' political interests (Kevill, 2002).

Where Blumler might be in more agreement with this section's conclusions is with the perceived systemic impact the BBC specifically and the values of public service broadcasting more generally have had in delivering 'profoundly civilizing consequences' in the UK (Blumler and Coleman, 2010, p. 149). For compared to US broadcast news in particular, they argue, public service broadcasting 'has (so far) protected political communication in Britain from some of the worst features of other countries' media' (ibid., p. 149). As this section suggested, the overarching values of public service broadcasting have maintained a relatively serious policy-driven agenda in the UK compared to the US's more commercialized landscape. And the 'civilizing' impact can be evidenced not just in the BBC's continued rapport with the general public, but in the continued demand for broadcast news to remain a highly regulated and impartial service. In the United States, by contrast, the free market approach has delivered precisely the opposite. Since 1987, broadcasters are no longer required to present news impartially, and several channels have become more openly partisan. In some respects, US news providers – notably cable television channels – are beginning to resemble the historically partisan nature of many UK national newspapers, which operate without any formal public service obligations. We now turn to exploring UK newspapers.

UK newspapers and the corrosion of public service values

Three developments have prompted concerns about commitments to public service values in UK newspapers, nationally and locally. First, the intensely competitive markets for readers and advertisers have prompted newspapers to increasingly foreground entertainment-oriented copy above 'hard' news (Franklin, 1997 and 2005b). Second, shortages of editorial resources have reconfigured journalists' sourcing practices, which in turn have encouraged 'churnalism' rather than 'journalism' (Davies, 2008). Third, developments in digital media technologies have (in the short term) undermined the funding of a sustainable and democratic journalism and challenged key elements in journalists' professional identity (Franklin, 2013).

Newszak, compact editions and the democratic deficit

Reith's priorities for public service, which articulated a mission to inform and educate above the requirement to entertain, have been reordered since the 1990s, when collapsing circulations and the increasingly frenzied search for sales and advertising revenues triggered striking changes in the editorial priorities of newspapers (Franklin, 1997, pp. 15–21). In broadsheet newspapers, an emphasis on entertainment increasingly replaced the provision of information, measured judgement gave way to sensationalism, a focus on trivia replaced discussion of weighty issues, and celebrity news achieved greater editorial salience than the coverage of significant international issues. Journalists' traditional news values became undermined by new commercial values that were primarily motivated by market needs rather than the kind of public service interests Lord Reith championed. 'Infotainment' (an emphasis on 'lifestyle journalism', health, travel, finance and features) became the new editorial priority, as human interest supplanted the public interest, with journalists seemingly concerned to report stories which interest the public more than stories which are in the public interest.

The judgement that broadsheet news was little more than 'newszak' or 'McJournalism' (Franklin, 2005b) seemed vindicated in 2003/4 when the UK 'quality' press became 'compacts' and assumed a very similar appearance to the tabloid or 'red-top' papers (Cole, 2008, pp. 183–91). As news disappeared from editorial pages, it was replaced with 'views', and columnists' opinionated commentary began to replace journalists' factually based reportage. Simon Kelner, the editor of the *Independent*, who led the broadsheets' charge to 'compact' format in September 2003, accordingly designated the *Independent* a 'viewspaper'; Rusbridger's preferred term for the *Guardian* was a 'broadloid' (Franklin, 1997, p. 7).

Significantly, these changes in journalism have contributed to a growing democratic deficit in the UK. Journalists no longer deliver the same degree of surveillance of the local, national and international communities they serve, and they fail to deliver the economic, social and political information necessary for readers to exercise democratic accountability over governments (Franklin, 2011a, pp. 2–3); newspapers seem increasingly ill-suited to the role of fourth estate. The same democratic shortcomings of newspapers are evident in the United States (Starr, 2009, p. 28).

One consequence of 'newszak', for example, has been the striking decline in coverage of foreign news, which is costly to sustain with shrinking news budgets (Sampson, 1996; Hamilton and Lawrence, 2012). Nationally, broadsheets' legendarily comprehensive and critical reporting of Parliament has effectively disappeared; perhaps predictably the humorous sketch tradition is flourishing (Franklin, 1997, pp. 233–49). Even sceptics acknowledge that some part (no matter how small) of the democratic life in the UK is enacted on the floor of the House, but it is no longer reported for readers. Finally, the same editorial neglect is evident in the local political arena, where newspapers' coverage of 'courts and councils' is much reduced. When there is coverage, this too often reflects journalists' 'repurposing' of press releases crafted by local government press officers (Franklin, 2011b, pp. 90–107). Although early in their careers, online citizen public affairs sites show little sign of redressing the deficit, with a study of 48 US sites concluding that they 'are, at best, imperfect information substitutes for most newspapers' and that 'few citizen journalism sites outside of large metropolitan cities covered local government' (Fico et al., 2013).

Churnalism, sources and the 'news factory'

Blumler identified two aspects of the crisis facing newspapers in the UK: a crisis of financial viability 'threatening the existence and resources of mainstream journalistic organizations' and a crisis of 'civic adequacy' which is 'impoverishing the contribution of journalism to citizenship and democracy' (Blumler, 2011a, p. xv); both are addressed in *Guardian* journalist Nick Davies' critical study, *Flat Earth News* (2008).

Drawing on a political economy analysis of media, Davies argues that as newspapers try to maintain profitability in the context of declining revenues and job cuts, a static or reduced editorial staff must sustain, or more likely increase, their output of news stories to fill the paper's editorial columns. Squaring the circle of publishing more stories with fewer journalists demands a growing reliance on 'pre-packaged news' bought from news agencies or free-to-use public relations materials issued by government, major corporations and interest groups. Lacking time and resources, hard-pressed journalists increasingly rely on these 'information subsidies' (Gandy, 1982) not merely to stimulate thoughts about possible stories but to set their editorial agenda and actually deliver stories which directly shape their editorial copy. Davies argues that this is not journalism but 'churnalism'. Journalists are no longer gatherers but merely 'passive processors of whatever news comes their way, churning out stories whether real event or PR artifice, important or trivial, true or false' (2008, p. 59).

A study by Cardiff academics offered empirical endorsement for some of Davies' argument. Comparing published news stories with press releases and agency materials revealed that across a sample of 2,207 published domestic news stories, 60% were wholly or mainly derived from PR/agency sources, with a further 20% being a variable balance of these sources. Only 12% of news stories had no evidence of journalistic reliance on pre-packaged news sources (Franklin, 2011b, p. 101). Some stories offered unashamedly verbatim replications of PR materials. *The Times'* 'George Cross for Iraq War hero', for example, a 24 March 2006 report attributed to journalist Michael Evans, simply reproduced a Ministry of Defence press release. To add insult to journalistic injury, deadline pressures mean that there is no time to check the factual accuracy of such press releases; Machill and Beiler found that journalists spend only 'eleven minutes [per working shift] checking sources and information' (2009, p. 183).

But how do these changes in journalistic practice contribute to the crisis of civic adequacy? First, and highly significantly, Davies illustrates the dominant, skewed and unrepresentative access enjoyed by corporate, governmental and other established voices in public debates hosted by newspapers. When the origins of PR sources cited in press stories were analysed, the corporate sector dominates, with 38% of sourced references, followed by public bodies (police, NHS, and universities – 23 %), government and politicians (21%), NGOs/charities (11%) and professional associations (5%). Perhaps most shocking is that while corporate and government voices account for 60% of cited sources in press reports, the opinions of ordinary citizens account for only 2%. In such an uneven public debate, loaded against the public interest, *vox populi* is readily overwhelmed by a deafening din emanating from board rooms.

Second, the emergence of digital media and more participatory forms of journalism signal the promise of a more plural sourcing of news, but in the short run offer little democratic comfort. Research suggests that as news sources proliferate, their credibility becomes more difficult for journalists to establish, tempting them to consolidate their existing reliance on the 'tried and tested' sources in news agencies and public relations (Phillips, 2010, p. 99).

Digital media; decreasing journalism

The emergence of digital media has been crucial to the radical restructuring of all aspects of news gathering, writing and reporting, including who writes the news and the converged and increasingly mobile news platforms which are used for its production and consumption. Currently six billion people have access to a mobile device, which is greater than for any other medium but also exceeds access to networked electricity (Westlund, 2013, p. 22). This last point underscores the massive promise and potential of digital media to enrich the number and range of news sources but also the originators and citizen authors of news. Citizen-derived reports of the Arab Spring, the Japanese tsunami and the Occupy Wall Street movement confirm their ability to inform and their cosmopolitanising potential (Chouliaraki and Blaagaard, 2013).

But in the short term, digital media have exacerbated both aspects of the crisis identified by Blumler: financial viability and civic adequacy. Online journalism has won readers and advertisers from newspapers, devastated their funding, prompted job cuts and the closure of hundreds of local and regional newspapers, reducing the independent sources of civic and political information necessary for meaningful citizen engagement, as well as the oversight and accountability of elites (Franklin, 2011a, pp. 3–4). Worse, no alternative business model has emerged to sustain a viable and democratic journalism as newspaper groups experiment with various mixes of pay walls (Franklin, 2011a), advertising on mobile devices (Nel and Westlund, 2012), the sale of newspaper apps (Franklin, 2012), crowdfunding (Carvajal et al., 2012), co-creation (Aitamurto, 2013), levies on corporate profits (IPPR, 2009), public subsidies (Downie and Schudson, 2010), or a voucher scheme which allows citizens to choose which news organizations will enjoy funding (McChesney and Nicholls, 2010). Political theorists will surely struggle to conceptualize a viable scheme for democracy that excludes independent and financially viable newspapers.

Other concerns emerge as electronic publishing exacerbates existing editorial problems. Davies' worries about *Flat Earth News* (2008), for example, in a digital context may lead to what Phillips calls 'creative cannibalism' with news editors requiring journalists to 'cut and paste' news from rival papers, repurposing the plagiarised story with a redrafted opening paragraph, but no sign of the original journalist's byline (Phillips, 2011, p. 289). Similarly, the emergence of the 'citizen' or 'participatory' journalist, whose endeavours increasingly complement or replace (Neuberger and Nuernbergk, 2011, pp. 235–48) the education, training, professional experience, identity and news contacts which the professional journalist brings to news gathering and writing news, is less likely to generate news which is well sourced (in terms of numbers and authority of sources) or informed by the same bedrock professional values and concerns with accuracy, verification and objectivity.

Undoubtedly the most urgent question arising from the continuing decline of newspapers is 'Who will now originate the news?' Broadcast media have always been indebted to the prints for their news agenda (listen to R4's *Today* programme in bed and then read the *Guardian* over breakfast); newspapers' online editions typically replicate stories from the printed pages. Creative cannibalism is rife, and 'infomediaries' such as Google News simply 'aggregate' (replicate) and distribute; they don't originate news (Bakker, 2012, pp. 627–37). Ultimately, news is a commodity, and someone must pay for the production cost to enjoy the highly valued democratic benefits.

Conclusions

In assessing the history and development of the UK's broadcasting and print media, this chapter has suggested that the regulation of newspapers may be required as much as for broadcast media. In our view, this would mean that the values long entrenched in public service broadcasting would inform the production of news in the public interest alongside, but superior to, the influence of the marketplace. Lord Justice Leveson, charged with a review into the culture, practices and ethics of the press, inquired who might 'Guard the Guardians', but our argument here has been that some form of regulation is key to delivering public service and thereby meaningful democratic engagement. It may well be that we need a regulatory mechanism which allows the public via statute to guard the guardian of the Guardians and ensure news and information about public affairs which sustains and nurtures citizen information, understanding and engagement and thereby a democratic polity. These values, after all, represent the enduring presence of public service broadcasting, and for all their continued vulnerabilities (Blumler, 1992a), they remain at the heart of what the fourth estate can achieve.

7
Political Communication Research in the Public Interest

Denis McQuail

Preamble

This chapter is guided by indications of a direction for research and policy that may be derived from the large and diverse corpus of Jay Blumler's work. Before setting out, some opening words are called for on the founder of this feast of ideas. It cannot help also being a somewhat personal account, given a close early collaboration at what was a formative moment for me as well as for him, on his journey from political theorist to virtual doyen of empirical political communication research.

My earliest collaboration with Jay after his arrival in 1963 at what was then the Television Research Unit at University of Leeds was in our study of the impact of campaign communications on the UK general election of 1968, resulting in the publication of *Television in Politics* (Blumler and McQuail, 1968). Leaving its content and findings aside, several features of this work offer clues to subsequent research choices. These include a preference for new thinking and innovation in research rather than for replication; a framework of theory (albeit of the 'short range') to give coherence to the research design; a sensitivity to changes in the environment (political and media-system related); a strong focus on the perceptions of audiences (as citizens and voters) of their own needs and interests as well as on the goals of the 'communicators', whether in politics or the media; an intention to learn lessons that could have democratic political benefits; a firm foundation in empirical data, both quantitative and qualitative, with a concern for 'media effects'; and finally, and not least, an underlying normative concern with a broad 'public interest', transcending the purposes of the different sets of participants, voters, politicians and professional communicators.

What follows is an elaboration of some of these principles, as they were further developed, applied and modified. The main purpose is to map out a set of values and principles that can still serve to guide political communication research and, indirectly, policy action, in what seems an entirely different communication era to that of the formative years.

The changing environment for political communication

The larger theme which this chapter intends to take up relates not only to changes in the means of public communication, but also to other shifts in the context and conditions of politics and of media structure which call for continuing attention to the manner in which a democratic public sphere can be sustained and strengthened. Significant elements of the institutional arrangements of early television days no longer apply, and it is in the light of changed circumstances that we try to look at and draw guidance from Jay Blumler's earlier work. This was carried out at a time when broadcasting was under close public scrutiny, if not control, with its political roles largely ascribed and circumscribed. The more dominant (having more freedom and higher status) political medium of the newspaper press was much politicized and divided according to relevant constituencies of allegiance, contrary to the broad national unity promoted by broadcasting, with its large and largely undifferentiated audience.

The conduct, or management, of the notional 'public sphere' was primarily in the hands of political parties, trade unions and a variety of organized movements in pursuit of public support for their goals. The flow of political communication was predominantly 'vertical' – from leader to follower, centre to periphery – although horizontal at the level of elites. Individual attention at 'lower' levels to the flow of public communication was still quite high by later standards, but controlled 'from above'. Participation was typically direct and in person (as audiences and crowds). The pattern described had legitimacy and was less rigid than it sounds, with flux and change in response to events and new ideas.

Skipping ahead 50 years to the present leads to a different picture, even though the basic political institutions and the principles of democratic government have not changed. In that time, many of the supports for the various communication roles discernible in the previous description have been removed, and new opportunities have opened up for either constructive alternatives or damaging competition for public attention.

There has been a loss of much of the protective environment given by public regulation as well as a decline in public acceptance of the arrangements. Changes in media and media markets have demoted the claim of politics to privileged treatment. It cannot be asserted that the public sphere has been transformed, but it does seem as if it is looser, more fragmented, more varied and less directly involving. It appears both more engaging for an active minority and more neglected by the majority.

Societies have undergone a distinct secularization, with goals of prosperity and consumption now paramount, and citizen concerns, as well as ideology, seemingly relegated in salience. For media owners and controllers, economic motives have become more pressing, while pursuing openly political goals or operating a public service for democracy carries less weight. The concerns of politicians are self-regarding, and short-term advantage often defeats noble aspiration. Techniques of advertising and marketing are freely used, and political communication becomes less challenging, revealing and interesting. The general implication of these brief remarks is that the potential of new means and systems for enhanced communicativity is largely being left to chance and the market.

On the credit side, there has been a vast expansion in opportunities to acquire and share information and ideas by way of online media, even if the possibilities are only in the course of unfolding and their impact is still uncertain – but certainly uneven. According to one interpretation, we should welcome a more flexible, active and truly responsive and interactive sphere of flow and debate on all manner of issues, with opportunities to bypass restrictive 'gatekeepers' and bottlenecks that often had a stranglehold in the original system of democratic political communication. This has now shifted to a system of multiple and diverse networks structured both horizontally and vertically. The age of competing ideologies and mass propaganda has faded, and the seeming losses just noted have to be seen as an inevitable reflection of changed times, not a retrograde step. Broadly, this interpretation presumes that, freed from restraints, the system will somehow respond to the wishes and needs of the many in their various roles, including that of democratic citizens. Much faith is placed in the benign hand of market forces.

This comforting version is still quite hypothetical. More sober and reformed reflection might also suggest that things are neither black nor white, nor are they simple. The institutions and machinery of organized politics have not greatly changed, nor have its methods of organizing communication. Many the same goals of political persuasion are being pursued for many of the same reasons by many of the same people and organizations, perhaps with greater sophistication and skill. The motives that led democratic states to treat the original 'mass media' with caution, and to set limits to their activities in the name of fairness and 'public interest', by way of regulation, subsidy and reward, are not necessarily obsolete when it comes to ensuring meaningful participation by the many rather than just the active few. The original normative impulses for research into the role of broadcasting are still valid, even if in need of adaptation and supplementation.

A provisional orientation

The range of ideas to be found in Jay Blumler's work is wide, and their application goes well beyond the circumstances of election campaigns. Coherence is given, firstly, by a notion of a political communication system, as was developed during the 1970s (Blumler and Gurevitch, 1975), that concerns the needs of a society (social system) and its various component groups (not further elaborated upon here). Secondly, there is the idea of 'public interest' as in the chapter title, used widely and diversely, sometimes misused and escaping an agreed definition except in very general terms (as a notion of the welfare of the public or society as a whole). However, Jay Blumler did suggest (1998) a fairly clear view of what it would mean, in terms of three key features: it refers to a vision of what is good for the many as instituted by some form of legitimate democratic authority (as are certain other functions in society, such as government or the justice system) and having an element of public responsibility as a consequence. It is an idea that requires a long time span, which takes into account the long-term needs and effects, thus of future as well as present generations. In addition, the notion of a public interest has to recognize conflicts of interest and of perspective in implementation; it must permit compromise and adaptation to the realities of the time and place.

All of this leads to a view of political communication as having certain desirable aims or effects. These relate in particular to 'surveillance' to discover and diffuse relevant and reliable information; social cohesion in some significant measure; the serving of varied institutional needs for public communication; facilitating adaption and change of the society; and providing the means of accountability for those who exercise the most power in the society. These needs are neither coextensive with the territory of political communication nor exclusive to it, but there is a significant overlap in each case. Finally, we are reminded of the need for a normative vision: value choices and judgments have to be incorporated. Without a minimum quota of such thinking, the framework of ideas falls apart, and it is hard to design fruitful research for any purpose beyond the limited requirements of sponsors or paymasters.

From 'public interest' to 'democratic public sphere'

The very broad idea of a public interest leads to the more specific topic of democratic politics. Here the concept of a 'public sphere' has gained currency as the most useful formulation of widely shared ideas of how a political system maintains its roots amongst the general population, opening political action to the many and ensuring a healthy relationship and exchange between 'leaders' and 'followers'. The public sphere, in this view, consists primarily of an open 'space' in society, equivalent to the public square or 'agora' of classical democracy, where, notionally at least, all citizens can participate in the business of decision-making for government, whether as 'listeners' or 'speakers'.

For this situation to be realized, or just approached, several key elements are required: a continuous supply of reliable information available to all concerning events and issues that need to be decided, opportunities for debates and exchange, and the formation of both broad public opinion and the organized views of interest groups, experts and advocates of all kinds. The spaces for this type of intercommunication and interaction have to be accessible to all and free from imposed or insurmountable obstacles to participation and speech, or any forms of manipulation and control. Such ideal conditions are hardly attainable in extensive modern societies but, nevertheless, all are presumed to be attainable in some measure.

In the 'age of democracy' there has been an increasing reliance on the 'mass' media to deliver the conditions for a meaningful substitute for personal interaction. It is now supposed that this can and will be even more effectively achieved, even for a large majority, by the Internet in its many applications. There is even a case for considering the term 'mediated public sphere' as appropriate for the contemporary version of an old idea that has not changed in substance, but has changed in form and means of attainment.

Most versions of the public sphere concept, as here, have tended to deploy a 'generic' version based on the writings of Jürgen Habermas (1962/89), along the lines summarized. However, we are reminded that there are different versions of the basic concept, reflecting differences of culture, history and traditions. For instance, Downey et al. (2012) have pointed to the existence of at least three different versions: one as discussed; another stressing representation of public opinion and needs by way of a leading elite; and a third, a participatory form, in which the widest possible involvement of citizens in debate and decision-making is sought. The main point is not to choose among any of the three variants, or others, but to recognize that the various changes noted above may also have been accompanied by a shift in the political realities on the ground, not least in the content and manner of conduct of political communications. The key task of theory, therefore, is to re-assess this matter and adapt the concept to current circumstances.

A coherent set of principles is required for responding to the challenges posed in seeking to realize the 'public sphere' conditions as outlined. The most general requirement to be satisfied is that of 'publicness', and this can be accounted for according to different criteria, especially the following:

- *Universal coverage* – Receivers of essentially the same range of information on matters of potential debate, including information about diverse reactions and opinions, should represent as wide a representation as possible of the whole relevant population of a nation, city, and so on, should be able to receive essentially the same range of information on matters of potential debate, including information about diverse reactions and opinions. This contributes to the ideal of a cohesive polity, as opposed to an earlier fragmented, alienated vision of a 'mass society', or the contemporary more individuated society encouraged by consumerism and the 'pull' media which cater to the personal interests of each individual media user. A key element must also be a concern with that largish sector of a population at risk of de facto exclusion because of limited education, low income and aspirations, plus other sources of marginalization.
- *A diversity of voices* – A wide range of perspectives, ideas and opinions relevant to politics and public life will be available without restriction or difficulty.
- *Access to channels* – At issue here is the accessibility to all of 'channels' to reach others, whether as fellow citizens or leaders, and the realistic possibility of engaging with others in some form of open dialogue or debate. This principle requires a realistic assessment of the typical imbalance of possession of, and access to, the main means of public communication, an imbalance that is subject to little chance of correction within an unbridled free market media system.
- *A multi-perspectival concept of audience as public* – The core of this principle is the recognition that all involvement in, or avoidance of, the public sphere will be driven by a variety of motivations and needs.

The benefits and satisfactions on offer from the media and other sources of communication are diverse, and citizens will vary greatly in the appeal they might have. Differences in motivation and interest have many, often unaccountable, roots and have to be charted and accounted for empirically.

* *Recognition of competing source interests* – In particular, the view from one of two main positions has to be taken into account: that of a 'political source' (whether contender, office holder or advocate) who originates ideas and information selectively, and that of the professional communicator (mainly editors, journalists, and owners/controllers of media) who originate information and cannot act simply as messenger or mediator. Within both categories there are further relevant divisions. In the case of professional 'communicators', for instance, there is a key distinction between what Blumler called the 'sacerdotal' and the 'pragmatic' outlook on the task (Blumler, 1966). No less significant is the rise of active lobby and pressure groups using their media market power, or just economic muscle, to buy an increase of direct access to the public as their audience and media users.

Each of the conditions mentioned is closely implicated in the transition to the 'mediated' version of the public sphere, as noted above.

Emerging problematics of the 'mediated public sphere'

A central theme of theory and research by Blumler and others (for example, Blumler and Gurevitch, 1995; Capella and Jamieson, 1997; Blumler and Kavanagh, 1999) concerns the heightened degree of cynicism and negativity about politics, running counter to democratic ideas of active and informed citizenship. Media reporting practices have represented politics in a negative, venal and trivial light, and the goal of gaining attention has replaced that of the communication of information and ideas. This happens in response either to journalistic imperatives or commercial self-interest in a very competitive environment, or it follows what is often supposed to be 'what the public wants'. The actions of politicians and political parties, in their self-oriented marketing strategies, have only reinforced these negative tendencies.

In the light of this pessimism, the most effective restorative of the traditional democratic role of the press has been looked for in the new, interactive forms of communication that are at the same time embedded in a multitude of interpersonal online networks for broad social uses.

Before assessing the chances here, the central idea of 'public sphere' as sketched above has to be reassessed. At the very least, some revision is needed in recognition of the emerging conditions of society and politics as well as of media. There are new grounds for uncertainty about the appropriateness of the 'traditional' concept of the public sphere. Instead of a majoritarian system rooted in the implementation of broadly based public opinion on key issues, the 'networked' public sphere seems as if it is characterized by a much more active and intense 'layer' of debate and action that is open to all to participate in, but in practice is not chosen by the many. A much stronger role is also being played by what could be called an 'expert sphere', which may also be penetrated by the well-funded efforts of professional lobbyists. The 'new' public sphere is not the preserve of elites of any specific kind, nor is it dominated by large bloc politics; it is fragmented in the ways mentioned and loosely structured around issues, movements and, maybe, charismatic figures. But democracy in the end requires origination in the will of the people and submission to majority approval in the end, and this is likely to be competed for by the older strategies of persuasion and propaganda, albeit by way of more diverse and more sophisticated means than in the preceding 'mass media' era.

The earlier (mid-20th century) version of the public sphere required a voluntary dedication by leading media of communication, plus a strong element of public protection (or sponsorship) for a 'function' that is essential to the society, by way of an ultimate guarantee of 'space' for public use, free from market and competitive pressures (essentially this was the role of broadcasting). Both of these are much less in evidence, with little chance of reemergence. Future strategies for supporting the public sphere have to take this on board as well as present some vision of working possibilities. The divergent versions of the public sphere sketched here may overlap a good deal with the earlier 'ideal types', but they lead in rather different directions.

Revising ideas of the 'functions', content and shape of political communications

After two decades or so of accelerating media change in an unsettled political environment, certain effects are beginning to show up. The general 'functions' of political communication remain much the same, anchored as they are by persistent elements in both the political and media institutions, but several things have changed. Hypothetically, these changes involve a broad shift from so-called 'push' media to 'pull' media, that pass the initiative to 'users'; a general fragmentation of the overall 'audience' into many smaller, often very small, groupings; a multiplication of channels, types of platform, sources, and genres; the loss of large 'captive' audiences delivered either by popular content or 'mass channels'; the 'escape' of large sections of potential provision from regulation or supervision; the delocalisation even if not globalization of much media supply. There is more going on, but enough in all this to suggest that we are likely to lack any reliable overall map of the terrain of practice, despite the newfound capacity of online media for the monitoring and registering of all manner of use.

Based on a mixture of evidence and conventional wisdom, it might seem that public motivation to engage in political action is, on average, lower and weaker than in the past, for a variety of reasons. In respect of media roles, the balance of outlook has shifted away from partisanship and a media willingness to facilitate the purposes of political actors. Both the impulses of professionalism and the demands of the competitive market lead this way. Even the democratically desirable (and newsworthy) role of increasing the accountability of office holders by way of criticism has declined, partly for economic reasons.

Realism is called for about the chances of holding back such forces of change, but the first necessity is to have an empirical basis for any normative guidance that might be derived from research. This means identifying the forms of presentation and transmission that have the best chance of achieving the goals of democratic communication. The engagement of interest is likely to be a condition for all this, if the well attested to ambivalence and even resistance of the audience to political communication is to be believed. Realism requires recognition of the fact that there is not a lot of incentive for media systems and organizations to look far beyond the measure of ratings.

Future research on media and the democratic public sphere

Much research has already been, and is being, carried out in relation to the potential effects of new online media on public sphere issues. Even so, there is as yet no settled pattern to Internet uses or effects, either on the part of the public or actors in the public sphere, and this has stood in the way of firm conclusions, even of a general kind. Perhaps there will never be a settled state, or no dominant one, unlike that which seemed to characterize the 'reign' of the newspaper press in respect of politics and then of broadcast television in a more broadly informational role at its zenith.

With these thoughts in mind, we turn to the matter of the role of research, adopting a firm normative stance, but concentrating on what is realistic to achieve or simply practical in application. For this purpose, several of the principles characteristic of Jay Blumler's work are still very serviceable, especially the following:

* Start with certain declared normative guidelines.
* Base inquiry on firm prior evidence.
* Look for factors of change and possible effects.
* Prepare by way of observation and qualitative inquiry.
* Ensure attention to alternative perspectives and preferences.
* Give preference to a comparative research design.

These 'principles' are not at all unfamiliar, but they merit reiteration in circumstances where expectations and judgments concerning change across a wide front are overabundant: in societies and cultures, in media and communications, and in political beliefs and movements. The 'online' media have seemed to provide unprecedented opportunities for testing ideas and collecting data with ease and speed, often doing violence to established rules of methodology (for instance in respect of generalization beyond the cases and reliability of information from unknown respondents). Innumerable small studies have yielded little guidance to what the future will be when online media and adapted 'old media' finally 'bed down' in established ways in respect of political institutions (if they ever do).

Following on from the general recommendation made earlier for conceptual clarification and a comprehensive empirical mapping of the terrain on the ground, some suggestions for research directions and priorities can be made. One dimension of variation is that of the national differences of system and circumstances. The broad sketch of change offered above, based on the UK and similar places, will certainly not apply everywhere, even if the forces of change will not vary much. These are already matters of extensive investigation, drawing certainly in the pioneering work of Hallin and Mancini (2004a; 2012a) on the relation between political system and media system.

A second entry point for tackling the problem is by way of the notion of generational change. There is a large literature on political socialization and much contemporary evidence of differences between the generations in uses of and attitudes to the 'new media' carried by the Internet and mobile devices (especially perhaps by 'social media', blogs, online news, search engines, YouTube and similar sites). Direct comparison with the past is not possible, but current links between the media experiences and habits of the current youth and their political concerns would be instructive. It cannot just be assumed that habits of media use characteristic of early years will persist in the face of changing life circumstances.

Thirdly, the territory of the communicator role needs to be explored in new and more relevant ways that are only gradually emerging, as communication activities are adapted to fit the new means (or vice versa). New forms of online publication have reshaped the long-established pattern. To some extent, a new beginning is called for here, with a new 'map' of the relevant roles and fresh set of role concepts to apply to sources, mediators and audiences/users. The extension of inquiry into the highest levels of control of media systems is also clearly desirable, as difficult as it has always been in comparable situations. The 'non-political' actors also need to be included, as far as possible. Independent observers and researchers are not welcomed for the usual reasons, but this does not mean that indirect methods of scrutiny cannot be applied, and much clear evidence of conduct can be assembled that might shed some light on motives and likely outcomes.

In conclusion

This short overview of a long and eventful period has tried to establish certain lines of continuity in what is going on in political communication and something of what needs attention from theory and research. We are fortunate that it is a period spanned by the efforts of such a productive and creative scholar, and fortunate, too, that the underlying instincts driving this work have kept democratic ideals and goals at the very centre of attention.

8
Journalists, Journalism and Research: What Do We Know and Why Should We Care?

David H. Weaver

This chapter draws on nearly 40 years of journalism and media research that I have conducted at Indiana University with many colleagues and students. This includes four major national surveys of US journalists; studies of media and voter learning in five US presidential elections; studies of media agenda setting in elections; and other research on newspaper readership, foreign news coverage, foreign correspondents, and press freedom in various countries.

The four national surveys of some 3,700 US journalists were based on an earlier 1971 survey of about 1,300 print and broadcast journalists by sociologist John Johnstone and his colleagues at the University of Illinois at Chicago. In the preface to their 1976 book, *The News People*, Professor Johnstone wrote that 'perhaps the main reason for being interested in the characteristics of newsmen and how they go about their work is that these may tell us something important about the nature of news.' (Johnstone et al., 1976, p. viii)

We have tried to remain true to this purpose in our surveys of 1982, 1992, 2002, and 2007 by attempting to link the characteristics, attitudes, beliefs, values and working conditions of individual journalists with the kind of reporting they do (Weaver and Wilhoit, 1986; 1996; Weaver et al., 2007; Beam et al., 2009). This interest in studying journalists has spread beyond US borders, and many of these studies have been modelled on Johnstone's and ours. About 15 years ago, I compiled and compared the findings of such studies in 21 countries in a book called *The Global Journalist* (Weaver, 1998). And in May of 2012, a second edition of this book with findings from more than 30 countries was published as *The Global Journalist in the 21st Century* with colleague Lars Willnat as co-editor (Weaver and Willnat, 2012).

My original interest in studying journalists grew out of a perception in the 1970s that most mass communication research was focused mainly on media messages and their effects, rather than on the producers of these messages. As Jay Blumler put it more than 30 years ago, the study of journalism and mass communication is like a 'three-legged stool,' with the three legs being message producers, messages themselves, and the uses and effects of these messages (Blumler, 1981, p. 44). A holistic view of the mass communication process requires knowledge about all three legs of research.

And that leads to another side of my research, namely the studies of agenda setting and voter learning, which have focused on the *effects* of news media on the public and on policy makers.

Since 1972, when I was a doctoral student at the University of North Carolina working with Maxwell McCombs and Donald Shaw on a presidential election agenda-setting study in Charlotte, North Carolina, I have sustained an interest in media effects, especially agenda-setting effects, as well as the antecedents and consequences of these effects, and the conditions under which they are more or less likely to occur (Weaver et al., 1975; Weaver, 1977; Weaver, et al., 1981; Semetko, et al., 1991; McCombs et al., 1997; Weaver, et al., 2004; Coleman et al., 2009).

There isn't space here to discuss all these studies in detail, so I will summarize the main findings of some of them and then speculate on their implications for journalism and its role in serving democracy in these uncertain and challenging times. I begin with what we have learned about US journalists in the four national surveys that we have conducted from the early 1980s until 2007, then move on to the studies of the agenda-setting and other effects of journalism, and then to the implications of these findings for the present and future of journalism and its democratic contributions in the United States and other countries.

Journalists – what do we know?

First, our surveys show that the number of fulltime journalists working for mainstream general interest news media in the US increased dramatically from 1971 (about 69,000) to 1982 (about 112,000) and reached their highest point in 1992 (about 122,000), declining to about 116,000 in 2002, and almost certainly to less than 100,000 today. At the same time, the US population has grown substantially since 1992, when it was about 257 million, to 2009, when it was about 304 million; an 18 per cent increase, while the number of fulltime mainstream media journalists has declined by about this same percentage. Thus, the number of journalists in the US has dropped from about one for every 2,100 people to about one for every 3,000 people, at the same time that the country has grown considerably larger and more complex.

The majority of US journalists have been employed by newspapers, especially daily newspapers, as compared to other news media such as radio, television, news magazines, news services, and websites. Daily newspapers have consistently employed half or more of all fulltime US journalists during the past 40 years, and when coupled with weekly (or less than daily) newspapers, this number rises to between two-thirds and three-fourths of all US journalists. I will return to this finding and its implications later.

The educational backgrounds of US journalists have become less diverse since the early 1970s when less than 60 per cent had a college degree, compared to the present when 90 per cent or more do, and twice as many of the college graduates today have majored in journalism or communication (53 per cent) as in 1971 (27 per cent). The most significant change has been in the percentage of college graduates. In this day and age, an undergraduate college degree is the minimum educational requirement for becoming a journalist in the US.

The level of freedom that journalists think they have to get important subjects covered and to choose stories to work on has been declining since the early 1980s, and this decline has accelerated in the past decade at newsrooms experiencing buyouts or layoffs, and also at news organizations where profits are considered a higher priority than the quality of journalism (Beam et al., 2009). In short, declines in perceived freedom of journalists tend to be linked to declines in the resources in news organizations, which have become much more serious just in the past few years.

Even in 2007 we found that roughly a third of the journalists in our study worked for organizations that had experienced layoffs or buyouts. Half were working in newsrooms that were smaller than the year before, and this situation has become worse since then. Given that the conditions facing many US news organizations are predicted to worsen in the near future, it seems likely that the professional autonomy of journalists will continue to erode, which cannot be good news for anyone who believes in the value of free and independent journalism in a democratic system of government.

On a more positive note, our most recent surveys have found that public service journalism remains a core professional value for US journalists, even in these troubled times. More than 90 per cent in 2007 still believed that it is very important for news organizations to produce journalism that serves the public interest, and more than 80 per cent said the same is true for serving all socio-economic groups in their communities (Beam et al., 2009). And two-thirds thought their news organizations were doing a very good or outstanding job of informing the public – so there was still considerable journalistic idealism out there when we did our last study. We completed the data collection for another national survey of U.S. journalists in December 2013 and are analyzing the data.

Another more optimistic finding in the 2007 study was that there was no indication that large, publicly held media companies were less likely to support public service journalism than smaller, privately held ones. It seems that we cannot make sweeping generalizations about the impact of ownership on news content. Organizational goals and values mattered more than anything else as predictors of a commitment to public service journalism.

Managers with a commitment to doing good journalism counted more than type of ownership or staff cutbacks in predicting journalists' views about how well their news organizations were informing the public or how committed they were to serving the public. Emphasis on high profits, on the other hand, undermined this perceived commitment to public service journalism, and so did working for an organization that had recently reduced the size of its news staff.

Our studies have also shown that the two most widely endorsed roles for journalists over the years have been investigating government claims and getting information to the public quickly, but the neutral information disseminator role has declined significantly and the interpretive role has increased notably, leading some to say recently that we have a journalism in the US that is increasingly one of views more than news, and that tendency seems to be reinforced by the various TV talk shows and internet blogs.

In our most recent study in 2007, we found an increase in support for nearly all of these roles, especially analyzing complex problems, being an adversary of government, and concentrating on news of interest to the widest audience. These are encouraging findings, but we have to wonder how many journalists can actually carry out these roles, especially the analysis of complex problems, given the shrinking newsrooms and resources that are so common these days.

Another finding from our latest study is that journalists who write blogs are more likely than others to favour investigating government claims, pointing out solutions to social problems, and helping to set political agendas – but there is a question of whether blogs have the impact on the public and policy agendas that more traditional news media have had. I will have more to say about this later, when I review what we have learned from the agenda-setting studies.

In our two most recent surveys done in 2002 and 2007, we found significant *decreases* in the numbers of journalists willing to use ethically questionable reporting methods such as paying for information, claiming to be someone else, getting employed to obtain inside information, and using personal documents without permission (Weaver et al., 2007; Beam et al., 2009). These findings can be interpreted as positive, suggesting that journalists are becoming more ethical and principled, but they can also be regarded as an indication that US journalists are becoming less aggressive. This 'less aggressive' interpretation could be seen as consistent with declines in the perceived importance of analyzing national policies and international developments, and with declines in perceived freedom to choose stories to report.

But overall there were some signs of increased professionalism of US journalists in the latest two studies in addition to their views on the ethics of some reporting practices. These included more college graduates, better pay, increased job satisfaction, and more support for investigating government claims. And journalists' descriptions of their best work emphasized serious reports reflecting long-term news values of public service rather than entertainment and celebrity gossip. The most common reasons that journalists cited for their best work included public service, a broader social context, unusual information gathering, and serious problems such as child abuse, homelessness, lack of affordable housing, and decreasing quality of education in government-run schools.

So, as mentioned earlier, we have some indications from our studies of journalists that public service values are still alive and well in the minds and hearts of many US journalists, but there are also serious concerns about all the closings of newspapers, the layoffs and reductions in the size of newsrooms, the declining levels of professional autonomy, and the ability to keep idealistic young men and especially women of various backgrounds in journalism.

Let me turn now to some of the findings from the studies of agenda setting and voter learning that I have worked on over the years.

Agenda setting

One of the most popular approaches to studying media effects that emerged in the early 1970s is known as the agenda-setting function of mass media. First tested empirically in the 1968 US presidential election by University of North Carolina journalism professors Maxwell McCombs and Donald Shaw, this approach originally focused on the ability of the mass media to tell the public what to *think about* rather than what to *think* (McCombs and Shaw, 1972). This was a sharp break from previous media effects studies that had focused on what people thought – mainly their political opinions and attitudes – and on behaviours such as voting.

Since this initial study of media agenda setting, there have been hundreds of studies carried out by scholars in the US and other countries, including Germany, Great Britain, Israel, Italy, Japan, The Netherlands, Spain, and Taiwan. Most of these studies have focused on the relationship between news media ranking of issues (by amount and prominence of news coverage) and public rankings of the perceived importance of these issues in various surveys, a type of research that has been called *public* agenda setting to distinguish it from studies that are concerned mainly with the influences on the media agenda (*media* agenda setting) or the impact of media agendas on governmental agendas (*policy* agenda setting) (Dearing and Rogers, 1996).

The evidence from scores of such public agenda setting studies is mixed, but on the whole it tends to support a positive correlation – and sometimes a causal relationship – between media agendas and public agendas at the *aggregate* (or group) level, especially for relatively unobtrusive issues that do not directly impact the lives of the majority of the public, such as foreign policy and government scandal, and also for those people who have what we call a high need for orientation (high interest in a subject coupled with high levels of uncertainty about it) (Weaver, 1977; McCombs, 2004).

Recently I have worked with one of our former doctoral students, Yue Tan, on a study of agenda setting among the media, the public and Congress from 1946 to 2004, a time span of 58 years (Tan and Weaver, 2007). Using annual data from *The New York Times*, Gallup polls and Congressional hearings, we found a small but definite correlation between *The New York Times* agenda and the public agenda, but we also found that the correlations were *decreasing* over time. We found a substantial correlation between *The New York Times* agenda and the Congressional agenda, and this correlation *increased* over time. We found almost no relationship between the public agenda and the Congressional hearing agenda over time.

As we wrote in the conclusions to this study,

> Generally speaking, the bonding between Congress and the media is stronger than the media's relationship with the public and Congress's

connection with the public ... The findings suggest that the public has the least power in this triangular relationship. Under no circumstances did the public agenda direct Congressional attention. (Tan and Weaver, 2007, pp. 740–1)

Since then, we have done another study of *state-level* agenda setting in 18 US states from 1984 to 2006, and we've found similar patterns – a moderately strong correlation between the agenda of the state's most popular newspaper and the public agenda, a strong correlation between the newspaper agenda and the policy agenda, and a weak correlation between the public agenda and the policy agenda (Tan and Weaver, 2009).

Both studies, then, suggest more newspaper influence, or reinforcement, of the policy agenda than the public agenda, and only a slight correlation between public and policy agendas.

Another study that I worked on with a former doctoral student found that media attention to a particular presidential candidate, and selected attributes of a candidate, influenced the candidate's standing in the polls cumulatively rather than immediately (Son and Weaver, 2006). And a third study found that increased salience of the issue of federal budget deficits was associated with public opinion and behaviour regarding this issue (Weaver, 1991).

All of these studies, as well as many others done in the past 40 years, suggest considerable power on the part of news media to influence, or at least to reinforce, public and policy agendas and even to affect public opinion regarding political candidates and public issues.

Voter learning

Dan Drew and I have also found evidence of *more detailed* learning of candidate issue positions from news coverage in surveys of Indiana residents during the five presidential elections from 1988 to 2004. We found that watching television news and televised presidential debates was associated with more knowledge of the issue positions of the two leading candidates. We also found in 2004 that visiting news websites and paying attention to information about the campaign on the internet was a significant predictor of knowledge of candidate issue positions in that election (Drew and Weaver, 1991; Drew and Weaver, 1998; Drew and Weaver, 2006; Weaver and Drew, 1995; Weaver and Drew, 2001).

Paying attention to news about the presidential campaign in *newspapers* (but no other news medium) was a significant predictor of intention to vote as well as of higher interest in the campaign. The importance of newspapers to political participation was also supported in a 2009 study of the effects of the closing of the *Cincinnati Post* by two Princeton University economists. They found that the next year after the closure on 31 December 2007, fewer candidates ran for municipal office, incumbents became more likely to win re-elections, and voter turnout fell in the suburbs most reliant on the *Post* (Schulhofer-Wohl and Garrido, 2009).

In our studies of voter learning, we also found that paying attention to campaign news on radio, on television, in televised debates, and on the internet was associated with higher levels of interest in a presidential campaign, which is contrary to some studies that have suggested that paying attention to news media causes people to become more cynical and less interested or involved in politics (the so-called 'videomalaise' hypothesis) (Patterson, 1993; Holtz-Bacha, 1990; Mutz and Reeves, 2005).

In short, these studies suggest that the news media *do matter* when it comes to setting public and policy agendas, informing citizens about the issue positions of political candidates, and raising interest in political campaigns. These are only the main findings from a few key studies, but they are similar to those from dozens of other studies that I and others have worked on over the past 40 years.

Why should we care?

Having briefly reviewed the main findings from a few of the studies I have worked on over these years, I want to turn now to the second part of this chapter: why should we care about these research findings regarding journalists, agenda setting, and voter learning?

I think that we should care mainly because these studies suggest that journalists and the news media are important influences not only on the public but also on government policy makers. And they also suggest that the independence of journalism and the ability of journalists to do investigative and analytical reporting are declining.

This should be a concern to anyone who believes that an informed public is vital to the proper functioning of a democratic system of government, and to the solving of serious social, political and economic problems. In many cases, unless journalists and the mainstream news media report about certain problems and issues, they will not receive much attention or resources from the public or policy makers.

There are those who argue that this bad news about US journalism is mainly about newspapers, and newspapers are an old medium that is in decline while the internet is the wave of the future, along with citizen journalists, bloggers and tweeters.

For example, Michael Kinsley, a columnist for the *Washington Post*, wrote in April of 2009 that, 'Few industries in this country have been as coddled as newspapers.' And he added that, 'more people are spending more time reading news and analysis than ever before. They're just doing it online.' He concluded, 'If General Motors goes under, there will still be cars. And if *The New York Times* disappears, there will still be news' (Kinsley, 2009, para 11).

And in March of 2009, Jack Shafer of *Slate*, the online magazine, wrote, 'I can imagine citizens acquiring sufficient information to vote or poke their legislators with pitchforks even if all the newspapers in the country fell into a bottomless recycling bin tomorrow' (Shafer, 2009, para 5).

He cites a Pew Research Center poll released earlier in March 2009 that shows that fewer than half of Americans 'say that losing their local newspaper would hurt civic life in their community "a lot"' (para 7)... 'On those occasions that newspapers do produce the sort of work that the worshippers of democracy crave, only rarely does the population flex its democratic might', Shafer (2009, para 9) writes.

My research on agenda setting, and that of many others as well, suggests that Kinsley and Shafer are missing an important point about the effects of newspaper coverage – namely that newspaper agendas often have more impact on politicians than on the public in general, and also that politicians and policy makers often respond to newspaper coverage as if it *were* an accurate representation of public concerns. In other words, they use newspaper agendas as a shortcut measure of public concerns.

I have not seen much convincing evidence, however, that policy makers respond to blogs or tweets in the same way, or that websites are employing journalists in anything like the numbers that newspapers have over the years.

In addition to the concerns about the number of journalistic jobs being lost, some agenda-setting research, known as intermedia agenda setting, suggests that newspapers are more often than not the agenda setters for other news media, including television, radio and the internet, because newspapers employ more journalists than any other medium, because they have had more resources to devote to news-gathering, and also because they are more respected and trusted than some of the other news media. In other words, they have more credible 'brands' or names compared to some newer media (McCombs, 2004; Weaver et al., 2004).

So research suggests that the loss of newspapers is *not* just about the loss of one method of delivering news, or even the loss of jobs for journalists, as important as that is. It is also about the loss of *influence* on politics and policy makers as well as on the public and on other news media.

I do not see any new journalistic medium waiting in the wings that has this kind of influence or the kind of resources to challenge the powerful institutions of government that can tax and jail citizens and wage wars. I doubt that the internet presently has this ability to challenge the most powerful institutions in our society.

As Donald Shaw would say, newspapers and television news are 'vertical' media, designed to reach the general public with general information, whereas most magazines and websites are 'horizontal' media designed to reach only certain segments of society (Shaw et al., 2006). Whereas newspapers historically have been aimed at entire geographic communities, magazines and many websites are designed to reach people with certain specific interests regardless of where they live.

Thus these 'horizontal' media tend to fragment geographic communities rather than unite them, but politics and political power are still based largely on geographic communities and boundaries, and the horizontal media based on interests rather than location do not have the kind of political influence that more 'vertical' media, mainly newspapers, have had.

Conclusions

What can be done to save influential news organizations and high-quality journalism?

There have been a number of different proposals in recent years, including making newspapers nonprofit organizations, asking foundations to fund investigative teams and foreign bureaux, requiring that websites that aggregate or use the news from other websites be made to pay for this news, and requiring that readers of news websites should have to pay a fee, as is the case with our own local newspaper in Bloomington, Indiana, *The Wall Street Journal* and now *The New York Times* (Kosterlitz, 2008; Perez-Pena, 2008; Perez-Pena and Arango, 2009).

So far, none of these proposed remedies has proven very effective, but some combination of them may in the future. For now, I think we should be concerned that the medium that has traditionally been the source of most of the news we get online, on air, and on paper is in serious financial trouble. My research, and that of many others over the years, has suggested that journalists, who have been employed mostly by newspapers, are important to a democratic system of government, and that news matters to policy makers as well as to the public.

We need to find a way to keep paying journalists to keep reporting on what our local, state, and national governments are doing, as well as to keep monitoring increasingly powerful corporations who can afford to spend great amounts on messages that promote their own often narrow interests.

Although my own research has focused mostly on who journalists are, what they think, and what they do, as well as on the effects of their work, I think that more research needs to be done in the future on the economics of journalism, including the development of new models for funding high-quality journalism. If not, I fear we are in increasing danger of not knowing what we do not know, in spite of the vast information resources of the internet.

One seemingly positive development in the United States is the rise of web-based news operations that do investigative reporting, such as VoiceofSanDiego.org, MinnPost in Minneapolis, Crosscut.com in Seattle, Chi-Town Daily News in Chicago, Gotham Gazette in New York City, St. Louis Beacon, and ProPublica, a nonprofit investigative reporting centre in New York City. Although these ventures are encouraging and seem to be doing worthwhile investigative reporting for much less than the cost of publishing a comparable printed newspaper, online advertising alone does not seem to be able to sustain a newsroom of any size. As Robert Giles, curator of the Neiman Foundation for Journalism at Harvard University, said in a *New York Times* article in 2008, nonprofit news online 'has to be explored and experimented with, but it has to overcome the hurdle of proving it can support a big news staff. Even the best-funded of these sites are a far cry in resources from a city newspaper' (Quoted in Perez-Pena, 2008, p. A1).

Some of those who are involved in these news sites agree with Giles about this, such as Andrew Donohue, one of two executive editors at VoiceofSanDiego, who is quoted as saying, 'We can't be the main news source for this city, not for the foreseeable future. We only have 11 people' (Perez-Pena, 2008, p. A1). Even one of the best-funded news websites, MinnPost, which has a $1.5 million start-up fund and a $1.3 million annual budget, is concerned about enough revenue to achieve self-sufficiency. Its founder and chief executive, Joel Kramer, former editor and publisher of The Minneapolis *Star-Tribune*, was quoted in the *National Journal* magazine in November 2008 as saying, 'It's hard to get enough ad revenues to sustain high-quality journalism' and 'it's impossible to charge for subscriptions.' 'The market has spoken: People do not want to pay for news' (Kosterlitz, 2008).

So, it is still not clear how high-quality journalism of the future will be paid for and whether the nonprofit news sites, funded by foundations and donations, will have sufficient long-term funding to be viable journalistic institutions of the future. Whatever happens, it seems that high-quality journalism is too important to democratic forms of government to let it wither away.

As Jay Blumler and Michael Gurevitch (1995, p. 97) have argued, democracy requires that the media provide a number of services for the political system, including surveillance of the sociopolitical environment, meaningful agenda setting, platforms for intelligible advocacy by politicians and others, dialogue across a diverse range of views, mechanisms for holding officials accountable, incentives for citizens to learn and become involved in the political process, a principled resistance to forces outside the media to subvert their independence and integrity in serving audiences, and a sense of respect for the audience. Some of these points have been echoed by Bill Kovach and Tom Rosenstiel (2001, p. 193) who call for 'a journalism of sense making based on synthesis, verification, and fierce independence' that is not 'subsumed inside the world of commercialized speech'. Past research suggests that such journalism is a necessary condition for democratic systems of government to function properly, and that its continued existence is in jeopardy in these uncertain times. Future research should focus on how to make quality journalism economically viable.

9

Democratic Political Communication Systems and the Transformative Power of Scandals: Phone Hacking at the *News of the World* as a Critical Juncture in the Regulation of the British Press

James Stanyer

On 4 July 2011, an ongoing British police investigation into the hacking of phones of prominent celebrities and politicians by the press revealed that a Sunday tabloid newspaper, the *News of the World*, had illegally accessed the voicemail on the mobile phone of a murdered London school girl, Milly Dowler. In the following days, public outrage grew as more revelations emerged that journalists at the *News of the World* had been listening to the voice messages of other members of the public, including the parents of missing child Madeleine McCann, the parents of murdered Soham school girls Holly Wells and Jessica Chapman, and some of the victims of the 7/7 bombings in London. The resulting opprobrium not only led Rupert Murdoch to close the *News of the World,* but also to the announcement of an inquiry into 'the culture, practices and the ethics of the British Press' led by Lord Justice Leveson. The inquiry lasted over a year, reporting in November 2012 with a range of significant recommendations for regulatory oversight of the press, which are currently in the process of being implemented.

Over recent years, there has been some interest in the power of public scandals to bring about reform of public institutions and practices. These studies have shown how scandals in the world of politics, finance and law and order, to name a few areas, have acted as a catalyst for reform, changing institutional behaviour, initiating regulatory over-sight and improving actor performance (Agrawal and Chadha, 2005; Sherman, 1978). However, in political communication and media studies, while there has been an increased interest in political scandals and their coverage in the media, the power of scandals to reform media organizations and professionals' behaviour and that of political communication systems more generally has been rather overlooked. Indeed, research that has examined media policy formation has tended to be incrementalist, focusing on government's response to technological, economic, political and social developments over time rather than to a specific event such as a scandal (see for example Van Cuilenburg and McQuail, 2003). This chapter focuses on scandals as points in time with the potential to affect political communication systems or subsystems, in particular, to bring about regulatory oversight which has the poten-tial to benefit democracy. In this sense, it situates the power of scandal within a wider framework of evolving political communication systems and the consequences of system *change* for democracy.

One of the many significant contributions of Jay Blumler and his colleague Michael Gurevitch to political communication research was the introduction of a systems perspective (1977). The evolution of polit-ical communication systems has been a recurrent theme of their work (see Blumler and Gurevitch, 2005, for example), as has the concern about the potential of developments to 'undermine the capacity' of the system to serve democracy (see Gurevitch and Blumler, 1990b). Their work has identified a range of system constraints which make necessary reforms difficult. This chapter argues that scandals and the subsequent reactions by the public may in certain instances overcome these constraints and lead to reforms which can change the behaviour of system actors or even alter the rules of the game by improving the ability of the system to serve democracy. It focuses specifically on the *News of the World* phone hacking scandal in 2011, and how this is leading to greater regulation of the British Press (this process was still very much ongoing at the time of writing). It examines the response of the government to the scandal and the pressures for reform of an almost unregulated tabloid press – for so long a section of the national media uninterested in serving democracy. The chapter starts by defining scandal and examining its transforma-tive power. It then looks at a history of the transgression of journal-istic ethical standards by the tabloid press in Britain and the response of the authorities to these scandals. It goes on to examine the hacking scandal and the policy recommendations of the Leveson Inquiry and the response of the newspaper industry. It concludes by looking at scandals as important examples of critical junctures (or critical moments, see Stanyer, 2013) in political communication systems, when constraints are overcome and a new regulatory regime can emerge that may improve media performance.

Scandal and concerns about press standards

Before exploring the impact of scandal on press regulation, it is worth briefly examining what is commonly meant by scandal. A scandal in simple terms is the exposure of 'transgressions (or alleged transgressions) of certain values, norms or moral codes' (Thompson, 2000, p. 62). Contemporary political scandals are more than mere revelations, though; they are media events, unfolding in the 24-hour news environment as information seeps into the public domain (Thompson, 2000).

So what about the impact of scandals in terms of bringing about regulatory reform? This is an area than has been less fully explored, but it should be said from the start that not all scandals bring about change. The scandals that have influence are those that can be described as major scandals. These have certain features in common. They tend to involve significant political figures, like a president or a prime minister, or involve widespread malfeasance by those in public life. The nature of the transgression or transgressions is seen as so serious as to trigger an investigation and prosecutions and provoke widespread public opprobrium and pressure for reform. This is not to say that all major scandals start out as such; some start off as small incidents and snowball into major national controversies over a long period of time. The public mood in particular is a key ingredient. Public disapprobation, amplified through the media and public opinion shown in a series of polls, places pressure on government to tighten existing rules or to introduce new laws to prevent such transgressions happening in future. With major scandals those in authority seem compelled to react and to be seen reacting to the outrage which is generated by the revelations of norm transgressions in the media. This response can be seen in relation to some recent political scandals. For example, British newspaper exposure of MPs' receipt of payments to ask questions in the House of Commons in 1994, the so-called cash-for-questions affair, prompted public opprobrium and the establishment of a committee of enquiry into standards in public life. The Nolan Committee made a series of recommendations which were enacted, including greater oversight by a parliamentary commissioner for standards, a code of conduct, and a register of members' interests (Thompson, 2000). Of course, authorities might be compelled to react to scandals on similar issues time and time again. For example, the early 20th century saw a series of laws introduced to eradicate corruption amongst politicians, and there have been more recent scandals around MPs' expenses (Thompson, 2000). The transgression of moral standards by politicians continues to be an issue which triggers outrage and regulatory reform in Britain and many other democracies (for examples from Italy, Japan and the US, see Donovan, 1995; Shiratori, 1995; Thompson, 2000). These examples from politics show major scandals have the power to transform institutional practice and individual behaviour for the better.

Press reform and resistance

Concerns about newspaper standards have a long history. For example, the 17th century playwright Ben Jonson attacked the rapidly expanding news culture of the day, comparing the false information it provided with the truth of poetry (Williams, 2010, p. 10). Those concerns have continued, from the late 19th century onwards, becoming focused on the 'muckraking journalism' of the mass circulation popular press. The behaviour of the tabloid press and its salacious reporting has produced regular calls for reform. However, these calls have been counteracted by a strong reluctance on behalf of governments to regulate, in part the result of the entrenchment of liberal theories of press freedom. Bingham (2007) argues that 'liberal theories of press freedom remained powerful in British political culture and peacetime governments were generally reluctant to encroach on the privileges of the fourth estate' (p. 81). These ideals also need to be considered alongside a pragmatic realization of the importance of the electoral support of the press and a fear that regulation might undermine this. Between the 1860s and the end of the so-called taxes on knowledge and the setting up of the First Royal Commission on the Press in 1947, the press was free of any regulation (O'Malley and Soley, 2000). Indeed, the First Royal Commission was set up by government under pressure from a range of actors, including politicians, unions and other civil society groups, to reform press standards (ibid.). Despite the calls for statutory regulation, government did not legislate, and the First Royal Commission led instead to the formation of a voluntary press tribunal, the Press Council (ibid.). By the early 1960s, concerns about press standards surfaced once more, provoked by privacy intrusion and inaccurate reporting (ibid.). Again there was criticism that the industry had not embraced the spirit of the original recommendations of the First Royal Commission. A Second Royal Commission was set up in 1961 to examine the performance of the Press Council. The outcome was a series of recommendations to beef up the council. Similar complaints through the 1960s and 1970s led to a Third Royal Commission of the Press to examine the whole system of self-regulation. Its recommendations for further reform, published in 1979, were also ignored (ibid.).

Efforts to strengthen self-regulation were made in 1990 after a decade which saw continued intrusion and sensationalist reporting by the tabloid press. The growing disquiet with the tabloids prompted a series of Private Members Bills aimed at protecting the public from press intrusion, and although none were successful, the government of the day once again felt pressure 'to be tough on the press' (Bingham, 2007, p. 80). The need to act was made all the more important in February 1990 when journalists of the *Sunday Sport* gained unauthorized access to British actor Gordon Kaye as he lay in hospital intensive care. Kaye's subsequent attempt to sue the newspaper failed as there was no law preventing intrusion of privacy. In 1990, the Thatcher government appointed David Calcutt QC to chair a committee to look into privacy and related matters. One of the key recommendations of the Calcutt Committee was to further strengthen self-regulation by replacing the Press Council with a new Press Complaints Commission (PCC), an 'authoritative, independent and impartial' body which 'should publish, monitor and implement a comprehensive code of practice' (ibid., p. 82). Although Calcutt argued for statutory regulation if the PCC did not work, the government of the day was in no mood to introduce statutory reform. It was extremely reluctant to depart from the self-regulatory regime given its political fragility (ibid., 2007, p. 82). The PCC began in 1991, and whilst initially not proactive and dominated by the newspaper industry, by the mid-1990s, the self-regulatory regime had evolved. Lay members were in the majority, its code of editorial conduct had been updated, introducing new clauses on bugging and long lens photography, and it had instituted a helpline in response to the death of Princess Diana (ibid.). However, complaints about tabloid press reporting continued. This is not to say that the PCC was without its critics, but there was no impetus for further reform of the press by the Blair or Brown governments. In sum, over the postwar period there have been continued attempts to find ways to develop a regulatory system that could ensure high journalistic ethical standards. However, these attempts have been met by strong opposition from within government, parliament and the newspaper industry, and those demanding reform have been unable to overcome this. There were plenty of transgressions but only small incremental changes in response to demands for fundamental reform. There was no profound change and nothing seemed on the cards until the phone hacking scandal broke in July 2011.

Phone hacking at News of the World

The phone hacking scandal put press regulation back on the political agenda. The sheer scale of the transgression of ethical norms involving the tabloid press was much greater than before. The scandal developed over a five-year period, starting with the arrest and jailing of the *News of the World*'s royal editor and a private investigator for hacking into the mobile phone messages of members of the royal family in 2007. Despite claims that such practices were widespread, this was denied, and initial investigations by the police and the PCC failed to find any evidence to the contrary. The claims continued, prompted by revelations of damages being paid to celebrities by News Group Newspapers (the parent company of the *News of the World*), and by investigations by the *Guardian* and the *New York Times* and the House of Commons Culture, Media and Sports Committee. The police investigation, however, was not reopened until January 2011. 'Operation Weeting' identified 6,439 possible victims, 829 who had actually had their phones hacked (BBC, 2012) including family members of high profile victims of crime. This caused particular public disgust and triggered widespread public concern about tabloid press behaviour. A YouGov poll commissioned by the *Sunday Times* in the immediate aftermath of the initial revelations, in July 2011, indicates the level of public concern. It found that 78% of respondents thought the tabloid press was 'out of control'; 86% thought there should be a public inquiry into phone hacking; and 61% felt that the PCC should be replaced by a formal authority to regulate the press (YouGov, 2011). Indeed, the police's seeming reluctance to reopen the investigation further fuelled public outrage.

The government was unable to ignore the anger and demands for change. In response, David Cameron expressed his disgust and announced a two-part inquiry under Lord Justice Leveson. The focus of part one of this inquiry was 'the culture, practices and ethics of the press', and the committee's main aim was to produce recommendations for improved press regulation to encourage the highest ethical standards (see www.levesoninquiry.org.uk). The Leveson Committee lasted over a year, took evidence from 650 witnesses and was highly visible, becoming a news event, with highlights of the hearings regularly making the early evening news bulletins (Greenslade, 2012). It exposed the practices of tabloid newspapers in shocking detail. The phone hacking scandal (and the following inquiry) represents a significant moment of change. The barriers to significant regulatory reform of the press have been weakened.

The arguments put forward by those who resisted press oversight have seemed hollow when set against evidence of widespread malfeasance at *News of the World* and the wider tabloid press. The next section explores the recommendations of the Leveson Committee and the response of the industry and government.

The tightening of press regulation: the recommendations and responses

The report, released late November 2012, criticized the press, particularly the tabloid press, for turning a blind eye to widespread phone hacking even though it was illegal; recklessly 'prioritising sensational stories, almost irrespective of the harm that the stories may cause and the rights of those who would be affected'; deploying 'surveillance, blagging and deception in circumstances where it is extremely difficult to see any public interest justification'; 'the publication of private information without consent and, again, without discernible legitimate public interest'; and having a 'significant and reckless disregard for accuracy' (Leveson, 2012, pp. 9–11). The report made a series of recommendations, the key one being the formation of a new regulatory system for the press overseen by a body of appointed members independent of the newspaper industry, parliament and government. The report stated that this body would develop a new standards code which would cover press conduct, privacy matters and reporting accuracy, and would oversee the regulatory scheme (ibid.). The new board will hear and decide on complaints if no agreement has been reached, but in the first instance, complaints about breaches of the standards code are expected to be handled effectively by the press, each newspaper having robust complaints procedures (ibid.). Unlike the PCC, the new body would have the power to take a series of steps to ensure that appropriate measures are taken in response to a breach of the code, including demanding apologies and imposing fines of up to £1m (ibid.). Further, there would also be an arbitral process as an alternative to the courts, providing affordable and quick justice. The new regulatory scheme would be an opt-in, open to all. It would be underpinned by statute, and the press would be offered incentives to join, with certain advantages for those who did, such as a set limit on the amount of damages that could be paid in comparison to the courts. The press regulator would be overseen by Ofcom, which would conduct regular reviews. These reforms, the report argues, are necessary to provide a 'recognized brand of trusted journalism' (ibid.).

David Cameron's response to the recommendations was widely interpreted as a rejection of the proposals; indeed, his reaction provoked anger from those campaigning for statutory press regulation. However, Cameron did not rule out statutory regulation; he merely gave the press a 'limited' period in which to find a way to implement the scheme proposed by Leveson, without the government resorting to such regulation, as he noted in his speech in the Commons: 'While no one wants to see full statutory regulation, let me stress: the status quo is not an option' (*The Guardian*, 2012). Although the prime minister did not accept some of the proposals, his Liberal Democrat deputy prime minister, Nick Clegg, was convinced by Leveson's plan, as was the opposition Labour Party. In March 2013, parliament voted for a royal charter on press self-regulation, the first step in implementing Leveson's recommendations. The impetus for change has been reinforced by an ongoing campaign by victims of press intrusion. Even though the press has largely been opposed to the Leveson recommendations and has mounted a vehement campaign against the report and its implementation, there is clearly no going back to the PCC or even weaker industry-led oversight. While a majority of newspapers have rejected the idea of being subject to a charter-compliant self-regulator, they have put forward plans for an alternative regulatory body more powerful than the PCC. I would argue these disagreements are about the detail of self-regulation post-Leveson rather than a dismissal of the principle of much tighter self-regulation. The previous commissions and reviews in response to transgressions of press standards had some, albeit limited, impact, but the scale of, and response to, the phone hacking scandal has been such that it might overcome vested interests and their defence of the status quo in a way previous scandals could not.

In sum, over the years, exposure of the tabloid's transgressions of journalistic norms of privacy and accuracy has generated calls for reform. Attempts to introduce significant change have been thwarted in part by powerful vested interests and by the entrenchment of liberal theories of press freedom amongst the political elite; the outcome has been a widely criticized system of weak self-regulation. What took place over the postwar period were small incremental steps to drive up standards prompted by the publicized excesses of the tabloid press, but attempts to make bigger alterations failed. However, the phone hacking scandal has transformed the regulation of press standards in a more significant way. The next section reflects on what this case study means for theorizing regulatory reforms of democratic political communication systems and subsystems.

Political communication systems, media performance and scandal: a long-term picture

Claims that the popular tabloid press fail to serve the wider goals of the British political communication system are not surprising. The tabloid press has had little regard for the health of the body politic. Instead of living up to democratic ideals, it loudly vocalizes its right to publish salacious gossip and argues that invasions of individual privacy are necessary in pursuit of the public interest. All too often, though, tabloid newspapers' claims to be operating in the public interest are nothing more than a cover for catering to the prurient interests of their readers. However, despite deep concerns about the transgressions of journalistic ethical standards, attempts to provide regulatory oversight have been fiercely resisted. Indeed, some of the key players within the system have fought any attempt to regulate such excesses despite concerted pressure. Previous attempts at reform have led to compromise and a highly criticized system of weak self-regulation. This chapter has argued that the phone hacking scandal has fundamentally undermined the positions and arguments of those actors who have sought to maintain the status quo. Faced with overwhelming evidence of malfeasance, they have found it more difficult to argue that things should remain the same or that only the smallest of changes should be made. Those seeking reform have never had a more favourable reception from government or more support from the public. The victims of press intrusion, including members of the public and celebrities, have also been effective at making the rational and emotional case for reform and keeping the pressure on government. The hacking scandal may lead to a regulatory environment with greater oversight of press standards than at any time in the past 150 years. The tabloid press may finally be held accountable for their performance in a way they have not before.

What does this small case study mean for understanding regulatory reform of democratic political communication systems? While scandal might have negative connotations, major scandals can have a positive regulatory impact. They can shake established regulatory order, overcoming the resistance of vested interests and improving the performance of the media. Major scandals, such as the one examined in this chapter, can be seen as important moments or critical junctures which can open political communication systems or subsystems to regulatory change. Critical junctures are 'trigger events that set processes of institutional or policy change, in motion' (Hogan and Doyle, 2007, p. 885). The notion of critical junctures has not received the attention in political communication research that it has in other fields. There are exceptions: see, for example, McChesney (2007) and Pickard (2011) who look at critical junctures in the context of US media policy. Major scandals like phone hacking at the *News of the World* can be considered a critical juncture or what Jones and Baumgartner (2012) call a punctuation of the existing policy equilibrium (the policy status quo). Their punctuated equilibrium thesis (PET) is a way of understanding scandal and policy change that is particularly pertinent. Although developed in the specific context of US politics, Jones and Baumgartner's thesis can be easily grafted on to the existing idea of dynamic evolving political communication systems put forward by Blumler and Gurevitch (2005). In any system or subsystem, new policy results from both incremental adjustments by policy makers to changes in the environment and from 'non-incremental, punctuated change' when demands for change overwhelm a subsystem (Jones and Baumgartner, 2012, p. 4). Non-incremental punctuated change can bring about quite significant transformation in a relatively short time. They suggest policy making in democracies is characterized by a stick-slip dynamic. Policy in a particular subsystem may remain relatively unchanged, or change only in small increments, in part due to the constraints that prevent adjustment, but it can also change in a short, significant burst. They use the metaphor of the earth's tectonic plates 'which are held in place by a retarding force' – 'the friction of the plates' – while the 'dynamic processes generated by the activities in the earth's core' push those same plates. At some point, when 'the forces acting on the plates are strong enough, the plates release, and rather than slide incrementally...slip violently, resulting in an earthquake' (ibid., p. 8). They observe systems 'remain stable until signals from outside exceed a threshold, and then they lurch forward' (ibid., p. 8). Although they do not say it, major scandals can act as a point of policy punctuation where the forces retarding change are overcome by overwhelming force. In this sense, PET provides not only a means of understanding the *News of the World* scandal and attempts to regulate press standards in its wake, but also a way to help us theorize the potential positive regulatory impact of major scandals on political communication systems and subsystems in advanced industrial democracies.

10
Morals and Methods: A Note on the Value of Survey Research

David E. Morrison

Nicholas Jankowski and Fred Wester, in their overview of qualitative research and its contribution to mass communications research, note that during the last years of the 19th century and the first decades of the 20th century 'as social issues became topics of academic study, virtually all research was of a qualitative nature' (1991, p. 46). Indeed, Paul Lazarsfeld, the seminal figure in the development of academic survey research, saw fit to remind that Weber was 'periodically enthusiastic about quantification making many computations himself' and that Tönnies invented 'a correlation coefficient of his own' before adding that it was nevertheless the case that before 1933, empirical research had failed to acquire sufficient prestige to find a home in European universities (Lazarsfeld, 1972, p. 328). True, the development of modern empirical techniques is of European origin. Sampling techniques derived from Booth's massive London surveys and factor analysis from the Englishman Charles Spearman, while family research emphasizing quantification owes itself to the Frenchman Frederic Le Play. Gabriel Tarde stressed the necessity of attitude measurement along with communications research, and earlier, during the French Revolution, the notion of applying mathematical models to voting was carefully worked out by the Marquis de Condorcet. His contemporaries, Pierre La Place and Antoine Lavoisier, both undertook social surveys for the revolutionary government. Yet, as noted, Europe failed to develop a critical mass of social researchers to provide a reciprocal reference group sufficient to gain recognition and support by universities.

Even though the basics of empirical social research techniques may have been a European development, the actual formal development of university based empirical social research is of American origin. The University of Chicago, founded in 1890, was conceived as a research university. The Department of Sociology, established in 1892 under the leadership of Albion Small, was the first in the world, and the joining of Robert Park to the department in 1913 and then Ernest Burgess in 1916 saw the city of Chicago transformed into a social laboratory. Chicago sociology grew out of, and addressed, the problems of city life there – immigration, poverty, the flophouses and slums, along with the marginal characters that inhabited the city (Shils, 1970). Chicago sociology, which dominated the field until the 1940s, was undoubtedly moral in the manner in which the plight of the individual was central to its operation, and in the manner in which the individual featured as a 'voice' in the research.

As famous as Chicago sociology became for its fieldwork and case studies, even by the 1930s it could not escape the debates between the quantitative and qualitative proponents of sociology that were afflicting the rest of the social research community. Indeed, the encroachment of quantification upon the hitherto dominance of qualitative thinking saw the establishment of a separate division within sociology. Nationally, the victor in the methodological struggle was that of quantification. Indeed, 'the Chicago case study had all but disappeared as a mode of social science by the 1950's. Survey research had become the method of the social science' (Jankowski and Wester, 1991, p. 48). In short, the audience began to become the statistical audience.

Methods and morals

Methods, or the language of research, to use Lazarsfeld's phrase, crucially form the nature of the conversation possible between researcher and the audience. At the methodological level, then, it is reasonable to say, as David Morgan does, that 'anything that a technique does notably well is done, at least partially, at the expense of other things that can only be done poorly' (1988, p. 20). It is immature, therefore, to consider one method superior to another without reference to its object of study. The rise of surveys as a predominant method of the social sciences is not, therefore, to imbue it with special qualities or attributes, but to recognize the sense in which it has played a particular part in making sense of the social world.

What survey research did, or rather the application of sampling to survey research did, was to allow conversation with large populations. At its furthest reaches, it opened the possibility of talking to an entire nation. However, the eclipse of Chicago sociology, with its emphasis on field studies, by that of Columbia University, with its emphasis on survey research, was not simply the result of an intellectual fight over the nature of knowledge, but a shift in appreciation of knowledge and how it was to be defined by business, government and social agencies. Whilst the features of Chicago – its slums, influx of migrants and so on – had not entirely vanished by the 1940s, nevertheless, shifts in American society had made urban life more ordered. As a result, the issues addressed by Chicago sociology were no longer as pressing as they had been. At the same time, New York became the centre of the emerging communications industry, advertising industries, and national marketing companies. Thus, rather than questions of local community problems capable of address by ethnographic methods typified by Chicago, national level research problems such as the effects of mass media came to the fore, which called for methods capable of generalization to populations as a whole: that is, survey research. Columbia University in New York was perfectly situated for Lazarsfeld, as director of the Bureau of Applied Social Research attached to Columbia, to exploit the funding possibilities offered by this situation. Columbia came to dominate American sociology and by extension sociology itself, especially due to its training of researchers.

Given the space available, this is not the place to examine in any detail the intricacies of Lazarsfeld's survey research and methods, nor the criticism against Columbia sociology as being one-sided and restrictive, or the scathing attack by C. Wright Mills (1959) for its abstracted empiricism. Indeed, to raise the latter is to misunderstand Lazarsfeld's survey work; his perfection of polling methods was precisely to rid them, by way of contextual analysis, of their atomistic and individual character. As Raymond Boudon (1972, p. 425) rightly notes: 'The respondent is defined not only by a number of individual characteristics (age, sex, opinion on various questions, educational level, occupation, etc.) but by the variables from which he comes'. The intention was to lose the atomistic character often promoted by opinion polls (see Herbert Blumer's 1948 attack on opinion polls) to 'regain the macro sociological tradition typical of Durkheim' (ibid.). Lazarsfeld's interest was in methodology, not people. The substantive nature of a study was always of secondary interest to him.

What must be stressed is that I am not examining the moral qualities of the individual or individuals conducting types of research, but rather the nature of the concerns upon which the research rests or is driven. Of consideration here must be whether the coming to dominance of a method acts as an overseer of moral concerns. In this case, whether or not survey research, the technical aspect of performance, removes, so to speak, the individual audience member as a moral actor as he or she is transformed into a statistical finding. As noted in discussing contextual analysis, survey research does not intrinsically mean the abstracting of the individual from the social context of their living: only to say that the method, as often used in audience research, views the individual as a respondent rather than an actor, to even become at times, as in the case of the application of factor analysis, the product of the statistical technique.

The survey method does not of itself swamp the moral by the technical need to 'force answers' or do so by removing him or her from the experiential setting of their everyday life. Apart from covert participant observation, then, no method in the social science is natural in the sense of not interfering with, or disturbing, that which is being studied, and that is so for focus group research favoured by qualitative researchers studying the audience. Focus group research, whilst capable of providing the range of opinions in the population, cannot give the distribution of those opinions. For that, survey research is required. Survey research, however, grows out of appreciation for a type of knowledge considered necessary for particular administrations or social organizations.

The organization of thought

Survey research methodology grows out of administrative thinking, the rationality associated with advanced industrial societies and the bureaucratic management of resources. The type of responses demanded by questionnaires may make little sense to cultural groups not affected by industrialization. Oral cultures, where a high emphasis is placed on storytelling and the non-literal expression of meaning, would find it perplexing to answer in pre-fixed categories of response. To complete a questionnaire is to be part of the logic from which that questionnaire comes; indeed, one has to be locked into the grammar of the rationality so that thoughts can be organized in a way demanded by the questionnaire. In other words, the respondent must be able to summarize experience in an arithmetic or quantifiable manner. The use of scaling in survey research only makes sense if one can think in terms of scales: that is, separating out thoughts and allocating strength to the parts that have been separated. In survey research, one is being asked to compartmentalize experience for the sake of quantification, but with the recognition that such compartmentalization is not an unfamiliar process for the respondent. The ability to be able to do this occurs because the administrative form of thinking which permeates survey research rests on structures of thought that are an integral part of the structure of modern advanced industrial society.

The administrative and the moral: the text and the survey

It was Lazarsfeld who coined the term 'administrative research' and not, as often assumed, Theodor Adorno in response to his shock of being confronted with 'a practical orientated kind of science' whilst working for Lazarsfeld (Adorno, 1969, p. 343). Adorno was concerned about what he considered to be the reified methods of American empirical sociology. For him, the statistical average of respondents' opinion remained, despite the seeming objectivity of the data, at the level of subjectivity (ibid., p. 347). However, such criticism of American empirical methods (Morrison, 1998, chapter 3) did not stop him moving from New York to Berkeley to produce, through elaborate scaling techniques, the huge 'Authoritarian Personality' study, but the question so far as this paper is concerned is whether survey methods as applied in audience research, and which owe their development to an administrative setting, entail the loss of the moral. Was there in the pursuit by the industry to know its audience a loss of the moral in the sense of how the individual came to be viewed: the transforming of the individual to that of a respondent, the aggregate of which became the audience? In other words, was the individual as individual lost to sight in the search for a type of knowledge useful to the industry and government agencies, and which then, especially in the effects tradition, came to frame much of audience research?

In terms of the individual as a moral actor I would argue that much audience research did, and still does, lose sight of the individual as a moral actor. On the whole, empirical investigation of the audience carried the seeds of moral disassembly wherein the individual had little say in the presentation of their experience. It is here that a link with Blumler's research on the understanding of audiences, and his wish to give voice to them as moral agents, can be made. Hynek Jeřábek, in an insightful article on the collaboration between Lazarsfeld and Robert Merton, draws attention to one of the 'fire-house projects' (2012, p. 7) conceived by Lazarsfeld and undertaken by Merton – namely, a study into the buying of war bonds in September of 1943 as a result of a series of radio programmes by the popular radio star Kate Smith (see Merton et al., 1946). Jeřábek observes that by 'identifying one of the main reasons why people bought war bonds (people's search for sincerity) Merton introduced and laid out an interpretive model' for understanding the audience – a model, he adds, which '23 years later was used by Jay G. Blumler and Denis McQuail in their television research' (Jeřábek, 2012, p. 9; Blumler and McQuail, 1968).

The connection between Merton and Blumler, as identified by Jeřábek, is not misplaced, especially in consideration of the individual as a moral actor. The insistence is on understanding the audience as people with experiences that, although sociologically patterned, nevertheless provide an identity that is not to be subsumed under, or operationalised by, the notion of a collective whole. Blumler, for example, writes in defence of a 'uses approach' to understanding the audience that 'uses and gratifications authors have always been strongly opposed to "mass-audience" terminology as a way of labelling the collectivities that watch television shows, attend movies and read magazines and newspapers in their millions' (1979, p. 21). Earlier in the same paper, in reflecting on traditions of research, he makes his position quite clear concerning his approach to audience studies:

> The uses and gratifications approach came most prominently to the fore in the late 1950s and early 1960s at a time of widespread disappointment with the fruits of attempts to measure the short-term effects on people of their exposure to mass media campaigns. It reflected a desire to understand audience involvement in mass communications in terms more faithful to the individual user's own experiences and perspectives than the effects tradition could attain. It sought to replace the image of the audience member as a passive victim, thought to be implicit in effect studies, with one of a person who could actively bend programmes, articles, films and songs to his own purposes. (Ibid., p. 10)

The above offers very clear insight into Blumler's methodological frame for understanding the audience. Behind the methodological frame, however, stands a moral outlook that locks his work, and this of course includes his survey research, into a humanistic tradition of social enquiry. He mentions that in the period under discussion 'functionalism lost its charm' to the point where uses and gratification researchers 'could no longer situate their work within a comprehensive Weltanschauung' (ibid., p. 11). However, such a loss of anchorage, as far as Blumler is concerned, was no ground for castigating the uses and gratification approach for any lack of theorizing. As he says: 'Is the lack of this form of grand theory all that deplorable?' He answers his own question, and in doing so provides entry into, if not exactly moral thought, then a political positioning that carries with it a commitment to a set of democratic values. He writes:

> After all, it is the distinctive mission of uses and gratifications research to get to grips with the nature of the audience itself, which is ever in danger of being ignored by (a) elitists who cannot partake of it and (b) grand theoreticians who believe they understand the significance of such experiences better than the poor benighted receivers themselves. (ibid., p. 12)

The above displays an irritation that is political, but nevertheless stands as a methodological reminder that without entering the world of the viewer, listener, or reader, one cannot capture the meaning of communications for people. To approach the empirical audience as mere receiver of information, of something that is acted upon, has already been dismissed, but in the above, so is any approach to the audience by cultural analysis that removes people from actively exploring the meanings of communicative material. To this end, Blumler singles out Herta Herzog's (1941) work on radio soap opera listening, which first appeared in the Frankfurt School's journal, *Studies in Philosophy and Social Science*, in the last issue before its demise, as an example of early gratifications research that involved both text and the meaning audiences extracted from the text as result of social position and structural location. Although appropriate to claim such work as an early approach to the audience using a uses and gratifications frame, it is perhaps even more appropriate to see it as an example of critical theory, and therefore fitting that it first appeared in the Frankfurt School's journal. It is a piercing critique of a society which saw the women fans, due to their structural location and status, 'borrow' from storylines in the soap operas to address the situations and problems that they faced in their everyday lives. However, as much as cultural studies scholars may wish to point to Herzog's work as one of confronting the empirical audience, they should not look to Adorno's work, also produced in the same volume of the journal, to say much, indeed if anything at all, about the audience.

The answer is not in the text

Lazarsfeld always blamed himself for Adorno's failure to produce anything on audience reception of music, for which Lazarsfeld had employed him, believing that he should have supported him more in an effort to marry critical theory to empirical social research (Lazarsfeld, 1969, p. 325). He is unduly unkind on himself (Morrison, 1978). Adorno personified the traits noted by Blumler at points A and B in his above defence of uses and gratifications. Adorno was preposterously elitist. Secondly, he considered that he knew the significance of the musical experience had by the audience better than the audience itself did. In part, this is due to Adorno's elitism, but it is also a product of singular dependence on textual analysis and theoretical reasoning flowing from such analysis. Adorno's writing on the place and reception of music are perfect examples of how textual analysis operates as a substitute for empirical examination of actual functioning (Adorno, 1941a; 1941b; 1945).

The problem of going from text to audience without including the audience directly is not something that remains the domain of cultural theory, media studies or even aesthetics, but in a hidden way surfaces in one of the historically main strands of communication research, namely content analysis. One can say nothing from content analysis about the audience, only that which is on offer to people. Yet, failure to project, or imagine, what the content might mean for an audience robs the findings of their full power; hence, and in similar fashion to focus groups research and the projection of findings onto populations as a whole, it is invariable that a connection between content and audience reception will be made. To speak on behalf of the audience in such a way is not only methodologically unsound, but morally cruel, in that it assumes a knowledge of the audience without ever bothering to understand those that are spoken about.

A moral ending

It is worth noting, by way of conclusion, that practically all those involved in the early days of the founding of social research addressed not simply the problems associated with rapid social and economic change in a technical sense, but the moral consequences for those experiencing the transformation in living. The work of Weber on rationalization, for example, Tönnies on community, Simmel on the metropolis, Durkheim's concern with social solidarity and anomie, and, somewhat earlier, Marx on alienation, all demonstrate the workings of moral concern: the fate of the individual as a consequence of changes in social organization and association (Nisbet, 1966). It is in this tradition of moral concern, I would argue, that Blumler's work can, and ought, to be seen. Indeed, his political research is similarly rooted in a concern for the individual as a consequence of political organization. The moral dimension, however, enters via his interest in examining the individual not so much as being acted upon, but rather the individual as an expressive actor. His insistence on recognizing that the individual in democratic theory is supposed to act and not merely be acted upon, as in some totalitarian systems, extends the normative to a methodological principle. In this way, methodology becomes a matter of moral principle and not mere practice, and as such manifests itself in his theorizing and his empirical research on audiences.

Part III

Public Culture and Mediated Publics

11
The Dream Machine? – Television as Public Culture

John Corner

In this chapter, I want to pursue some questions about television's character as public culture, questions which turn on matters both of cultural form and of content as well as on broader questions of the television economy and the institutions and structures which affect policy and practice. I want to do this by taking as my principal reference point a 50-year-old television programme, directed by the distinguished documentarist, Denis Mitchell, which took the social identity of television as its subject. It was called *The Dream Machine*, made by ATV and broadcast on the British ITV channel on Wednesday, 11 November 1964. I want to look at the questions it raised about the nature of television and the kind of tentative answers it offered. Not only the programme's treatment of its topic but also its own design and delivery as a piece of television are clearly of interest, since it is an example of the very phenomenon it sets out to investigate. My approach will require quite extensive citation from the programme, but I hope this will prove readable and illuminating.

The choice of a programme from the mid-1960s is perhaps particularly apposite given that this was the period in which Jay Blumler moved to a Granada Research Fellowship at the University of Leeds (in 1963), publishing in 1964 the article 'British Television: The Outlines of a Research Strategy' in the *British Journal of Sociology* – an original and concise little 'manifesto' to which I will return (Blumler, 1964). The programme was also broadcast some two years after the Pilkington Report on Broadcasting, which raised questions about the direction and quality of 'independent' (or 'commercial') television in Britain and led to political and public debate, often heated, about what television should be doing across its range of output and what structures might be the best for it to achieve its aims and serve its audiences (see Curran and Seaton, 2009, for a discussion and further references).

Television values: terms of divergence

When talking about *The Dream Machine* in a much later rebroadcast, Mitchell noted his belief that 'you see in my film the beginning of a sort of divergence between the dream and the reality' regarding television. In previous writing about Mitchell (Corner, 1991) I have suggested that he can be usefully seen as a kind of 'social impressionist' within television documentary, paying very careful attention to the texture and phrasing of speech as well as the content of what is being said, and often using various disembodied voices in montage fashion to create, through their combination with his images, an engagingly unstable flow of meanings. Alongside this, he is also very much an 'observationalist', using his camera to overlook and overhear social interaction for quite extensive periods in a manner quite close to those directors who attracted the 'fly-on-the-wall' label, although Mitchell also wants to mix his scenes, use voices over them, and regularly move them across time and space in ways which the more intensive kinds of observationalist work usually avoid.

The basic structure of the programme is simple. Two people with very different relationships to television are chosen: one a television entertainment producer and the other a university lecturer who is running a seminar course on television for his undergraduates at Durham. The programme offers the viewer brief glimpses at how television figures in both these working worlds, keeping commentary merely for introducing the two principal participants and working thereafter largely through overheard speech and observed actions. Such a structure is a key part of Mitchell's own ideas about how television documentary should operate – encouraging the viewer to look closely, listen and consider the possible meanings of what they see and hear. He also presents viewers with a strongly humanistic picture of people in social settings and within social interaction.

However, the programme starts by setting up its theme more directly. After a lengthy opening sequence showing some of the spaces, equipment and processes involved in making television – studios, control desks, editing suites – a number of different voices are heard making pronouncements about the medium over the continuing visual flow. This runs as follows. I have numbered the separate elements here for ease of subsequent reference.

1. *... tinged with GL4 ...* (brief voiceover extract of TV advert for shampoo, stressing scientific properties of product)

2. *Television is and will be a main factor in shaping our society.*
3. *...perfect shampoo*
4. *Dear Sir, give me wrestling every time. You've got something to think about for the rest of the evening.*
5. *A choice of eight gorgeous...*
6. *What some people regard as the herd, we respect as the human family.*
7. *If you gave people what they wanted, the programmes would be deplorable.*
8. *You don't necessarily make more money in television if you provide a better product.*
9. *It's untrue to say that because people are unaware of what they're missing, they're not missing it.*
10. *The living reality of a twelve million audience is absolutely compelling. How can one not want passionately to write for it?*
11. *...Anyway, isn't television rather...you know...*
12. *Television is not for people like us.*
13. *Oh we only keep it for the* au pair *girl of course.*
    ...Of course.
14. *Clocks everywhere, time pressures, time passing, nothing permanent, all transient.*
15. *Television is a means by which the creative artist makes a quick buck. A kind of mechanical whoring.*
16. *Immortality is what we care about, and there's no immortality on the box.*
17. *But surely if the thing lives on in people's memories, that is immortality.*

This assembly of voices is arresting because of the very different types and 'angles' of relationship to television it indicates. It not only offers a variety of voices (both male and female) and accents (with their class implications) but a variety of judgements about television and about how television fits within broader ideas about culture.

Segments 1, 3 and 5 are taken from television advertising, with their attempts at promotional allure, discernible in the speech tones as well as the phrasing. 2 is a direct affirmation of the 'shaping' importance of television, one which looks towards the future. 4 is an expression of a viewer's choice of programming (spoken by a woman), while 6, 7, 8 and 9 cut more deeply into the complexity of evaluating television. There is a rejection of ideas of 'the herd' often introduced into discussion of 'mass media', but there is also the proposition that popular demand would lower standards. This latter, provocative point is indirectly reinforced by the idea that making money out of television is not directly related to the quality of the material offered. The comment about 'awareness' and 'missing out' connects with central questions of cultural choice in relation to available cultural options, and the awkward issue of what we might or might not want to call 'cultural deprivation'. Segment 10 affirms the possibility of television as a medium of artistic achievement while 11, 12 and 13 dramatize the class tensions and class anxieties that surround it, leading among other things to a certain dishonesty of attitude among the middle class. Segment 14 (using a voice which is that of the film's commentary) establishes the importance of time to the world of television. Segment 15 presents a strong view of television's cultural status as undercut by its identity as a means of economic exploitation (the 'quick buck'). 16 reinforces this by emphasizing the transience of the medium, its inability to confer immortality, but 17 articulates a more sympathetic approach, challenging established notions of artistic immortality by invoking the values which follow from having a place in popular memory. This last comment interestingly shifts the focus (in a way which would be quite certain to get Blumler's approval) from the programmes themselves to the contexts and consequences of viewing.

Altogether, this is a subtle and suggestive sound sequence, close in many respects to the imaginative best of BBC radio features (in which Denis Mitchell had first worked) and has something of modernist poetry about it in the way it assembles the fragments of formal and casual phrasing into a larger, intriguingly disharmonious whole. It is a good example of a *stimulating* start, creating spaces and disjunctions around its utterances, which have to be connected, contrasted and deliberated upon by viewers themselves.

Two biographical settings for 'Television Today'

A commentary voice briefly introduces us to the two people whose activities the programme will follow. The television producer (Francis Essex) leaves home for the studio and begins his hectic round of phone calls and discussions with colleagues as he prepares a production to be called *Six Wonderful Girls*, in which well-known women from the world of show business will be brought together for a show of sketches and songs. The lecturer, Roy Knight (one of the pioneers of film and television studies in Britain) is first seen coaching a student rowing crew on the river below Durham Cathedral, and then leaving his study and walking across a college green, with the cathedral in the background, for the first of his seminar classes on television.

The sections on the producer are able to work mostly in an indirect manner to suggest what television 'means' for him, as he is observed going about his busy routine. The sections on what television 'means' for the lecturer, however, although they also use observation, include his direct statements about the medium to the students in his class. Rather than following the film as it moves regularly between television studio and seminar room, I think it might be best for my analysis if I concentrate first on the lecturer's comments, which effectively constitute the *spoken core* of the programme, and then turn to the presentation of the producer, where scenes of preparation, rehearsal and performance constitute what can be seen as its *visual core*. In doing this, however, it is important to note just how much the regular cross-cutting between the two spaces, with the consequent sense both of simultaneity and contrast it produces, is an important part of programme design and impact.

The lecturer

All the sequences below are delivered to a seminar room of seated undergraduates (there is regular cross-cutting to their faces during the address). The lecturer speaks from a chair while smoking a cigarette. I have edited the transcript in the interests of space and relevance, although I have been careful to try and avoid any distortion of argument or judgement as a result of this compression. Again, I have numbered the separate sections for ease of later analysis. In the programme, these sections are separated by shifts, of different duration, to the television producer at work in his office and studios.

1. *We're beginning a course. We are going to spend a whole year looking at television and talking about television...*
2. *I suppose something like 40 million people on any given night are looking at television and probably about half those people the following morning are talking about it. Therefore we are not doing anything unusual in looking at it or talking about it. How do we do this? Everybody talks about it, but usually from some biased point of view. They talk about it as entertainment, talk about it as big business, talk about it as a mass medium, talk about it as communication. And of course it is all these things, and something that we have very much got to bear in mind is that we mustn't try and split them off ourselves. We can't separate art and communication; we can't separate entertainment from big business. All these things are involved in television and whenever we think about one thing we need to think about the others.*

3. *I want to go back a good way in history to think about a time before the invention of the press when people then had a culture based on what they'd heard. I suppose we'd call it an oral culture, a spoken culture. They'd listen to stories and then talked about those ... Then we moved to a very different culture – a literary culture in which people were reading. They were reading novels, they were reading pamphlets, they were reading poetry. And this was the basis of the discussion and the culture and criticism of that period.*

4. *Now I think we are moving, and what's more we are moving very rapidly ... moving to another stage of culture ... No one culture excludes the others; we add another layer. We are moving now I think to a visual culture, in which people are much more concerned with the things they look at.*

5. *All that you can say really positively is that we get the television that we get, and this really means that we get the television they want us to have.*

6. *At the receiving end of television is perhaps a couple of people, or a family group or a group of friends sitting around the TV set watching a programme. It's not a mass audience, and until television producers and directors realize this, they are never going to produce television of a sufficiently high standard.*

7. *Why isn't television better than it is? There are reasons for this, and let's think about them for a moment.*

8. *It's new – it's still new compared with film, compared with literature or anything else.*

9. *And therefore we couldn't expect great talents to have arisen within it.*

10. *And therefore I think it is amazing that TV is as good as it is ...*

11. *So much of television seems to have behind it no real purpose, no real beliefs.*

12. *And so much television seems solely designed to fill time and to have no other purpose whatever.*

This sequence of comments exposes the viewer to a particular academic perspective on the medium they are watching. There is an emphasis on not making sharp classificatory divisions when attempting to determine the medium's identity but to consider the many-sided complexity of it. There is a brief historical context developed, with reference to the strengthening role of the visual. Segment 5 suggests that television is in the service of a power elite which determines what is offered ('they'), but this is a point left undeveloped. Criticism of the idea of the 'masses' is offered (in a way which connects with the writings, both contemporary and later, of Richard Hoggart and Raymond Williams). There is, perhaps, some apparent inconsistency of judgement: Television is too new for great work to have been produced within it, and it is amazing that it is as good as it is. Nevertheless, its tendency is towards lack of purpose and beliefs, towards mere time-filling.

It is interesting how the broad position being advanced is one in which television has cultural and artistic promise as part of broader cultural change. This is absolutely not a decisive academic put-down of television, nor is it a view which sees the information functions of the medium as being more important than its broader cultural functions. However, around television a number of questions are seen to gather, relating to the fulfilment of its cultural promise within present arrangements and contexts. In later comments, the lecturer develops his point by pointing to the relative lack of interest then shown by newspapers in 'serious' television criticism, and the tendency even in programmes devoted to viewers' comments, such as the BBC's *Points of View,* for a degree of trivialization both of topic and treatment to occur. He also contrasts unfavourably the freedoms given to the BBC in its charter ('to do what it wants') with the limitations placed on ITV by the Television Act (perhaps the fact that the programme was made for an ITV company influenced this emphasis, running counter to the one usually made in intellectual circles at the time).

The TV producer

The presentation of the TV producer can be handled more briefly, not because of its lesser importance but because, as I indicated earlier, it works primarily through the viewer eavesdropping on the various preparations being made for the programme *Six Wonderful Girls,* alongside other more routine business. Discussions with several members of staff occur, plans are drawn up in relation to times and dates, including those for rehearsal. The central matter of inviting six participants and getting confirmation that they will be free for the required period produces a good deal of time on the phone and one or two setbacks. Set designs are produced, and both sketch routines and songs are worked upon. Compared with the intercut scenes in Durham, there is almost a marked frivolity on display here: in the everyday humour of the exchanges between producer and staff and the kind of 'theatrical' language used in the phone calls ('Hello, Milly darling...'). Of course, the very title of the piece under development indicates the commitment to 'fun', but the detail and intensity of the planning offset this with more 'professional' values and a sense of 'hard work'. On one occasion, the producer makes direct comment about the values of his work to someone who appears to be a colleague. This occurs in a scene which has them both standing at a bar, a scene in which the silent companion, holding his drink, is shown in cutaway shots (thereby producing a rather uneasy naturalism).

> To entertain means to amuse and to give pleasure. But there's a faction of well-meaning and sincere people who think it is very right indeed to give education and give information but then very wrong to give pleasure. And the first thing they will do is to deny that you are doing what you say you're doing. They will insist on putting something into your thoughts which in fact isn't there. If you do a sketch on some political subject, they say, you are making a social comment, and in fact you're not: all you're doing is just setting out to get your laughs.

This comes across, of course, as a calculated 'case for the defence' rather than anything credible as bar chat. The 'other' identified here is the *mistaken* 'well-meaning and sincere people', a group perceived to combine elements of cultural elitism with elements of political radicalism, although the formulation and tone are too vague to deliver a more precise analysis. There is a rhetorical use of overstatement ('very right', 'very wrong') in pursuing the claim of innocence in relation to the charge of 'social comment'. As so often in discussion of television, questions of *intent* and questions of actual *function* become a little confused. Although this comment cannot but connect across to what has already been said in Durham and what will be said later, it does not provide a direct contrast, since, as I have noted, the lecturer's presentation, whatever its expressed concerns, has its own complexities of judgement, which certainly do not translate into 'it is very wrong to give pleasure'.

The producer has one more direct statement to make about his own perspective on television values. This he makes to the newspaper television critic Philip Purser, then working for *The Daily Telegraph*, who takes a quite important role in the final section of the programme, where he is seen to be researching a piece for his newspaper. In response to a question from Purser, the producer says,

> I feel it's my job to take a man's mind off whatever it's on. I don't require him to contribute in any way. He doesn't have to even think.

Whatever the positive positioning which the programme accords the speaker as a successful professional, it is hard not to see this statement as appearing seriously open to question (leaving aside the casual sexism which is cultural-historical rather than personal) and to be so in the context not only of what we have heard from Durham but in relation to the emerging and implicit evaluative framework of the programme itself. This tends to be confirmed in a subsequent scene, discussed below.

Television on television: some issues summarized

Lengthy scenes of the hectic activity, including at the studio control desk, involved in the performance of *Six Wonderful Girls* before a studio audience form the closing sequence of *The Dream Machine*. They are immediately preceded by shots of Philip Purser composing a newspaper article ('Only Entertainment') which refers to his discussion with the producer. As he types away, we hear the words of his developing piece:

> He sees his task purely as one of distraction and diversion. If escapism is wanted, and why not, the superficial, undemanding programme is least likely to provide it. Lastly, I hold that the idea of an inert, gaping audience is not only immoral but impossible. You can't crack a joke, sing a song, tell a story or make any sort of statement without calling upon someone's acquaintance with life or without adding however minutely to someone else's.

This critical statement, essentially making a point about the 'essentially active audience' and attacking superficial programming, gets as close to being the 'verdict' of the documentary as anything in it, and it is to some extent developed further by the final words which, following the shots of the studio production, return us to the Durham lecturer:

> We can't afford not to be as deeply concerned about it – television – as we are about our own jobs. I fear and I think that at the moment, neither inside television nor outside it, are enough people anything like enough concerned.

Thus, in its final minutes, the programme is able both to affirm the professional and technical achievement of television as it goes about the business of giving pleasure, and also strongly to suggest the need for 'concern'.

Placing television – documentary accounts and academic inquiry

I have taken *The Dream Machine* as a piece of television posing questions about television (itself a rare enough occurrence) in ways which have not only their own qualities as documentary inquiry but which connect us back to a much earlier period of television's social and cultural identity, even though elements in the evaluative frame are still very familiar. As I have noted, the programme works subtly, and often by counterpoint, rather than by direct proposition, although the seminar address to the Durham students introduces an element of direct and vigorous claim-making which allows other parts to work more expansively. This is particularly true of the visual portrayal of studio life, where the programme is allowed to be an exploration only loosely controlled by expositional purpose, giving the sequences more space to fascinate the viewer through the overheard exchanges and observed activities of 'putting a TV show together'.

There are some obvious limitations to the treatment, one of which is the absence of a clear sense of genre – the fact that television does news, documentary, drama, variety shows and countless other things. The taking of the main example from light entertainment skews the account of what television is currently *seen* to be doing, and perhaps makes the connection with the Durham arguments less sharp than it might be. But there are also, as I suggested, clear advantages from staying with just two people as the core 'cast' of the programme, articulating their two very different versions of the medium, joined by what is finally a quite crucial third version (moderate in tone but firmly critical) spoken and typed by Purser at the end. This is, I think, an example showing at its best the potential of television as an agency of 'public culture' at the same time as it raises questions precisely about what might progress, and what might impede, the full realization of such an idea.

I want finally to refer across to Jay Blumler's paper of the same year, mentioned at the start, in which, with his characteristic clarity, an outline of a 'research strategy' for British television is put forward. He notes the way in which debate about the medium's social and cultural identity is too often the victim of 'fact-starvation', showing more about 'the anxieties and needs' of intellectuals than about 'the place of the mass media in the lives of most of the public' (Blumler, 1964, p. 224). He calls for a 'spotlight of attention upon the uses which ordinary people make of the mass media' (ibid.). A central section of his paper is given over to the question of 'realism'. He suggests that we need to know more about 'the processes involved when people distinguish television materials they regard as "true to life" from those they deem implausible' (ibid., p. 227) and asks how questions of social class are implicated in the criteria employed here. He thus raises a number of issues for the attention of empirical research, about the positioning of television in everyday life, about 'escapism' and what he calls the world which the 'entertainers, themselves, have created' (ibid., pp. 231–232). These questions can, I think, be seen nicely to connect with the fragments and glimpses, the points of critique and of defence, offered us in Mitchell's richly indirect and provocative film. The 50-year gap between then and now has not invalidated either account.

12

Audiences and Publics: Reflections on the Growing Importance of Mediated Participation

Sonia Livingstone

As part of the task of understanding how our world has become increasingly media saturated lies a conceptual uncertainty regarding ordinary people. Through much of the 20th century, they were called 'audiences' – in academia and in everyday discourse. In relation to specific media, they were – and still are – referred to as 'readers', 'listeners' or 'viewers'. In the jargon of contemporary regimes of governance, they are called 'consumers' or 'citizens'. As the media environment diversifies to encompass interactive and networked media, the language of 'users' has gained prominence. But although the notion of audience remains the most commonly accepted collective term for people's relations (now pluralized) to the media in all their forms, this does not bring consensus. Most importantly, audiences are still commonly distinguished from the main collective term for ordinary people in a modern democratic society, that of 'the public'.

In *Audiences and Publics*, my colleagues and I explored the intellectual and empirical complexities of the relations between these two terms in order to illuminate the role of the media in advanced democracies (Livingstone, 2005a). 'The audience', especially in the English language, refers in everyday discourse to a casual, private and largely inconsequential engagement with media as part of leisure time, usually in the home, even to the extent of ridiculing the audience as mindless 'couch potatoes'. Meanwhile, ordinary uses of the term 'public' in relation to the media generally focus on how the media offer a public service, meet a public interest or result in a public good. Academic discourse has built on this opposition, theorizing the mass audience from a critical political economy perspective as constructed to serve the interests of the corporate mass media within an individualized, even alienated, certainly consumerist, mass society. This can be seen in the classic views of, first, Adorno and Horkheimer (1977), then Smythe (1981) and, more recently, Ang (1990). In parallel, scholars from the liberal pluralist traditions have argued for the necessity of an independent media as the fourth estate, able to inform and enlighten citizens (Blumler, 1992a; Schudson, 1995; Swanson and Nimmo, 1990). These scholars have documented that citizens positively want such enlightenment, seeking out news media to support their civic engagement in ways that may be enabling or resistant of the state (Barnhurst, 2000; Gamson, 1992; Graber, 1988).

Jay Blumler has long been a firm advocate of the audience as public. His research reveals an audience keen to seek out quality media and to become informed and engage in deliberative discussion with others. He has examined the conditions which most effectively support audiences as publics, in relation to the press, television and internet, and developed theoretical frameworks by which to understand these (Blumler, 1970; Blumler and Katz, 1974). Yet somehow he and many others in this tradition, and I include myself here, often seem to be swimming against the tide of a discourse that resolutely positions audiences as passive rather than active, withdrawn rather than engaged, consumerist rather than civic, selfishly motivated rather than public-spirited. As I shall argue in this short chapter, far from 'the audience' being obsolete in the age of digital 'users', it is this pejorative discourse that should be left behind, both for its underestimation of audiences' motivations and public concerns, and for its conceptual separation of the private and domestic from the public sphere of action and political significance (relevant here is Elliott's [1974] famous but misguided critique of uses and gratifications theory for its supposed reductionism and individualism; see Blumler, 1979).

Persistent misconceptions of audiences arise partly for linguistic reasons. In *Audiences and Publics*, European scholars explored the relation between 'audience' and 'public' in different languages and traditions, observing that it is only in English (albeit the dominant language of international media and communication research) that 'audience' is an everyday term for the readers, viewers and listeners of mass media. Elsewhere, it is often the Latin word 'publicus' that is used – as in the French *public/publique* or the Danish and German *Publikum* (Meinhof, 2005). In such cases, a stark opposition between passive, commodified audiences and active, reflexive publics does not arise. In French, for instance, 'audience' is a purely technical term used by media ratings agencies to refer to measures for reach and share; it is not the term by which ordinary people refer to themselves when watching the news or going to a cinema. Nor, incidentally, was this word so used in Britain until the 20th century: when charting the history of audiences in the 18th century, McQuail (1997) refers to the 'reading public'. Similarly, the term 'public' has been variously interpreted across cultures and contexts, and need not be given the highly rational and ideal reading common in (especially English-language) media and communication theory – as in Habermasian conceptions of the bourgeois public sphere (Outhwaite, 1996) or as the self-knowing and deliberate agency of the public articulated by Dayan (2001).

However, this is not to say that audiences (or media publics) are not denigrated for their mindlessness across the non-English-speaking academy, for the problem is also one produced by the elite status of the academy itself. Academics the world over have reproduced their elite status in society by their common disdain for popular culture, including the mass media and those who enjoy it or rely upon its views (here Bourdieu, 1999, and Hoggart, 1957, represent classic cases). In *Meanings of Audiences*, Richard Butsch and I invited researchers around the world to reflect on the discourses (academic, state, media industry, popular) within which people's relations to media are framed. Inspired by Blumler's claim that comparative research 'can pose challenges to scholars' preconceptions and is liable to be theoretically upsetting' (Blumler et al., 1992, p. 8), one purpose was to de-centre the Eurocentrism of much media theory (Kraidy, 2011). It became apparent from this project that the concept of 'public' itself is an uncomfortable fit beyond the West, reflecting the people's very different relation to the state in non-democratic cultures. For example, where a Marxist or communist tradition has been dominant, the masses may be regarded positively (as the spirit of the nation or the vanguard of revolution) even as they are subject to direction and control. Further, pre-modern conceptions of 'community' remain strong in many countries, and this, too, gives today's conception of 'the people' a positive cast. But at the same time, every society that we examined discursively divides its 'elite' from the 'masses', often with a small group in the middle serving the elite. Mass media, by and large, are associated with the lowest stratum of society, with audiences castigated for their supposed limitations – including by academic theory; thus elitist interests in maintaining control generally outweigh democratic efforts to educate.

As will be apparent, I think academic concepts do political as well as intellectual work. By defining audiences normatively rather than through independent empirical investigation, such discourses can become a means of social control, especially of subordinate groups. In the West, framing audiences as publics attaches Enlightenment values to audience activity and sets a positive standard of an ideal audience. But when audiences are characterized as crowds, masses or even the mob, positive expectations of audiences are undermined and anxieties about audience inadequacy or misbehaviour come to the fore. It is no accident that throughout history, concerns over media audiences have centred on regulating the tastes and behaviours of women, children and the working classes (Butsch, 2000). However culturally and historically contingent, it seems that discourses about audiences are used to justify and sustain status hierarchies and regulate access to power and privilege even as they obscure their effects by normalizing their assumptions as the common sense operation of both formal institutions and the practices of everyday life.

There is one further reason why audiences are denigrated even in media and communication theory, surely the body of knowledge best positioned to understand them. This is the curious reluctance on the part of the academy to investigate empirically the nature of people's motivations, beliefs and actions in relation to the media, both as individuals and collectively (Livingstone, 2010). If the highest ideals are asserted of publics while little is known of audiences, it is easy to presume a too-strong opposition between audiences and publics as is common in English-language scholarship. If, further, it suits the aspirations of an elite academy to maintain a comfortable relation to state power, or to prefer investigation of powerful organizations over messy living rooms, or sophisticated film texts over ordinary chat about reality television, then again audiences will be obscured by the lens through which they are (inadequately) viewed.

This was precisely the motivation for an 'exciting phase' in audience studies (Hall, 1980) that opened up in the 1980s–90s, drawing on German reception-aesthetics and American reader-response theory to reveal the interpretative work (Katz, 1996) that audiences do in completing (or renegotiating or contesting or disrupting) the circuit of culture. This extraordinary moment of intellectual convergence, in which diverse streams of thought (temporarily but productively) coalesced to generate a new and fundamentally empirical project, illustrated Blumler et al.'s call for research to 'reach out' across the bifurcations of political economy and cultural studies, or administrative and critical, or text-centred and audience-centred, or qualitative and quantitative approaches that have long divided our field. Since I was, at that time, completing my doctorate on audience reception of the soap opera (Livingstone, 1990), and since Blumler was my external examiner, it seems apposite to recall this moment as a spur to my present argument.

The importance of empirical investigation is clearly illustrated by audience reception studies' success in revealing people's diverse and contextualized responses to a range of genres (soap operas, news, reality television, comedies, documentaries and more). The findings challenged prior assumptions of textual meanings (from which audience responses could supposedly be inferred), strong claims regarding media effects (thus joining with the findings of minimal effects from persuasion and social cognitive studies of influence) and implicit notions of a homogenous or mass audience. Thus we now know that audiences are plural in their decoding, that the cultural context of viewing matters, and that one cannot read off their response from textual analysis (or the claims of the producers). As the television audience once again risks being stereotyped as passive by comparison with the new forms of activity prominent among interactive and online media users, this body of knowledge remains pertinent.

But audience reception studies had a bigger ambition than merely making visible an audience too often devalued, marginalized or presumed about in academic and popular discourses about media. This concerned the relation between audiences and publics as part of the wider inquiry into the possibilities for, and normative demands of, democratic participation, especially in complex networked societies. One might read the whole history of political communication research as seeking to understand how addressing people in their role as audiences can advance (or undermine) democratic purposes, it being precisely the intersection of audience and public that must be mobilized as publics become too large for face-to-face interaction (that is, ever since democracies expanded beyond the city state) and as states become too little trusted for representative elites to be left unaccountable to the electorate. Indeed, the more that society makes contradictory demands for, on the one hand, transnational engagement and global responsibility and, on the other hand, individual citizen rights to participate and be heard, the more the media are required to mediate and, therefore, the more the public is also an audience.

It is interesting but unsurprising, therefore, that audience researchers increasingly focus not merely on active audiences but on participatory audiences (Livingstone, 2012), seeking to understand when and how media can enable audiences *qua* mediated publics to participate, with participation apparently overtaking earlier concerns with interpretation, identity or resistance (Carpentier, 2009) and mediated citizenship now of greater interest than mediated consumption (Schrøder, 2013). This academic interest includes far more than the traditional concerns of political communication, for the scope of the political has been extended to cover (almost) every dimension of everyday life and, in consequence, (almost) every media genre and platform. So too, of course, has the scope of the media – as Silverstone (2002, p. 762) put it, mediation is 'the fundamentally, but unevenly, dialectical process in which institutionalized media of communication are involved in the general circulation of symbols of social life.' Thus, interest in participation is not simply on audiences' participation *in* media as on their participation in society *through* media – in other words, participation in media is increasingly the means to a grander end. Mediatization theory is helpful here, for it is less interested in the effects of media on an audience, in a situation or for an institution, than it is in the fact that people and institutions now act in situations that include media or that have been shaped by media among other historical influences (Krotz, 2007; Schulz, 2004). Arguably, even the distinction between participating in media and participating in society through media is disappearing, as ever more institutions and practices in society become 'mediatized'.

In our *Public Connection* project, Nick Couldry, Tim Markham and I explored such claims in relation to ordinary people's life experiences (Couldry et al., 2010). Extended diaries kept by a diverse set of individuals revealed that audiences do indeed engage with media as a means of connecting with the wider public realm. It is not that media engagement leads people to go out and take direct political action, for this requires political efficacy reciprocated by responsive institutions but, as Peter Dahlgren puts it, it can enable that 'reservoir of the pre-or non-political that becomes actualised at particular moments when politics arises...[for] the political and politics are not simply given, but are constructed via word and deed' (2003, p. 155). But sometimes people use those same media to disconnect and – for mediatization is far from overtaking all spheres of society as yet – they still have other means to public connection also that are not, as yet, significantly mediated.

Moreover, to whatever extent people are motivated or engaged in processes of participation, this can only become significant if the opportunity structures for participation are institutionally respected – voices must be not only expressed but also heard. Herein lies a problem for any collectivity brought into being or mobilized through media engagement – as Herbert Blumer (1946/1961) observed many decades ago, crowds, publics and masses tend to lack an organic relation to the established structures of society (unlike, say, workers, congregations, students or electorates). Efforts towards mediated participation, in consequence, often fail, breeding disillusion and distrust rather than political efficacy and accountability.

Today we are witnessing a transformation in the nature and signifi-cance of audiences in a digital, globalized age that is matched by a burgeoning of new research. Audiences are now dispersed, networked, engaged with hybridizing genres and stepping over the hallowed production/consumption boundary to speak back, remix, navigate and share in familiar and new ways. In response, audience studies of many kinds are proliferating, enriching our understanding of people's rela-tions with media and, through media, with society. But I have argued that audience research cannot be parochial: it must connect with wider studies of societal structures and processes, and this is precisely how Blumler, the audience scholar, as well as the political communication scholar and comparativist, has always worked, and how he urges others to work also.

I will end by drawing on Habermas' conception of the relation between the everyday lifeworld of audiences and the wider structures to which media provide ever more chances for connection (Habermas, 1981/87; see also Fraser, 1990). As shown in Table 12.1, distinguishing system from lifeworld independently of the distinction between public and private allows a two-by-two table that illuminates the problematic and shifting terrain of audiences and publics with which I have been grappling in this short chapter. Habermas' wider purpose is to identify the key features that delineate four spheres of society. Comprising what he calls the 'system world', he distinguishes the state from the economy (which he sees as increasingly interpenetrating and so undermining the vital but 'relatively informal ways of life' of the lifeworld; Outhwaite, 1996, p. 369). Then he divides the lifeworld into the public sphere, which he specifically theorizes as a vital democratic/deliberative buffer between the private and the state, and the personal or intimate sphere, which he sees as generating the energy and interest for the public sphere. As Habermas puts it, 'By "the public sphere" we mean first of all a realm of our social life in which something approaching public opinion can be formed. Access is guaranteed to all citizens. A portion of the public sphere comes into being in every conversation in which private indi-viduals assemble to form a public body' (1984, p. 49).

Why do I end with this? Because it is precisely the ways in which audiences relate to larger social structures and processes that makes them significant, and because such a scheme helps us to think through the contrasts among different discourses of audience – popular and

Table 12.1   Approaches to audiences and publics

	Public Audience as citizen	Private Audience as consumer
System Audience as object	**The state:** specifies legal and regulatory frameworks for the media industry, including protection for 'fourth estate'. *Audience as object of media education and, through their vulnerabilities, of content guidelines and controls*	**The economy:** encompasses the media industry, characterised by the commercial logics of media, advertising, marketing and branding. *Audience as commodity or market, characterised through ratings, market share and unmet needs*
Lifeworld Audience as agent	**The public sphere:** demands that media serve as a forum for democratic debate, mediated community participation and public culture. *Audiences as active and engaged, informed, participatory and/or resistant*	**The personal or intimate sphere:** embraces media for providing the images, pleasures, habits and goods for identity, relationships and lifestyle. *Audiences as selective, interpretative, pleasure-seeking, creative in doing identity work*

Source: Livingstone, 2005b.

academic – and, thus, varieties of audience research. Critical scholars from a political economy perspective examine how audiences become enrolled in the systems of state and economy. They are particularly concerned about the capture of the state by economic processes – prioritizing market innovation over public value, for example. Still, the curious fusion of citizen and consumer approaches in contemporary governance regimes (Clarke et al., 2007) may, on occasion, also benefit audiences, as Peter Lunt and I have recently argued (Lunt and Livingstone, 2012). Those who work with audiences in their everyday lives are exploring the conditions under which the intimate sphere may support the public sphere and, in turn, how the public sphere may enable people to participate in larger processes of state and economy, provided these latter are responsive to the voices of ordinary people. Blumler's own work on audiences, interestingly, encompasses the diversity of these approaches. Consider, for example, how his work on uses and gratifications has been particularly concerned with the wider societal implications of personal motivations to engage with media. Or, note how his work on the civic commons online shows how participation from the lifeworld could inform and shape the actions of the system world (Coleman and Blumler, 2009).

I do not, therefore, divide approaches to audiences into these four ideal types in order to separate them. Nor am I simply motivated to prevent our talking at cross purposes about audiences differently conceived. Rather, I find that these distinctions help us grasp the complex contexts of late modernity within which audiences are positioned by the increasing interpenetration of the lifeworld by the system world (as Habermas put it at his most pessimistic) and yet, at the same time, in which audiences are sustained by the resources of the lifeworld to contribute, at least sometimes and with some purpose, to what can be – and could be further – a lively, diverse and deliberative mediated public sphere.

13
On Seeing Both Sides: Notes on the 2012 Presidential Debates

Elihu Katz and Menahem Blondheim

The term 'media events' refers to those live broadcasts of 'historic' occasions, whether ceremonial or disruptive, that mobilize an entire nation or the whole world. Normatively, the genre tells us that there is nothing more important to do than go home and watch television! The first such broadcast was the coronation of Elizabeth in 1953, when television was introduced (Dayan and Katz, 1994, pp. 31–2). Not long after, in 1960, there followed an equally compelling broadcast, the pre-election presidential debates between John Kennedy and Richard Nixon that were viewed simultaneously by almost two-thirds of Americans and have served as a model for subsequent debates in the United States and throughout the democratic world (Katz and Feldman, 1962 pp. 130–5).[1]

Britain long resisted, claiming that parliamentary and presidential systems are different and that ample free time is made available for party political broadcasts. John Major is quoted as saying 'we hold televised debates in the House each week' (Minow and LaMay, 2006, p. 82). But, say Coleman et al., increasing mistrust of politicians and increasing deterioration in the quality of political broadcasting led Britain to institute pre-election debates in 2010 (Coleman et al., 2011). Although each of the four scheduled debates was broadcast on only one channel – unlike the United States where the major networks and cable channels suspend all other programming – each debate was viewed by some 60% of the population.

According to Dayan and Katz (1994), these events – the ceremonial kind – divide into three types: contests, conquests and coronations. Coronations celebrate the rites of passage of the great – weddings, funerals, inaugurations. Conquests are 'great steps for mankind' in which the odds are against a daredevil hero (like Anwar Sadat), while sports and democratic politics take the form of contests. Indeed, for theorists like Michael Schudson, contests – not conversations – are 'the soul of democracy.' Dissenting from Habermas' ideal speech situation, Schudson (1997) insists that democracy is based on often-hostile argument and needs a referee.

Typically, citizens of a democratic polity hear only their own side. We have known this for ages, from studies of 'selective exposure' – and the same holds for studies of 'deliberative democracy' – one talks almost exclusively with those with whom one agrees (Mutz, 2006). It follows that the major function of presidential or prime ministerial debates is to overcome selectivity: that is, to see and hear 'the other side.'

If that were the case in the heyday of broadcasting, when television's news shows were designed for universal reach and appeal, today that function is even more important (Blondheim and Liebes, 2009). Given the likes of Huffington, FOX, or Rush Limbaugh – let alone Facebook groups and Twitter choices – exercising selectivity is hardly necessary: what one gets is one side, almost exclusively. In this environment, the function of presidential or prime ministerial debates in overcoming selectivity has become crucial. To illustrate, Mitt Romney, the 2012 challenger, may have won the first debate against Barack Obama simply because he failed to fit the bill of the imbecile version of Lord Voldemort that so many one-sided viewers had expected.

According to Dayan and Katz, contests (1) involve evenly matched opponents, (2) are performed in terms of agreed rules, (3) have a referee or umpire present, (4) declare a winner, and (5) give the loser another chance. While presidential debates seem to qualify as paradigmatic contests, the fit is a little more complicated. First of all, the two sides may not be evenly matched. The incumbent generally has an advantage. Ironically, if the betting is tilted against the challenger, an upset almost makes the contest into a conquest, as in David versus Goliath, Kennedy versus Nixon and Lincoln versus Douglas. Secondly, it is not clear who is empowered to declare the winner. Even if the public is supposedly the ultimate judge, the multi-dimensional 'spins' that are produced by the parties, the pundits, the focus groups – are important ingredients in deciding 'who won' and, often, in pre-empting the popular judgment.

Does winning a debate carry over into the polling place? The answer is 'rarely', but in the case of Kennedy, the answer seems to be 'yes', and Lincoln, an even longer shot, leveraged his debate victory and surprisingly narrow election loss to subsequent victory. In Israel, Benjamin Netanyahu outperformed Shimon Peres and won the 1996 election, according to Blum-Kulka and Liebes (1999). And if it were not for Hurricane Sandy, some pundits believe that Obama might have lost the election, given his performance – or lack of it – in the first debate of 2012. But, on the whole, research finds that viewers of debates emerge reinforced in their pre-debate intentions, even if many viewers say that the debates helped them make up their minds.

In this day of hundreds of channels, it is remarkable that the debates attract and hold such a large proportion of the population. Indeed, the four American debates in 2012, like most of the debates since 1960, attracted a majority of the population (Katz and Feldman, 1962, pp. 132–3). And the British case is even more remarkable in attracting some 60% of the population, given that the debates were rotated among the three major networks, one network per debate, and one could easily escape. A majority is freely forgoing entertainment for a civics lesson.

Of course, it is possible that the audience has not forgone entertainment, and expects the contest itself to be entertaining. And perhaps it is (except when it is not!). The most convincing evidence of this expectation is in the explosion of conversation, instant messaging, and amateur analysis of 'who won.' Indeed, all of these side shows – including the live tracking of approvals and disapprovals by undecided voters on screen and in the crawl, the interplay of social media, and the post-debate spins of party spokespersons and pundits – enhance the festive aspect of the occasion (Dayan and Katz, 1994, pp. 140–1; see also MacAloon, 1984). Some researchers, and some critics of presidential debates, think that the 'horse race' aspect – including the betting – constitutes the primary motivation of the viewers.[2]

Fortunately, however, from the very outset of interest in the roles of television in the electoral process, researchers have confirmed that the 'uses and gratifications' (Blumler and Katz, 1974) of the debates reach beyond curiosity about the race itself. In their study of the British elections, Coleman, Steibel and Blumler found that in the 'game-substance balance', audiences – in contrast to media – were more interested in the latter (Coleman et al., 2011, pp. 23–4; Blumler, 2011b, pp. 38–9). According to Blumler, among the 'gratifications sought', viewers seeking an 'enhanced surveillance of the political environment' significantly outnumbered viewers who wanted to 'enjoy the excitement of following the race.' 'To understand the problems facing the country better' and 'to see what some party will do if gets into power' far outstripped 'to pick the winner of the debate' as a motivation for viewing (Blumler, 2011b, p. 38). Importantly, the amount 'learned' from both sides was essentially equal. A sizable minority says, 'It helped me to make up my mind', and, objectively, as we have seen, sometimes these decisions persist to the end (Blumler, 2011b, pp. 35–54). Selectivity does prevail, however – not in exposure, or learning, but in perception of who won. Beyond these explicitly perceived functions, it is clear that the debates provide viewers with an agenda of issues, and American audiences even took to 'inspirational' elements of debates, alongside insights into the personality and character of the candidates (Katz and Feldman, 1962, pp. 136–7). As is well known, such rankings provide the frames in which one judges the candidates. Altogether, it is clear that the civic utility of the debates easily matches their role as contests.

The production of such debates involves not only attention to the audience, but serious legal and organizational concerns as well. Thus, in the 1960 debates, Congress had to suspend section 315 of the Federal Communication Act, granting equal time to all legitimate candidates, in order to limit the debates to the two major parties. New rules governing invitations to third parties are now in place, as is a Commission on Presidential Debates, which brings parties and broadcasters together, helps make decisions about where the debate will take place, who will moderate, what the staging should be like, how much the public is represented, and what the agenda will be (Minow and LaMay, 2006, pp. 65–6; 73–8). For their part, the broadcasters must arrange to pool resources, and to suspend all other programming. The parties, of course, seek to impose favoured conditions on the production, but, increasingly, they are overruled.

The cumulative history of these studies needs continuous updating, but the centrality of the institution remains unabated. Indeed, the option *not* to debate has virtually disappeared in the United States. Following the gap between 1960 and 1976, every national election in the United States has featured at least one debate between the two leading contenders. After each round, reactions of professionals and academics have been scrutinized in order to improve the quality of the debates. Over the years, the call has been for less formality, for more direct engagement between the contenders, for more direct dialogue between candidates and voters, and for different allocation of times to initial statements, rebuttals, and comebacks. Minow and LaMay discuss some of these suggestions, citing Kathleen Jamieson's ideas at many points.

We were among the viewers of the 2012 debates, although we did not undertake to study them systematically. Nevertheless, this seems an opportune moment to offer up some of our own notions about the debates in general and the 2012 debates in particular.

1. Like political campaigns in general, the American debates misrepresent the power of the presidency, at the same time exaggerating and

diminishing it. These misperceptions, and the inevitably unfulfilled expectations bred of the debates, may have negative implications on the trust of the electorate in the political process. The debates tend to inflate the expectations that the elected president will carry out the agenda, let alone achieve the goals, he charts in the debates. While a president has more power than a prime minister – who is more directly embedded in a political party – the debates exaggerate the ability of the president to enact the policies he proclaims, and hardly require him to explain how he would go about that. The skills and tactics required to implement a programme may be of no less importance than the proposed policy and its 'selling'. Certain issues may be addressed at the discretion of the president – but on the whole, the public deserves to be privy not only to the promises, but to the procedures and politics that are involved in governing.

2. Moreover, the real world of politics calls for reaching across the aisle, negotiating and compromising. The debates, merely by their framing as contests, tend to be agonistic, uncompromising affairs, in which a candidate is expected to score blows, not compromise or reach an agreement.[3] In this context, the public may find the inevitable postelection compromise a cynical, 'inside the beltway' ploy, featuring unprincipled deal makers or even corrupt operators deceiving the public.

3. Apart from the incumbent's salience (visiting China or responding to Hurricane Sandy, for example), the incumbent is generally assumed to have an advantage in the debates themselves. But there may also be a disadvantage. The equalizing factor is well known: having the president and a contender share the same podium, time allowance, and limelight. But at least as important is the talk-back factor. The significant power that does reside with the 'imperial' presidency is practically discretionary, and ergo, is never contested in the workaday political process. Unlike the parliamentary system, there are rare occasions in which the president is directly challenged by a peer. The White House press secretary has become the lightning rod for the president, and the president is practically immune from direct challenge by his equals throughout his presidency, save in the presidential debates. This heightens the significance of the debates, in which the future (and oftentimes past) president's positions are actually challenged, as they are presented. Indeed, some commentators saw Obama's awkward collapse in the first debate as a consequence of his being unseasoned in direct confrontation. Unlike the constantly challenged British prime minister, the American president leaves his

cocoon only after his first four years, should he make it to in the next presidential debates. This may or may not be a blessing in disguise for the president.

4. An even more elusive question is whether the staging itself delivers a message, or, in McLuhanese, whether 'the medium is the message'. Minow and LaMay count six different models (so far) of presidential debates ranging from direct confrontation – each man glaring at the other from his own podium – to being seated intimately with the moderator around a coffee table (Minow and LaMay, 2006, 105–8). One of the 1960 debates featured Nixon and Kennedy debating from two different studios, one in California, the other in New York (Seltz and Yoakam, 1962). More recently, the town meeting model has gained favour. Our question is whether the choice of staging for the debates – confrontational, Habermasian town meetings – might not symbolize enactments of different democratic ideals and serve as models for citizen interaction at the grass roots (Dayan and Katz, 1994).

5. The place of moderators – literally and figuratively – is also part of the staging. Their role is much discussed in the literature, and much negotiated in practice. Apart from keeping time, should there be moderators at all? Why not let representatives of the public ask the questions? Are well-known journalists the best choice? Should there be more than one? Do moderators put their own questions to the candidates, or do they present questions that are forwarded by the public? Should they follow up or even challenge responses? More fundamentally, who sets the agenda of issues to be discussed? Should moderators intervene in case of a blatant dispute over fact, as happened in the 2012 debates?

6. Both the Americans and British assigned domestic and foreign affairs to separate debates, and within these constraints, the moderator ranked the issues, presumably in order of importance. The primary issue of the first debate of 2012 was the American economy. A large amount of time was spent on this issue, but what if – this is a guess – most of the viewers were unable to follow? The issue was simply too difficult – maybe even for the candidates themselves – to be handled in the to and fro of the debate format. One got the sense that the two disagreed, and that they expected to enact different policies, but they (especially the Republican) certainly did not lay out their specific plans. Indeed, the arguments were so difficult to follow that one wonders how viewers were able to cope at all.

7. Since the debates are not real 'debates' anyway, one wonders whether there might not be some way to present the problem more elaborately

than in the form of a single question. One method might be by means of a mini-documentary on which the candidates comment as to their understanding of how the problem emerged, how to deal with it, and so on. Viewers could then better judge the candidates as communicators and as analysis and policy makers, and find themselves more enlightened citizens. This is a very tricky business of course, but the problem is a problem, nevertheless, and one to which we don't know the answer.

8. Another structural problem – this time on the production side – is how to allow the audience to view the candidate who is not speaking. In earlier debates, the number of so-called reaction shots was negotiated. That is, it was agreed between the sides that the cameras could switch away from the speaker to show how the opponent is behaving, whatever he was doing (smirking, dozing, writing notes, not reacting, and so on). Instead of reaction shots, the 2012 debates showed both candidates side by side, most of the time, on a 'split screen'. Yet another explanation of Obama's 'loss' of the first debate is widely attributed to his bowed head during much of the time he was not speaking, as if to say that he was tired, or depressed, or making notes, or arrogantly dismissing criticism generally and that of his rival in particular – or even worse – of his rival's sheer presence, rather than focusing attentively on his opponent and what he was saying. However unlikely, it does seem that the president was unaware of this simultaneity.

9. Classic 'media events' – the Olympics, the moon landings, the Diana funeral – transform the everyday of the salon, the all too familiar TV set and casual gatherings of family and friends into a ritual occasion, a joining of a nation, or the world, in solemn or festive communion, depending on the occasion. Traditionally, presidential debates fit this model. In recent years, however, the viewer finds himself not only a member of an 'imagined community' (Anderson, 2006; Gouldner, 1982; Katz, 2006), focused on a semi-sacred 'centre,' but an increasingly active participant in the event itself, even to the point of tailoring it, what Fiske calls 'audiencing' (1992). In addition to the new self-referentialities of the 'message' itself – portrayals of the speaker, reactions of his adversary, the graph of the responses of the focus group of undecided voters – we are seeing the first signs of a two-tier viewership model. In this model, the audience is both a dutifully attentive couch potato passively sharing the great unifying event on the ever-widening living room screen, and at the same time an involved and responsive web 2.0 performer, who likes, dislikes, talks

back, posts statuses, tweets and is tweeted to, and 'shares' his group members' reactions on Facebook. At issue here is much more than the death and revival of television and the two-screen or companion device model of viewing (TV plus tablet/smartphone). The issue here confronts Blumler and his fellows of the uses and gratification school, who see TV and other mass media messages as a cue to viewers to do their own thing with media event colleagues who see the live broadcast of history that the whole world watches as a cue to reunite and reintegrate and pledge allegiance. Put otherwise, can media events continue to assemble very large communities, or are we moving into a world of 'active' individuals and social networks? If the latter, will this new ecology reaffirm the viewers' role as fair arbiter between the sides, or will it reintroduce the tendency to attend selectively and join in only one of the sides?

Notes

1. Sweden, however, was the first country to hold televised debates, in 1956 (Minow and LaMay, 2006, p. 82).
2. Thus, Jamieson and Birdsell (1988) seek an institutional framework for the debates that would balance a broad canvas of the issues with performance and showmanship.
3. Kathleen Jamieson, however, holds that debating candidates are aware of the fact that agreeing is an audience-winning tactic and try to demonstrate their propensity to agree and be united in the debates.

Part IV

Changing Media, New Democratic Opportunities

14
Changing Societies, Changing Media Systems: Challenges for Communication Theory, Research and Education

W. Lance Bennett

The current era of economic crisis and political turmoil comes in the aftermath of 40 years of social and economic change, commonly lumped together under the heading 'globalization'. Critics of this era typically refer to its guiding ethos as neo-liberalism, which broadly refers to an ideology of market deregulation that was typically sold politically with the promise that individuals would experience great freedom of choice in an enhanced consumer marketplace. The political marketing slogan for this broad transformation of public and private life is typically a variation on 'free markets, free people'. The global trend to deregulate markets even touched many once protected public goods and services such as health care, education, public broadcasting funding and public utilities. As these policy reforms swept through various societies, they were accompanied by a number of secondary (and often unimagined) consequences, including the fragmentation of social institutions, the individuation or separation of people from those social institutions, and the gradual replacement of modern social structures based on groups, class, and common memberships and status with more fluid social relations, ushering in an era that has been described variously as 'liquid modernity' (Bauman, 2000) and the 'networked society' (Castells, 2010). Noting that these networked forms of social, economic and political relations are often made stable and effective through innovative communication technologies, Bimber (2003) has termed the emerging era a 'post bureaucratic society'. This paper explores how this reorganization of society and personal life affects communication processes and how we study them. The discussion addresses three broadly interrelated areas of change:

- The fragmentation of public life: This includes the breakdown of broad social membership institutions such as unions, churches, public education systems, and related shifts in political party loyalties. This fragmentation of mass society corresponds to the rise of large-scale networked publics, which contributes to ...
- Changing media systems and communication processes: New technologies and channels enable more fine-grained 'many-to-many' communication within fragmenting societies. Communication has become increasingly personalized, both in the way messages are framed, and how they are shared across social networks. Individuals become active agents in the production and transmission of information, which leads to ...
- Communication as political organization (that goes beyond messages, framing, and effects): Younger generations prefer networked participation that relies less on formal organization than on peer recommendation and peer production of ideas and plans. In these technology-enabled networks, communication often goes beyond message transmission to become an organizational process.

The extent of these changes varies in different societies. Some countries such as the United States and the UK have embraced them more fully than others, such as Germany, which still displays a higher degree of modernist social structure and communication. Current frameworks for comparing media systems note general similarities and differences (Hallin and Mancini, 2004a), yet the change processes transforming communication systems in the digital age are not yet well established in theory, research or teaching. Not only is the volume of public information in the so-called digital age unsurpassed in human history, but its production, distribution and consumption patterns are changing in ways that also outpace current communication theories and research methods, with a few notable exceptions (Bimber, 2003; Benkler, 2006; Coleman and Blumler, 2009). The following sections sketch the broad changes, illustrate them with examples from different countries, and show how they impact communication and journalism research and education.

The reorganisation of public life

As publics became persuaded of the merits of deregulated markets, consumer lifestyles and economic growth that seemed limitless before the financial crash of 2008, even many of the parties on the left rushed toward so-called third way thinking about reduced commitments to labour protections, public goods, and social welfare. In many cases, parties on the left actually led the way with market reforms in core public sectors such as social services, health care and education. The ironic result was a political boomerang that benefited centre right parties who charged the social democratic left (with some good reason) with becoming a pale imitation of the freedom-loving centre right. So the 21st century opened with the helpless drift of the legacy socialist parties in the UK, Sweden, Italy, Germany and elsewhere. The resulting race to rebrand seemingly empty political vessels led to further disillusionment with the political process for many younger citizens.

The separation of younger generations from guiding institutions such as political parties and the press (which derives a good deal of its content from parties and government) left citizens with few stable models for managing distress and confusion. As many social scientists observed, individuals experienced an increased sense of personal risk and responsibility for managing their own life chances during these times of rapid social change (Beck, 1992; Giddens, 1991). Cast adrift from broad party agendas, younger citizens increasingly attached themselves to issues connected to their lifestyles and personal values (Inglehart, 1997; Bennett, 1998). These shifting identifications produced a fluid politics that resisted easy ideological order: environmental protection might rest easily alongside human rights in Tibet and support for gay marriage, or libertarian values supporting free marijuana might combine with support for defence spending and fiscal austerity.

Coherent mass communication from parties and institutions becomes ever more challenging in the face of such fragmented and personalized politics. And once in power, governments face serious challenges to satisfy the personal expectations of the citizens who voted them in. As governments are perceived to be less capable of solving problems, individuals further shift their political repertoires away from programmatic orientations based on social position, class or ideologies, and toward concerns about issues that affect their lives in more immediate ways, such as the environment, education or health care. These lifestyle politics put further strain on the political parties of the left because they cannot mobilize resources and broad public support to solve problems, while parties on the right suffer under the suspicion that their preferred market solutions may have caused or exacerbated these problems in the first place. Under these conditions, the usual sources of information such as mass media news become increasingly doubted, and in the case of younger generations, abandoned. The result is a series of changes in media systems and how people use them.

Changing media systems

This fragmentation and personalization of social structures and political agendas – along with the proliferation of communication technologies and information sources – have changed communication processes in many societies. There are, of course, also important variations across those societies. In addition, the legacy media of modern society continue to exist, which may distract scholars from attending to what is changing. For example, there are still plenty of newspapers and television news programs carrying the messages from elite sources and the spin from legions of communication and image consultants that Jay Blumler and his colleagues associated with the last era of political communication (Blumler and Kavanagh, 1999). But those institutional authorities and their spin doctors face more challenging messaging and targeting problems due to less reachable and less responsive audiences in more dispersed societies, resulting in soaring costs and diminishing returns.

One explanation of the shifting logic of communication from modernist, mass communication-based systems to late modern, more fragmented systems is that technologies and information sources have multiplied. The result is that audiences are no longer captives of a few mass media channels (Prior, 2007). To this, it seems important to add that younger generations nearly everywhere have moved away from traditional news and political attention patterns and toward more lifestyle-oriented issue engagement facilitated by social networks and specialized online media. Those who think that younger citizens will return to more traditional patterns of civic engagement as they grow older have apparently missed the over-time generational studies showing that successive age cohorts attend to conventional information sources at diminishing rates. Audience studies also generally show that the media forms that are most popular among younger demographics seldom feature 'quality news' about public officials and their activities. These patterns appear in countries as different as Sweden (Hamilton, 2010; Sternvik, 2010), Norway (Høst, 2010), Germany (Best and Engel, 2011; Köcher, 2009), Japan (Wolf, 2010), the UK (Ofcom, 2009; Wolf, 2010) and the United States (Putnam, 2000).

This does not mean that younger generations are necessarily apathetic or cut off from important issues. However, they are less likely to seek information from official institutional channels and more likely to define their interests in terms of personal lifestyle values and related activities such as buying fair trade products or changing personal living habits to address environmental concerns. What seems to be missing in many nations is a natural connection between these lifestyle issues and conventional political attachments through parties and voting. In addition to finding more diverse information sources and political outlets, increasing numbers of citizens of all ages seek like-minded information sources (Bennett and Iyengar, 2008). The selective exposure pattern may hold more for the United States than other societies, but better research is needed on where scattered audiences are getting their political information.

Citizens seeking more relevant coverage of their personal issue clusters create growing strains on journalism, which, in most places, continues to deliver government agenda-driven news to broad audiences. The legacy modern press system persists of course, but it is followed mainly by older and more affluent demographics that support the old institutional order into which they were born. Meanwhile, younger citizens are turning to alternative sources of information, including nongovernmental organizations (NGOs) that create information-rich environments around their issues, and often personalize their communication through environmental policy messages using cute baby animals or fair trade and development policies pegged to endorsements from rock stars and actors. The emergence of vibrant issue communities on Facebook, Twitter, and other social media sites also suggests different kinds of information production and distribution than are commonly studied in conventional approaches to news production and framing.

Even when young people report following the news through publications or online zines, the communication formats typically involve narratives shaped around lifestyle concerns, rather than with reports of conventional politics, politicians and parties. For example, lifestyle zines such as *Neon* in Germany have captured large segments of the young audience demographic now being lost to newspapers and public service broadcasting. The *Neon* formula is an explicitly youth-oriented mix of music, shopping, technology gear, reader profiles, meeting places, and pages of direct video and photo blog posts from readers about the cool things they do. Interspersed in this lifestyle cocktail are selected political stories designed to tap interest in the world beyond. Timm Klotzek, a founding editor of *Neon*, explains what kinds of stories are interesting to his audience:

> We're searching for something to identify with, where people would say 'I like that' or 'this is like me or like I want to be'. ... We don't

have a policy of 'elected officials are a no-go'. However, I think that most young people are not interested in politics. They are interested in political issues or topics though. But in Germany ... there is a great distance and almost cynical attitude toward this party spectacle. ... A story such as 'The New Shooting Star of the FDP' – I think people couldn't care less. But political topics in general, dealing with problems in our society, do engage people very much. It's either the question of 'what has it to do with my life?' or 'I've heard so much about it, I want to learn a little bit more. (quoted in Wolf, 2010)

As noted earlier, longitudinal studies of generation cohorts show that conventional newspaper readership and television news viewership has declined with each generation in most of the OECD nations, particularly in public service and 'quality' journalism sectors. Despite persistent faith among journalists (and more than a few scholars) that younger citizens will acquire a taste for quality news when they grow older, most longitudinal cohort studies show that younger citizens do not return to the fold of dutiful citizenship later in life. These discouraging trends in public service broadcasting audiences provoked the CEO of Sweden's public television to proclaim on the front page of a leading Stockholm daily: 'Swedish Television has a problem with viewers between 25 and 55' (Hamilton, 2010). Similar concerns afflict the BBC, German public service broadcasting, and other systems that find their audiences for both news and entertainment fare aging and, even more alarmingly, dying off.

With the loss of audiences and related loss of advertising revenue or public budget support, conventional news organizations in many countries are in crisis. In 2010, the OECD issued a report on problems facing journalism in its member democracies, noting substantial circulation and revenue declines in all countries (led by the United States and the UK) compounded by long-term erosion of journalism jobs, with countries such as Germany and the Netherlands high on the list (OECD, 2010). The dramatic loss of journalism jobs led a prominent US journalism review to run this feature story: 'Is there Life after Newspapers?' (Hodierne, 2009). Indeed, the cuts in the United States have been staggering, estimated at 30% in 2011 alone (Mutter, 2011). While keeping a characteristically stiff upper lip in public, the BBC has also suffered huge revenue cuts, creating evident loss of quality, particularly in its international coverage. As journalism becomes spread ever thinner, reporting suffers in terms of breadth and depth. The 2013 Pew report on the state of journalism in the United States showed that after years of reductions in newsrooms and closures of news organizations, the spiral of audience defection has grown severe – ironically, due to perceived lack of quality and decreasing coverage of issues considered important by publics (Pew Research Center, 2013). Even the venerable *New York Times* announced the closure of its environment desk in 2013.

There is, of course, some evidence that young people encounter news online, but the trends are less than clear in terms of the quality and volume of the information. The modes of encounter may involve passing by headlines on the way through Internet service portals, or sharing relevant lifestyle issues with friends on Facebook. When I asked a large undergraduate class at my university in the United States if they had watched a nightly news programme recently, barely 25% raised their hands. When I asked if they had seen a YouTube video 'KONY 2012' about a mercenary army and child slavery in Africa, nearly all of them raised their hands.[1]

These shifting demographic trends in traditional information production and consumption have many implications for the communication processes we study and how we conceive of them. Among the most notable areas of change are the gatekeeping or authoritative filtering of public information, upon which much of the research on media effects, persuasion, cueing, agenda setting, and public opinion formation depends (Bennett and Iyengar, 2008). As publics invest less authority in officials, journalists, and professionally spun communication (which defined the heart of the modernist mass media public sphere), information is increasingly self-selected and constructed by social networks and shared via trusted recommendations from friends.

Some European scholars – particularly those living with still healthy public service broadcasters – tend to dismiss these trends as not applying to their countries. There are of course national variations, but few studies are able to explain the persistent shifts in the attention patterns of disaffected younger citizens. What often passes for defence of civic media traditions in some European systems are studies showing that quality journalism still exists, and that those who consume it continue to behave as ever before (Albæk et al., 2013). Yet both the audiences supporting these findings are aging and shrinking, putting the findings more in the service of reifying old modernist communication paradigms than helping to understand the new trends. The efforts to plug the dikes of multiplying information flows and fragmenting audiences are understandable, but they do not prepare us for handling change processes either theoretically or empirically.

As publics become more responsible for their own gatekeeping and authority schemes, the results are, not surprisingly, rather uneven. In

some cases, such as Wikipedia, the product is high-quality information on a larger array of topics than ever before found in one source or
previously shared across language and culture divides. In other cases,
however, information reaching large numbers of people reflects severe
political views bordering on delusion. Witness, for example, the years of
public discussion in the United States about whether Barack Obama was
really born in the United States, and in the view of those who doubted
the authenticity of his birth certificate, whether he was legally quali-
fied to be president. Such seemingly absurd beliefs can become magnified beyond anything that would have been admitted into the public
sphere in conventional modern press systems that kept the gates of
public information for much of the modern era. In the United States,
the controversies about the legal status of Barack Obama's birth raged
on the Internet and were carried regularly into the quality news by politicians and celebrities who recognized the ease with which they could
make news just by simply echoing the question. Other countries have
suffered similar breakdowns of gatekeeping. In Sweden, a racist, anti-
immigrant campaign ad by the Sweden Democrats in the 2010 election
was rejected for television broadcast as violating election communication standards, but it received more than a million views on YouTube,
and a similar volume of commentary online. These examples suggest
how the rise of digital networks can rival conventional media reach,
while undermining the old gatekeeping process.

As gatekeeping becomes less functional, one of the challenges to
traditional communication research involves the dissolving boundaries
between citizen-generated information and journalism. In many cases,
as in the protests following the 2009 Iranian elections, or the massive
uprisings in Tunisia, Egypt, Spain, and the United States in 2010–12,
direct citizen reports offer the best (or only) source material available to
journalists who must relax their usual standards of news sourcing and
adopt the role of curators rather than editors and reporters. In some
cases, news organizations settle into new hybrid information forms, as
when WikiLeaks shared anonymous and controversial source material
with prominent news organizations that added their editorial and distribution capacities in processing huge volumes of material (Chadwick,
2013). The many examples of changing genres of news and public information raise questions about the continuing role and status of old media
regimes (Williams and Delli Carpini, 2011).

Despite the many examples of new and divergent communication
processes, many media scholars continue to be caught in the sway of
ideas such as 'mediatization', which loosely suggests that much of social

order is bent to a singular, pervasive and somehow 'convergent' media logic that structures institutions and public behaviour. There is surely some merit to the idea that there are identifiable media logics, as anyone who has watched the shrinking news sound bite would agree. However, as Jay Blumler and his co-authors suggested long ago, those logics are as much shaped by the formulas of communication professionals and adopted as news formats, as the other way around (Blumler and Kavanagh, 1999). Moreover, the idea of a singular or convergent logic seems a poor account of the current era of digital media and networked societies, where many different media logics seem to be in play. Thus, imputing too much power to some vague media logic risks losing the variety of content and social organization produced by creative uses of personal communication technologies (Castells, 2012). Indeed, the more that people disconnect from legacy information systems, the more creative communication processes enable new patterns of participation and organization.

Communication as organization: beyond messages and effects

The changing information tastes of fragmenting audiences reflect changing styles of citizenship. Citizenship has changed historically, reflecting surrounding political, economic and social changes, and those changes have been expressed via different communication processes (Schudson, 1998). Citizenship is undergoing transformation in the current era as well, with the most evident changes occurring among younger generations that experience the full impact of the social, economic and communication changes described above (Bennett, 1998; 2008; 2012). Indeed, younger citizens in many countries are more averse to joining parties and other civic organizations, more inclined to choose personal issues to support, and more inclined to seek alternative channels of information and modes of engagement that mix information with the capacity to take action.

Communication theory has lagged in understanding new forms of political engagement, information acquisition, and public opinion formation. The recent period has witnessed a series of the largest direct actions in human history, from the global protests against the Iraq War in 2003 to many subsequent mobilizations pressing for stronger climate change policies, overthrow of corrupt regimes, fairness in finance and trade policies, and people-friendly solutions to the financial crisis (Bennett and Segerberg, 2013). Scholars locked into modernist frameworks dismiss these kinds of citizen engagement as somehow marginal compared to voting and other legacy participation categories. Yet many younger activists see the capacities of conventional party and election politics as closed to their demands as political parties and national sovereignty have become bent to the pressures of neoliberal economics and the overbearing influence of business on government. The disaffection from governance institutions also propels many young citizens toward massive direct action, from online petitioning (Earl and Kimport, 2011), to large-scale occupations. Those action varieties are often enabled by commonly available personal technologies from mobile phones to social networks. Not only are the communication processes underlying these mobilizations less centrally managed than most institutional communication, but the ways in which content is generated and how it travels over these digital networks requires new theories and methods to understand (Bennett and Segerberg, 2013).

An important development in understanding the properties of technology-enabled networks is to see how communication often becomes an organizational process rather than just messaging and information acquisition. Organization theorists have developed the idea that communication is constitutive of organizations (Putnam and Nicotera, 2009). However, there are broad areas of society beyond the bounds of formal organizations that also display organizational properties constituted importantly through communication networks. The idea of communication as organization means that networks anchored in hardware and software of various sorts enable people to stay connected to issues and to each other, sometimes with the moderating role of formal organizations, and sometimes largely through the coordinating capacities of crowds that develop intentionality and focus (Bennett and Segerberg, 2013). Among other things, the organizational capacities of crowds may alter how we think about public opinion formation, as powerful frames may emerge from crowds and travel virally within and across societies. This occurred, for example, with the 'We Are the 99%' meme that emerged during the Occupy Wall Street protests in the United States. This frame touched broadly across society and became a media topic that raised the long buried issue of inequality in social discourse. Not only did the issue rise on the media agenda, but it also rose on the elite agenda as well (Bennett, 2012).

By following the traces left by technology in crowd-enabled organization, we are able to see public opinion that arises outside of polling more clearly than ever before. Indeed, the organic qualities of technology-assisted association and information sharing become compelling to study, but often defy conventional analytical frameworks. Communication scholars may continue to use and adapt alternative frameworks such as Latour's Actor Network Theory (Latour, 2005). Yet the sheer scale and complexity of technology-equipped crowd organization suggests the need for new theories of crowd sourced information and related methods for handling the volume of 'big data' they generate. The very logic of communication changes in contexts of large-scale peer production (Bimber, 2003; Benkler, 2006; Bennett and Segerberg, 2013).

The increasing prominence of crowd sourced information flows invites the development of new models and standards for public communication processes. In some cases, crowds are prey to rumour and misinformation and may embrace them as fact. It may be prudent for journalism organizations to act as secondary filters on these crowd dynamics, helping to feed back outside perspectives into the crowd. This happened, for example, during the Occupy Wall Street protests in the United States, as millions of tweets revealed a balance between links to firsthand individual accounts and links to news reports containing pronouncements from political officials, police, and others outside the mobilizations (Agarwal et al., 2012; Bennett et al., 2013).

Figuring out how to connect news organizations with crowds is a challenging prospect for journalism education. How do reporters use social media feeds? How do they assess their credibility? What are the central tendencies and trends in rapidly changing public networks? These questions are more than just about standards and evaluation; they also contain implications for how journalists gather and process information. News organizations may need to become adept at gathering and processing big data and filtering crowd information flows in real time.

Despite the evidence of changing information systems, communication scholars lack much theoretical guidance for research and normative assessment of these processes. Yet reality does not wait. For example, a major journalism award (The Polk Award in the United States) has now been given to an anonymous citizen who used a phone to record events during protests following the 2009 Iranian elections, including the death of a young protester named Neda Agha-Soltan (Stelter, 2010). The 'Neda video' was posted on YouTube, where it received a huge global audience, and was subsequently amplified by numerous television and newspaper journalism channels. The growing importance of news from the crowd means that journalism is changing and that both scholars and journalism educators must update their thinking about just what counts as news and how to address questions such as sourcing, credibility, and the changing interface between news organizations and political actors.

Conclusion: challenges for communication research and journalism education

Few nations have escaped these patterns of social fragmentation, media market deregulation, dispersal of audiences, upheavals in party identifications and interests, and the rise of new technologies that merge information production with social and political organization. There are of course important national variations in these developments, but most nations are grappling with them. Media research is showing signs of shifting its paradigms as well, although there continues to be understandable reluctance to adjust the boundaries or yield the supremacy of legacy fields such as journalism, audience behaviour, media effects, persuasion and public opinion, among others (Bennett and Iyengar, 2008). Nonetheless, more attention is being paid to new information technologies, as they change the delivery and distribution of information and enable citizens to become producers of news and public information. However, with a few notable exceptions, this emerging research is largely descriptive and unguided by theory that captures the social, psychological and political contexts in which these technologies operate.

Despite the evident changes, the conventional wisdom is still that the mass media should be the centre of political communication research, based on the assumption that what elites say in the news establishes a feedback loop to citizens who vote for, or otherwise confer legitimacy on, those elites. This is an old notion of the public sphere in which a system of well-connected institutions (party, press, cultural and civil society organizations) maintain the information gates through with citizens receive news and ideas about who they are and how society is working.

In the current era, many citizens are actively creating their own channels and methods to communicate directly with each other and to make that communication increasingly hard for both elites and the mass media to ignore or marginalize. The emergence of networked public spheres involves rethinking the relationship between communication content and the organization processes that produce and distribute it. Put simply, communication processes are changing in ways that variously complement, compete with and, in some cases, replace the forms that defined modern societies. What is more challenging still is that both modern and late modern systems are in play at the same time, meaning that new models must take into account the interaction of both kinds of communication processes (hierarchical/bureaucratic and distributed/

networked) as they shape power, participation and public life in various societies. A fourth era of personalized, technology-enabled communication is clearly emerging, and our challenge is to understand it.

Note

1. 'KONY 2012' is a half-hour documentary framed around childhood in 'our world' contrasted with the nightmare of a mercenary army enslaving children in Africa. This video had received nearly 100 million views at the time of writing. Available online at http://www.youtube.com/watch?v=Y4MnpzG5Sqc, (Russell, 2012).

15

The Internet's Gift to Democratic Governance: The Fifth Estate[1]

William H. Dutton

Democracy on the line

Many administrations have launched major initiatives to put public information and services online. Increasingly, citizens and businesses can go online for many public digital government services. Similar initiatives have been tied to digital democracy, such as efforts to support democratic institutions and processes, policy consultations, and improved access to government documents and data. Nevertheless, many continue to view the Internet as a marginal, if not irrelevant, tool in political campaigns, elections and other democratic engagements. To many, it is more of a risk than an opportunity, such as in promoting direct forms of political participation – so-called point-and-click democracy – that lack adequate information and public deliberation. Nevertheless, most of these digital democracy initiatives are driven by an effort to maintain and enhance existing democratic institutions.

Politicians are increasingly seeking to use the Internet to engage with citizens, including new forms of contact with prospective voters and new sources of funding. The presidential campaigns in 2008 and 2012 saw the Internet being used to great effect in the campaign of US President Barack Obama and many of his opponents. Open government initiatives have been another force for support of democratic institutions, such as enabling nations to publish more information online in forms that the public can more easily access, and through innovations in open linked data. By making data, such as detailed departmental budgets, more accessible, this move supports greater transparency, enabling the public to hold politicians to account.

In contrast, the fifth estate identifies an emergent development that has not been orchestrated from the top down, but has evolved from patterns of Internet use that are creating what could be a new organizational form. Individuals who are online can create and source information and network with others in ways that are not tied to local or formal institutions. Networked individuals – not only institutions (Dutton and Eynon, 2009) – can be armed with the information and social support to hold politicians and mainstream institutions more accountable. Many institutional initiatives, such as open data, can support access to information and thereby the role of a fifth estate. But it is by virtue of emerging patterns of Internet use that this technology has made pluralistic democracies *more* pluralistic, by adding a new independent base of accountability – networked individuals of the fifth estate.

The communicative power of networked individuals

Since the turn of the century, Internet-enabled online social networking, e-mail, the web, blogging, texting, tweeting, and other Web 2.0 digital channels and services have provided the opportunity for networked individuals to reconfigure their access to alternative sources of information, people, services and technologies, such as when smart phones enable mobile access to the Internet. Networked individuals can then use the Internet to move across, undermine and go beyond the boundaries of existing institutions, thereby opening new ways of increasing the accountability of politicians, press, experts, and other loci of power and influence. This is representative of what I have called a 'fifth estate' (Dutton, 2007; 2009). This label is used to denote a comparable role to the press – the fourth estate – that arose in an earlier print era. Use of the Internet, like evolving uses of the printing press, augmented by the electronic mass media, is shaping new modes of governance across sectors of increasingly networked societies (Castells, 1996).

The fifth estate

The concept of 'estates of the realm' is usually traced to divisions in feudal society between the clergy, nobility, and the commons – the three traditional estates. It was the 18th century philosopher Edmund Burke who first reputed to have identified the press as a 'fourth estate', arguing (according to Carlyle, 1905, p. 104), 'There were Three Estates in Parliament; but, in the Reporters' Gallery yonder, there sat a Fourth Estate more important far than they all. It is not a figure of speech, or witty saying; it is a literal fact – very momentous to us in these times.'

The fourth estate has also been used in countries such as the United States to contrast the press with the three branches of government, implying that the separation of powers between each branch has been extended by another separate base of power – the fourth estate of the press. This characterization draws on Montesquieu's tripartite division of powers among the courts, monarch and parliament, which underpins the separation of powers in the United States constitution, rather than Burke. Nevertheless, the fourth estate has been almost universally linked to the independence of the press in liberal democratic societies, such as in the UK and the United States. The rise in the 20th century of press, radio, television and other mass media consolidated its role as a central feature of pluralist democratic processes, but it is being joined by another source of communicative power, the fifth estate, also with a degree of independence from the press and other estates.

I use the term 'communicative power' to put the influence of the fifth estate in a realistic frame (Garnham, 1999, p. 77). The fifth estate is not usurping power from government or other estates, but the relative influence of networked individuals in communicating with and about the other estates has been enhanced through their use of the Internet. That is, the growing use of the Internet, web, mobile applications and other digital online capabilities is creating another new 'literal fact': networked individuals can reach out across traditional institutional and geographical boundaries into what Castells (2001, p. 235) has called a 'space of flows', moving beyond a 'space of places'. This augments contemporary perspectives on governance processes that build on earlier pluralist models as 'hybrid and multi-jurisdictional with plural stakeholders who come together in networks' (Bevir, 2011, p. 2).

In concrete terms, people increasingly go online to find information and services. Most often, it is the first place networked individuals go. And when they go online, they more often go to a search engine, or take cues from a social networking site, to determine where they go online. They are not simply going to the same local and official institutions they might have gone before, such as to a specific organization's site or to a place, such as to their government, library, newspaper, university, or other geographically centred institution (Dutton, 2009). Their destinations online could be located anywhere – within a global space of flows.

Moreover, Internet users trust what they can find online at least as much as they trust broadcast news or the newspapers (Dutton, 2009; Dutton and Blank, 2011). Generally, the more experience people have with the Internet, the more they develop a learned level of trust in the information they find and the people they meet online. They remain skeptical, with more educated individuals relatively more so. They do not exhibit a blind faith in any source of information. However, those who are most distrustful of the Internet tend to be people who have never used this technology, suggesting that the Internet is an 'experience technology' (Dutton and Shepherd, 2006). As experience online has continued to build, more users have developed a learned level of trust, and rely more on the Internet as a source of information and expertise. These empirical findings explain why the Internet is playing such an increasingly central role in everyday life and work – the use of the Internet by users is reconfiguring access to resources (Dutton, 1999; 2005).

How the Internet reconfigures access is shaped by institutional and structural constraints, such as education, but also by 'digital choices' (Dutton et al., 2007). Outcomes of these changes in access are inherently unpredictable, at micro and macro levels, because they depend on the interaction of numerous strategic and non-strategic choices made by a pluralistic array of actors as they seek to shape access to and from the outside world. This is shown, for instance, in the strategies of government agencies, politicians, lobbying groups, news media, bloggers, and others trying to gain access to citizens over the Internet. The sum of these strategies and choices will reshape how we do things, such as how we get information, but also alter the outcomes of these activities, changing what we know, whom we know, whom we keep in close touch with, what services we obtain, what technologies we use, and what know-how we require to deploy them.

Alternative conceptions

The fifth estate provides an alternative to competing perspectives on the communicative role of the Internet. For example, many view the Internet as creating a 'public sphere' as articulated by Jürgen Habermas (1989) and discussed in contributions to this volume. This concept offers a valuable normative model, but is tied to a romantic view of the past and not able to capture the rise of an entirely new sphere of influence that is a mixture of public and private spheres. Likewise, the notion of an 'information commons' (Kranich, 2004) and its many variants are often used to characterize aspects of Internet space, especially the open sharing of information free or at low cost. However, the Internet and web contain much that is trademarked, copyrighted, licensed, or otherwise owned, in addition to its enormous range of free material, making the concept of a commons problematic as well.

Social science perspectives that the Internet creates a new 'space of flows' are supported across other disciplines. For instance, Tim Berners-Lee, and his Web Science colleagues describe the web as an engineered space creating a distributed 'information space' (Berners-Lee et al., 2006). They realize this space is being shaped by an increasingly diverse set of actors, including users, and for a wide range of purposes, some of which may not be those originally sought by its designers.

Within this information space, a fifth estate is being formed, but it is only one occupant of this information space. Institutional networks are also occupying this with others, from mobs to civil society. The interplay within the fifth estate and its interactions with other estates of the Internet realm is a key aspect of the pluralistic processes reshaping governance and social accountability in contemporary politics and society.

Politics of the Internet in society

The concept of a fifth estate challenges prevailing perspectives on the political role of the Internet in society, such that it is unimportant – a technical novelty or passing fad, or a technologically deterministic force for democracy (de Sola Pool, 1983) or as autocracy, as in George Orwell's 1984 vision of a 'surveillance society'. It also challenges the position that I have called 'reinforcement politics', where the Internet can support and reinforce many different forms of networking, each shaped by its context and stakeholders to reinforce or challenge the interests of networked individuals (Danziger et al., 1982). For example, Evgeny Morozov (2011) falls into this perspective, arguing that autocratic states have used the Internet to reinforce their control of citizens.

The fifth estate takes the Internet as a significant political resource that is changing patterns of governance across multiple sectors, though it does not view this impact as inevitable or an inherent feature of the technology. It is viewed as the consequence of a pattern of use observed over time, and one that could be undermined by key actors interacting in unpredictable ways across the other estates. In contrast to reinforcement politics, the fifth estate exists because no single actor can control the Internet and its political use and implications. Other estates of the Internet realm often want the fifth estate to disappear. A pluralistic interplay among an ecology of multiple actors has given rise to the fifth estate and its role in governance, but its continued vitality is no more certain than was its rise.

The social shaping of the fifth estate

The Internet's broad social roles have similarities with those of traditional media. However, the fifth estate crucially differs from traditional media in how it helps to open up opportunities for greater social accountability in the governance of important institutions, including the media. This contributes to significantly distinctive features of the fifth estate that make it worthy of being considered a new estate of at least equal importance to the fourth – and the first not to be essentially institution-centric. Two key distinctive fifth estate characteristics emerge from this viewpoint:

First, there are shifts in 'communicative power' of networked individuals and the institutions in which they are enabled (Garnham, 1999). This derives from the use of the Internet and related information and communication technologies (ICTs) to reconfigure access to information and social resources. Secondly, the fifth estate provides networks of accountability by enabling the creation of independent sources of information and collaboration that are not directly dependent on any one institutional source or any single estate.

Internet-enabled individuals whose primary aims in their networking activities are social can often break from existing geographical, organizational, and institutional networks, which themselves are frequently being transformed in Internet space (for example, local government officials engaging with individuals on community websites within and beyond their constituencies) to hold other institutions accountable. This results from the role networks can play in altering the biases of communication systems, such as by changing cost structures, eliminating and introducing gatekeepers, and expanding or contracting the geography of access (Dutton, 1999, pp. 60–8). Reconfiguring access can also reconfigure the geography of information and communication networks. It can help to both overcome geographical distances through virtual networks and make geography more important by enabling people to be where they need to be to have face-to-face communication.

Digital choices and divides and the significance of a critical mass

The Internet has become such a crucial infrastructure of everyday life that disparities in its availability and take-up are of substantive social, economic and political significance – placing great emphasis on reducing digital divides which often follow and reinforce socio-economic inequalities in society. Despite these continuing digital divides, networked individuals have become a significant force because the existence of a fifth estate does not depend on universal access, but on reaching a critical mass of users. This enables the fifth estate to play an important political role even in nations such as India, China or Iran with low proportions of Internet users.

Networked individuals and institutions across fifth estate arenas

There are complementary patterns to the use of the Internet in everyday life across various institutional arenas. The Internet is enabling networked individuals in various sectors of society to associate in new ways – creating a fifth estate that helps them to reconfigure and enhance their communicative power. Citizens, or civil society, achieve this, in general or as specialists in a particular sphere (for example, medical professionals and patients), by going beyond their institutional sphere to reach alternative sources and contacts over the Internet (Dutton, 2007). Of course, institutions rooted in the other estates are also using the Internet to maintain and enhance the communicative power of their organizations and institution, such as through the opening of new online communication channels by print and broadcast media. In addition, institutional networking is supporting strategic shifts in organizational activities, including e-government, e-commerce, and e-learning, but these are distinctly different from the activities of networked individuals. This is clearly the case in democratic institutions, where the Internet is being used to maintain and enhance key institutional structures and processes, such as citizen contacts with politicians, parliamentary consultations, and the crowd sourcing of expertise, to name a few. Institutionalized political movements are also utilizing the Internet and social media to help build their organizations and orchestrate activities, from call-ins to protests.

Governing the media and the fifth estate: freedom of expression

The Internet has been criticized for eroding the quality of the public's information environment and undermining the integrative role of traditional fourth estate media in society. This includes claims that the Internet is marginalizing high-quality journalistic coverage, such as by proliferating misinformation, trivial non-information and propaganda created by amateurs (Keen, 2007) and creating 'echo chambers' where personal prejudices are reinforced as Internet users choose to access only a narrow spectrum from the vast array of content at their fingertips (Sunstein, 2007).

Such views fail to recognize the two-edged nature of all communication technologies, including the traditional mass media's equivalent weaknesses (for example, a focus on sensational negative news stories, poor quality reporting and celebrity trivia). More importantly, there is often an unjustified assumption that the Internet will substitute for, rather than complement, traditional media. Many Internet users read online newspapers or news services, although not always the same newspaper as they read offline (Newman et al., 2012). In these ways, the Internet can be realistically seen as a source of news that in part complements, or even helps to sustain, the fourth estate. At the same time, citizen journalists, bloggers, politicians, government agencies, researchers, and other online sources provide a related alternative that is independent and often competing.

The enhanced communicative power of networked individuals has led to attempts to censor and control the fifth estate, even disconnect the Internet, in an equivalent way to tactics used against traditional media. The Internet's opening of doors to an array of user-generated content allows in techniques deployed by governments and others to block, monitor, filter, and otherwise constrain Internet traffic (for example, Deibert et al., 2008). These are typified by the Chinese government's efforts to control Internet content, by creating the 'Great Firewall of China', the Burmese government's closing down of the country's Internet service during political protests in 2007, and efforts by a number of governments to block Internet access and create a 'kill switch' to block the Internet. The arrest of bloggers and Twitter users is another growing concern that is evident in even liberal democratic nations, such as Britain.

At the same time, networked individuals are using the Internet to challenge attempts to control access, such as circumventing censorship. For example, www.herdict.org accepts and publishes reports from Internet users of inaccessible websites around the world, and the OpenNet Initiative and Reporters Sans Frontières support worldwide efforts to sustain and reinforce the Internet's openness.

The fifth estate's governance challenge

The vitality of the fifth estate within the space accorded by the Internet is not inevitable and can be undermined or sustained by the strategies of the other estates of the Internet realm. For example, the modern equivalent of the first estate –the clergy – could be seen as the public intellectuals and critics who undermine the value of the Internet by depicting it as a space overly occupied by an ill-informed, ill-disciplined cult of the amateur. The power base of 21st century nobility is reflected in economic elites, such as global corporations competing to dominate and commercialize Internet spaces. Traditional media are also competing with, co-opting and imitating the Internet's space of flows. Finally, there is the emerging major force of the lay public and civil society, empowered by networked individuals – a modern and dramatic contrast to what Burke might have called 'the Mob'. There may be mobs in contemporary society, and they can be enabled by the Internet, such as a group of hackers calling themselves Anonymous, who sought to attack institutions that did not support WikiLeaks in December 2010. Yet mobs can also have a positive role as in some spontaneous protests orchestrated online.

Questions about the governance of the fifth estate are likely to become more prominent as the realization grows that the Internet is a social phenomenon with deep societal implications. The greatest threat to the fifth estate's enormous potential as an aid to democratic participation and accountability will be from governmental policy and regulation – actions of the commons – such as if regulations, online gatekeepers and other controls constrain or block the Internet's original conception as an open, end-to-end network allowing a free flow of content.

Summary

Internet use can enhance the communicative power of networked individuals who can access sources of information and expertise independent of key geographically and institutionally based organizations, creating a new fifth estate that can contribute to greater democratic accountability. Whether this potential is realized in a particular context depends on myriad factors such as public policy and regulation that is shaping the choices of individual and institutional users. The Internet does not in itself cause people to be more or less strategic, but it can be used to reinforce and extend networks that support individuals and local communities as well as institutional actors.

The role that the fifth estate plays by enhancing the communicative power of networked individuals is likely to have profound implications for government and politics, but also for governance in nearly every sector of society. But the continued vitality of the fifth estate depends on preventing inappropriate regulation of the Internet and other media, which could undermine support for individuals to source information and network without fear of retribution. Regulation of the Internet, including innovations in self-regulation, such as typified by the 'peer production of Internet governance' (Johnson et al., 2004) and other self-governing processes where users participate in establishing and monitoring governance rules (for example as achieved with Wikipedia and the eBay online auction service) will be key to the future of this new estate of the Internet realm. Failures in self-regulation have created a momentum behind increasing Internet and press regulation, such as in the UK's response to phone hacking, which could undermine the independence of the fourth estate and the vitality of the emerging fifth estate.

Note

1. This paper further develops ideas on the fifth estate discussed in Dutton (2007, 2009).

16
Towards an Inclusive Digital Public Sphere

Gianpietro Mazzoleni

An interesting question worthy of address by political communication research is whether we are witnessing the reappearance of the 'romantic' features of the early Habermasian (1962/1989) idea of the 'public sphere' in today's global media ecosystem. In the theorist's imagination, it was late 18th century Europe's coffee shop environment that provided a locale where the public (mostly bourgeois) met informally to discuss issues of public interest, wherefrom eventually emerged public opinion. In the cafés, and other casual meeting places, later to become – when not disbanded by despotic regimes of the time – crowded squares and town halls, public opinion grew to become a critical force, both cultural (capable of questioning the foundations of the existing power systems) and political (able to challenge the power of the dominant classes).

To be true, Habermas' public sphere (like Arendt's 'public realm') is a normative ideal-type, only loosely traceable in the real world, as it presupposes the existence of a well-informed populace, actively interested in public matters – something that hardly existed in the Enlightenment times or afterwards.

In fact, most of the public debate in those early days was constrained by an elite-driven and hierarchical circulation of ideas. The press was the expression of the educated circles, and its readers were mostly confined to the same circles, leaving the unschooled masses excluded. It took almost a century to see the press becoming a mass phenomenon, thanks to the coming of the working classes and citizens to literacy and media consumption. Until then, one can hardly concede that the mass media accompanied the diffusion of democratic ideals and practices that were present in the embryo of the public sphere.

The decline of the mass communication age?

The age of mass communication has not been exempt from a limited realization of the public sphere where discursive confrontation of opposed views is the nutriment for democracy. Habermas, echoing Adorno and Horkheimer's contempt for the culture industry, blames the process of privatization and commercialization of the mass media that gradually transformed the information outlets from instruments of social dialogue (Dahlgren, 1995) into a fake world of images and of opinion control (Thompson, 1995). His pessimistic view about the demise of the 'ideal' of the public sphere (and of its spin-off, deliberative democracy) has been very popular, and it is still shared nowadays by many critics of mass society. They see in the action of modern, commercially oriented mass media, an impediment to the development of an informed and critical citizenship and active political participation – in a word, to the construction of a healthy democracy. Robert Putnam's thesis (2000) in this respect is well known. He unequivocally claims television content and television consumption to be the culprits of disconnecting millions of American citizens from public life.

Many other theorists, of course, have expressed more optimistic views, arguing that by means of the modern mass communication outlets, an expanded public space is brought about that surpasses the narrow boundaries of interaction among elites and also accommodates the uninformed in political life (Schudson, 1998). According to Meyrowitz (1985), the electronic media (television) have made possible a more accessible and democratic public culture and the traditional confines between public and private spheres have collapsed.

The arguments of pessimists and optimists cannot be dismissed simply as ideological preconceptions. On the contrary, their judgments of the role of (traditional) mass media in the polity acknowledge the inner nature of mass communication and the peculiarities of the close relationship between the media systems and political institutions in the historical context of Western democracies.

The process of mass communication is based on a one-to-many, top-down flow of information that forces the target public into a passive, receiving condition. This is indeed the primary insufficiency of traditional mass media to foster political participation. The media produce and disseminate important information for citizens, who eventually use it to make their own views of the world and political opinions, but the same citizens have no say in the production process nor do they have access to the control room. The theories (compare Fiske, 1987; Biocca,

1988) that claimed the existence of an 'active audience' tried to rescue the power of the members of the public of mass media in deciding whether or not to expose themselves to media stimuli, and in decoding the messages in aberrant ways with respect to the coders, could all but claim that the decoders can lay their hands on the coding process.

A further feature of mass communication is its restricted or concentrated ownership; the interests and ideology of those who control the means of communication have evident effects on its informational contents.

Finally, one trait contributes greatly to the structural inadequacy of traditional mass communication to fulfil the democratic ideals: its ubiquitous *liaisons dangereuses* with politics and the political powers. Media and politics are closely related, maintain privileged relationships in a great variety of ways, and exert influence on each other in different degrees and with different outcomes (Hallin and Mancini, 2004a). Historically, this has taken the form of an actual *conventio ad excludendum*, by which the third party of political communication, the citizen, is kept separate from the relationship. The press was postulated to be an expression of the citizenry and served as a surrogate for the citizens' voices, claims and opinions. It actually did this in several circumstances, and there have been positive examples of advocacy and watchdog actions in defence of citizens. However, this is all but active incorporation of the citizenry in the mainstream public discourse.

Some scholars have made a generous attempt to envisage the traditional mass media environment as the modern version of the 18th century-like picture of the public sphere. For example, Dahlgren (1995, p. 8) argued that 'the mass media have become the chief institution of the public sphere', and, according to Bennett and Entman (2001, p. 5), mediated communication fulfils crucial functions in the contemporary public sphere. In brief, a media-centred, media-driven public environment has long been thought to be the natural development of the early coffee shop locales, of the printed sheets that Habermas imagined as the initial spaces of modern democratic debate.

Dahlgren's and Bennett and Entman's arguments depict a 'mediatized public sphere', brought about by the diffusion of modern mass communication in societal and political realms. However, at a closer look, this mediatized environment appears to be an inner negation of the idea of the peer-to-peer exchange of opinions in the Habermasian view of the public sphere: where citizens engage in dialogue in a frame of 'publicness' (*Öffentlichkeit*). It is grounded on the sender-receiver asymmetry; it does not allow the real dialogue among citizens themselves or between them and political counterparts; it is conditioned by the not quite transparent symbiosis between media and political elites. In a word, it is an abstract representation of a public sphere that does not reflect the real state of unbalanced democratic participation in the mass media age. On the contrary, the escalation of the interactive digital media in the postmodern society is creating the conditions for the establishment of a genuine public sphere in the original, romantic, Habermasian sense, where all actors, on equal bases and with equal access to communication resources, can diffuse their ideas, voice their claims, compete in advocating policy solutions – in a word, shape the public/political agenda.

The rise of a global public sphere

The most evident difference between mass communication and what Castells (2009) labels 'mass self-communication' is the horizontal, many-to-many structure of numerous new media that the Internet has bred. The impressive diffusion of the Internet is accompanied by unprecedented (and largely unforeseeable) changes in all human activity domains, but especially in communication. A number of technological inventions made the birth of mass communication, which has radically changed the landscape of modern society, possible. The arrival of television was rightly saluted as a revolution in a) the ways people enjoyed leisure time that had considerably increased thanks to the improved labour conditions and the new lifestyles, and b) in the political arenas (Lang and Lang, 1968; Blumler and McQuail, 1969). Technology, once again, has made possible mass self-communication, which is the reversion of the one-to-many paradigm that has been dominant in the mass communication age.

It is hardly a surprising revolution, insofar as interactivity and circular communication have always been the natural modes of human exchange since the dawn of society. However, nowadays, thanks to an extraordinarily resilient platform such as the Internet, individuals can interact with potentially global audiences. This truly 'quantum leap' in communication – incomparably greater than any yet amazing revolutions initiated by the traditional mass media – prompted McLuhan to envision a 'global village', even if he could not foresee that it would substantiate into global communication networks known today as Twitter, Facebook, YouTube and the like.

One major effect of the establishment of the new communication ecosystem is the development of a global public sphere. The network society is by definition a global society, according to Castells (2009), because it activates and integrates a multiplicity of cultures. This impinges on the contours and features of the new public sphere, because it extends its boundaries to include in the global discourse players from virtually all paths of social, economic, cultural and political life, in a 'cyberspace', which is interconnected and interdependent. Any significant event in any part of the world nowadays is not only immediately made known, but it can prompt comments, criticism, and even consequential action on the part of large numbers of citizens in different countries. That was what happened in the 2011 Arab Spring, when the images of tragic events occurring in Tunisia, diffused by Al-Jazeera, triggered the mobilization of most sensitive sectors of civil society through the social networks in other Arab countries and eventually fuelled the uprising in Egypt. Watching the suicide of the Tunisian protester Mohamed Bouazizi would not have caused the spread of revolts if the crowds of young citizens of those Arab countries had not had smartphones and access to the web. This resource has made the difference: it empowered citizens to share impressions, emotions and propositions and generated change in society.

By means of the new interactive media, citizens create communal evaluations, collaborative communities, participatory environments, where they are no longer passive targets of hetero-produced contents but act themselves as '*produsers*' (von Hippel, 2005), capable of generating, remixing, relaunching and recoding new messages.

In classic views, the public sphere is essentially identified as an environment where people engage in discursive activities. When concrete action is involved, the public sphere leaves room for 'civil society': both concepts are ideal-types and largely overlapping, especially vis-à-vis the rapidity by which the new media spread ideas, beliefs, slogans and calls to action in the network society, and the promptness with which this cyberspace-based discourse converts into concrete actions, such as protests, sit-ins, political activism, rallies for or against government policies, and the like. In a word, civil society can be seen as the place where the people who have exchanged opinions within the perimeters of the public sphere eventually make their voices heard with real effects on politics and power holders.

This is not to say that intense debate and ensuing action in the mass communication age were politically ineffective. They have certainly been in several circumstances, like in the often-quoted American TV networks' critical coverage of the Vietnam War, which affected the mood of American public opinion, eventually forcing the government to put an end to the war. However, in the mass self-communication age, we can envisage the shaping of a public/civic Athenian *agora* where citizens debate and deliberate, finally unrestrained from the asymmetry of the traditional media-carried communication and unbound from the secular hegemony of the elites.

It is not necessary to espouse the positions of the cyber-optimists to see how beneficial to democracy this can be.

Implications for political communication: the rise of an 'enlarged digital polity'

Habermas describes the classic public sphere as a space lying between the citizenry and the state/government. With the ongoing transformation of the nature of the metaphorical and actual space where people meet and mobilize by means of the interactive media, and considering that technology dis-intermediates communication between citizens and government, as well as between government and citizens, the question is whether both the Habermasian public sphere and civil society can still be seen as 'separate' spaces or whether we stand in front of the building of a communal arena of discussion and confrontation by citizens, political institutions and the media. All the players use the new media in a variety of ways but basically try to influence each other and/ or impose competing and conflicting views, and to shape the agenda of public debate and of government decision. Unquestionably, we are observing the blurring of the traditional boundaries – and of related power balances – of the mass communication age.

Coleman and Blumler (2009, pp. 10–11) put forth three assumptions to explain the rise of a new form of citizenship: (1) 'the relations between the members of the public and holders of political authority are in a period of transformative flux'; (2) 'an inexorable impoverishment of mainstream political communication is taking place'; (3) 'interactive, digital media have a potential to improve public communications and enrich democracy'.

What is emerging from the paradigm shift in mass communication and the change from centripetal to centrifugal models (Blumler and Kavanagh, 1999) or, in Brants and Voltmer's words, from a 'decentralization' of political communication (2011, p. 10), is what we can envisage as an *enlarged digital polity* that encompasses the whole of communications and relations between the major and minor actors of the political game. The traditional portrayals of top-down, bottom-up flows of communication no longer represent the dynamics introduced by the interactive media. Most certainly, government maintains its prerogatives intact, but presidents, prime ministers, mayors, members of parliament, political leaders and politicians in general have all accepted to listen carefully to the voices coming from the web, not only to show that their communication is state-of-the-art, but principally because it has become crucial to sense the pulse of the 'real' citizens, a *sine qua non* for gaining and maintaining political and electoral consensus. Politicians still use opinion polls to measure the temperature of their electoral markets or of national publics. However, what the French scholars (for example, Wolton, 1995) have long considered the opinion poll (*le sondage*) to be – the 'third actor' of political communication, a proxy for the citizen whose wills could be registered only rarely (in elections) – is losing its clout in favour of new investigative tools like the 'Twitter sentiment analysis' that register and measure accurately what opinions, issues, threats and trends are boiling in the web communities.

Political actors engage themselves directly and personally in the web debate via social networks, responding to tweeters and bloggers. What was described as 'rhetorical presidency' by Tulis (1987) – that is, presidents bypassing the news media to establish direct communications with American citizens – has become a daily reality in the Obama years and is likely to become an institutionalized strategy of 'going public' (Kernell, 1986), alongside the traditional press conferences, participation in TV shows, photo opportunities and the like.

The recent deliberative turn of the democratic theory provides further interpretive elements. Borrowing from Chambers (2003), Kriesi (2012, p. 1) observes that the traditional 'vote centric approach' is being replaced with a 'talk-centric one' that explains, among other things, why 'responsive leaders use rhetoric ... in a way which facilitates public discussion, and ... are held in check by a public that is capable of assessing the validity of their talk' (Kriesi, 2012, p. 5).

Such trends bring along developments in the nature of public discourse. The dis-intermediation – that is, the end of the editorial filters, especially of the mainstream, independent news media – opens the way to a populist kind of political speech: 'Politicians have embarked on strategies to meet people where they are', and 'the considerable popularity and electoral success of populist leaders has forced established parties to adopt both stylistic and content-related elements of their populist rivals' (Brants and Voltmer, 2011, p. 11). We do not yet have sufficient evidence of the extent to which politicians' demagogic communication impacts the citizens of the enlarged digital polity. The impression is that the debate carried on on the web counterweighs the politicians' populist talk, so vast is the quantity of comments, reactions, critiques that make a sort of zero-sum effect. This is another sign that in the 'talk-centric', web-based public sphere, political communicators' power of influence is levelled to that of the larger citizenry.

Does the rise of the digital public sphere mean altogether the end of the 'old media regime'? In other words, are the new media the only champions of a real democratic dialogue?

Williams and Delli Carpini (2011), analyzing the changes in the American news media landscape, argue that the 'Age of Broadcast News' – characterized by 'its attempts to limit politically relevant media to a single genre ("news") and a single authority ("professional journalists")' (p. 282) – is being supplanted by a 'New Information Environment', strongly relying on the digital media, whose central qualities are 'multiaxiality and hyperreality' that clash with the traditional canons of journalism but not with a 'democratically useful media regime' (ibid., p. 286). This new regime, however, is not completely displacing the old regime of the newsmaking profession; on the contrary, it absorbs 'the best of the Age of Broadcast News while also making possible the reemergence of useful qualities found in earlier regimes' (ibid., p. 286).

The underlying assumption of their analysis is that the new media environment is more 'democratically useful' as long as it ensures 'opportunities for a wide variety of voices, interests, and perspectives to vie for the public's attention and action' (ibid., p. 324). They seem also to warn that the digital public sphere does not automatically construct democracy if it 'reduces public understanding, deliberation and/or participation' (ibid., p. 287).

Their warning is indeed accurate, because the risk of 'technological determinism' is often lurking when evaluating the impact of the new communication technologies on social and political realities.

Of course, there are ways to avoid a deterministic reading of the rise of the new global public sphere. One is suggested by Williams and Delli Carpini themselves: that is, not to consider the old media regime with its social, cultural and political architectures necessarily an obstruction to democracy. Even if traditional mass media were top-down means of communication, they did guarantee a wide dissemination of relevant information to the citizens, thus allowing them to make informed decisions even if they could hardly make their voice heard in the public space, still dominated by political and media elites. The traditional functions of the news organizations to gather, filter, and circulate information are still valid and recognized in the digital public sphere. Journalism is in fact undergoing a deep revision, not only of its traditional production models but also of its founding tenets. It will not be totally replaced by citizens' journalism, but it will have to come to terms with it and other forms of mass self-communication. This is something already happening with the increasing integration of print media outlets with the blogosphere and the social networks. An additional way to obviate deterministic accounts of the impact of the new media is provided by a sociological approach: that is, focusing on the measurement of citizens' attitudes, opinions, and behaviours in the new public sphere. If empirical evidence proves that the use of social networks fosters civic engagement, increases political knowledge, and favours the naissance of movements, then we can safely argue that it is not the smartphone that encourages democracy but its social use. This is indeed evidence that political communication research is abundantly producing, as witnessed by the large number of journal articles and books on the role of the web in general and of social networks in particular, in politics, elections, political discourse and the like.

Concluding thoughts

A final question – how can the digital media *better* serve the democratic public sphere? – still needs more reflection before being properly addressed. The limited success of movements like the *Indignados* and Occupy Wall Street, and the latest developments in the countries touched by the 'Arab Spring' stir many doubts about the real contribution of the new digital media that the optimistic arguments of Castells in his recent book, *Networks of Outrage and Hope: Social Movements in the Internet Age* (2012), fail to dispel completely. Morozov's (2011) pessimist views of the 'dark side' of the web, and the several attempts by governments – not only authoritarian – to bridle the activities in cyberspace (like in the United States versus WikiLeaks and China versus Google cases), all reveal that the equation of the Internet with-Democracy is far from being universally accepted political dogma.

On the other hand, nobody can negate the 'pre-political', educational function of such phenomena. Protests, even if eventually unsuccessful on the ground, diffuse a sense of empowerment in the participants, build strong identity and communitarian ties, and attract new followers and activists; in a word, they contribute to the development of democratic ideals perhaps more effectively and more rapidly than when citizens lived in a non-networked society. Not all the power holders encourage this global trend; indeed, they often portray it as a menace to the existing order. However, the best defenders are the 'netizens' or the 'prosumers' themselves, who can rely on potentially formidable communication tools to offset the attempts to suffocate the nascent digital polity: A polity that is buttressed by communication technologies virtually accessible to all and that assures the readiness of critical information via the old mass media and the new social networks. A polity that is (or can be) the realization of the old, romantic ideal of a 'public sphere'. This time certainly 'inclusive'. In theory and in practice.

17
Beyond the Po-Faced Public Sphere

Stephen Coleman

Willie Whitelaw, who served as deputy prime minister under Margaret Thatcher, once accused his political opponents of 'stirring up apathy'. This was, to be sure, an infelicitous construction: apathy – from the Greek *a-pathos; without feeling* – implies that something is absent – and to stir up an absence of feeling would seem to be an absurd enterprise. But there is a second sense in which Whitelaw's accusation should interest us, for it belongs to that tradition of thought which regards emotions as smouldering liabilities, constantly in danger of being kindled, inflamed, stirred up. Just as you 'stir up apathy', you ignite pathos – which then disrupts and disables its Aristotelian antithesis, logos. Politics, according to this discourse, entails quiet appeals to reason. The political becomes a project to protect logos from contamination by pathos.

My concern in this chapter is the damage that is done to democratic politics when the animating force of affect is regarded as a distraction – when there is a conscious effort to create a disjuncture between the diffuse energies and porous spaces of popular culture and the instrumental work of making decisions that affect the public. Democracy, I want to argue, suffers when it becomes encased within the well-managed boundaries of self-referential institutions and can only flourish when decision-makers breathe the same air and speak the same language as the people they claim to represent. This is not an argument against the existence of a division of political labour; otherwise, to paraphrase Oscar Wilde, democratic citizenship would take up too many evenings. My argument is that at the most common point of entry to democratic politics – the public sphere in which we share, discuss, challenge and act upon ideas about the common good – the repudiation of pathos should be rejected and an unapologetic reconciliation between logos and the terms of popular communication realised.

The chapter proceeds through three stages. Firstly, I reflect upon the normative claims of the democratic public sphere and suggest that these are largely unrealised, even in the most advanced and sophisticated national versions of democracy. Secondly, I outline a number of ways in which citizens have migrated from the official public sphere – or, more accurately, have found themselves faced with new conditions of publicness that refuse to be delimited by the aesthetic continence of rationalist discourse. Finally, I argue that while successful political communication in these new conditions increasingly depends upon who can attach credible symbols to pervasive feelings, there is still a resistance in significant quarters to the intrusion of pathos into the hallowed halls of logos.

Public aversion to the public sphere

For all of its normative significance as an inclusive 'sounding board for problems that must be processed by the political system' (Habermas, 1996, p. 444), the limited appeal of the political public sphere as a popular cultural space has proved to be problematic. Public indifference to its sombre allure has become a taken-for-granted feature of contemporary politics, making a mockery of its multivocal, democratic credentials. The vibrant chatter of competing testimonies, each proclaiming their warrant as public reason, is conspicuous by its absence. The contemporary political public sphere is too commonly conceived as a monument to dispassionate reason: a space in which members of the public are expected to be on their best behaviour, an arena of politely repressed performance. Historically shaped (or perhaps deformed) by an ascetic avoidance of animated and haptic distractions from unadulterated rationality, the late-modern public sphere has come to be characterized by a relentless search for sound sense and casual inattention to deep sensibility.

Why is it that the political public sphere, which is normatively rooted in principles of popular inclusion, has in practice become so exclusive and uninviting? How did places of public debate – from political parties to television studios – become so averse to the intrusive danger of the unscripted voice? What is it that has made the public seem like such strangers on their increasingly rare forays into the public sphere? While neither joking nor ranting are explicitly against the rules of the public sphere, they – and other visceral outbursts – have come to be frowned upon with the tacit force by which giggling in church or clapping at the wrong moment in a classical concert are deprecated by po-faced cultural guardians. Governed by an ethos of instrumental rationality that celebrates the analytical and eschews the pre-cognitive, 'proper conduct' in the public sphere is increasingly at odds with quotidian sociability. Why should this be so?

Firstly, because, while the public, as a constructed entity, is constituted by feeling, pulsing, sweating bodies, the collective body politic can only ever be a bloodless aggregation. The public is a collective entity that can only exist at the level of abstraction. The public sphere is the arena within which individuals learn to recognize themselves in the other (Habermas, 1996, p. 162) as experiential subjectivity is translated to a greater or lesser extent into civic integration. For Habermas (2004, p. 9), the enchantment of the public sphere lies in its 'mysterious power of intersubjectivity' whereby it unites 'the disparate without eliminating the differences between one and the other'. The work of ironing out stubborn disparities and producing a common 'we' out of a mass of strangers who need one another in order to coexist, but can never hope to know and fully understand one another personally, entails a language of generic abstraction. The kind of affectively rich and narratively nuanced expression characteristic of subjective expression is hardly achievable within the multivocal context of the public sphere. For in stretching intersubjectivity into the form of a public (body politic) that can speak for itself and be spoken for, the richness of experiential specificity must give way to the relative thinness of a shared and representable consciousness.

Secondly, the public sphere, which in its early form comprised a range of spontaneous and close-knit interactions between literate opinion leaders, containable within the intimacy of the market square, coffee house or the *salon,* has now become institutionalized. Replete with codes, protocols, records and institutional memories, the spaces of public gathering in contemporary mass democracies inevitably exceed the kinship of the lettered. The public sphere of contemporary politics is less a place or singular space than a web of connections: communicative entanglements between groups that cannot live without one another, but might never choose to speak to one another. It is a sphere of mediated relationships, populated both by physical face-to-face encounters and the gossamer presence of near and distant others whose claims cannot be ignored. The institutions responsible for mediating these relationships – the press, radio, television and increasingly a range of online curators and connecters – are faced with a set of social interactions that can never be represented or dramatized on a fully human scale, because the number and density of characters and actions constituting the public are too great to fit on a single stage. The public come to be described via generalizing statistics and indicative events. Knowledge comes to matter most when it relates to everyone and to appear irrelevant when it is merely the testimony of someone. In such a context, the scope for personal recognition is limited. The public sphere becomes a domain of social strata and forces rather than bodies and faces.

Thirdly, the guardians of the public sphere as a space that embodies and protects the most highly-valued symbolic features of democracy – the formation of publics; opportunities for cross-cutting discussion and deliberation; and the aggregation of mass preferences and values – see fit to demand for it a degree of respect that is widely assumed to be incompatible with the frivolity of popular culture. From the elite cadre of political journalists and spin doctors to parliamentary and congressional officials, there is an explicit expectation that *their* institutions will be acknowledged in ways that reflect their own views of their purposes, values and status. The assumption here is that the public sphere is not just any old space of human interaction – a football terrace, a theatre auditorium, a bar – but one in which 'the public organizes itself as the bearer of public opinion' and becomes the court before which is affirmed the legitimacy of all political decisions (Habermas et al., 1964, p. 56). If public will formation is to be guided by reason, dignity and equanimity, the model of the courtroom or scholarly seminar seems more appropriate than the boisterous tumult of emotive exchange characteristic of popular and inclusive spaces. Defenders of the decorum of the rational public sphere employ a subtle conflation between propriety and exclusion, closing the door on popular culture as a way of fortifying the public sphere against vulgar entrants. It follows from this that the performance of citizenship comes to be not only shaped by positive norms of what it means to be a rational-critical being, but also a set of expectations about how citizens should *not* act. Just as 19th-century theatre audiences had to be taught how to respond in a civilized fashion to the delicacies of high culture (Sennett, 1992), so members of the contemporary public are given to understand that civic performance, be it in the polling station, party conference or town-hall consultation, entails a certain way of speaking, standing, arguing, registering support and signifying disagreement. The protocols of public engagement appear to frown upon spontaneous speech and creative sense-making.

Historians will observe that democracy was never supposed to be like this. They might point to Justice Brandeis's famous summary of the outlook of the American Founding Fathers, which suggests that for them democracy involved more than occasional secret voting:

> They believed that freedom to think as you will and to speak as you think are means indispensable to the discovery and spread of political

truth; that, without free speech and assembly, discussion would be futile; that, with them, discussion affords ordinarily adequate protection against the dissemination of noxious doctrine; that the greatest menace to freedom is an inert people; that public discussion is a political duty, and that this should be a fundamental principle of the American government. (Brandeis, quoted in Bork, 1971, p. 24)

But in the contemporary public sphere, these principles do not hold true: 'noxious doctrine' is commonly disseminated by media organizations that are rich and powerful enough to drown out the experiential testimonies of the disadvantaged and marginalized. The manipulation and vacuity of much political debate plays to 'an inert people' upon whose weariness and disenchantment it has come to depend. The 'political duty' to discuss takes the form of off-stage muttering, rage and ridicule, while the bearers of 'political truth' have all too frequently ceased to even believe in their own rhetoric. Political parties turn into freakish cults of obsessive loyalists. Much media debate turns into the crudity of Punch and Judy. Opinion polls seek answers to sterile questions of interest to a shrinking minority of political junkies. Voter turnout declines. The public sphere begins to look like a wasteland. And yet ... and yet the transgressive energy of democracy is far from exhausted. Around, between and alongside the po-faced public sphere, agendas are being set, stories told, groups mobilized and collective action exercised in ways that interrupt and disrupt the old repertoires of politics. Might these constitute a bid for the soul of the atrophying public sphere?

The new publicness

The Habermasian model of the public sphere, in its original iteration at least, seemed to be tied to a place-based conception of political geography. From the Parisian salon to the Washington TV studio, the public would somehow gather in or around a centre that was imbued by an atmosphere of critical rationality. The defining feature of such nuclei was a certain sensibility: one went to the circus to be tickled to distraction, to church to have one's spirits lifted and to the public sphere to produce rational discourse. According to this model, acts of civic solidarity were typically coordinated by and within central spaces of undisturbed rationality from which publicness seeped out to the wider society. As in the surrounding industrial order, where economic value appeared to emanate from bounded centres of production, the civic value nurtured within the public sphere appeared to be the product of a kind of rational incubation; a safeguarding of public voice from the contamination of popular culture. As in economic theory, the public sphere was conceived as depending upon inputs and outputs: one went to the public sphere with ideas, agendas, proposals and demands and, through a process of discursive sorting, the output comprised forms of civic agency fit for a rationally enlightened society.

Post-industrial societies have tended to eschew this model of value-producing centres. As Castells and many others now argue, the structure of social coordination has shifted from hierarchical centres to networks of diffuse circulation. There is a growing acknowledgement – not without some resistance – that technologies of linear knowledge transmission are less effective than they once were. New ways of circulating information with a view to creating cumulative knowledge have assumed an increased social significance. The tension between industrially structured media distributing symbolic fodder for mass consumption by relatively monolithic audiences, and emergent patterns of pluralistic symbolic circulation across global nodes of digital connectivity is a conspicuous example of how networks have destabilized the shaping of public meaning and challenged the hegemony of the shrinking mass media. Media owners, editors and journalists have long regarded themselves as being trustworthy (though largely unaccountable) gatekeepers to the sacred centres of knowledge production and dissemination, but the Internet has opened up a space of circulation in which messages and memes regularly interrupt such domination. Citizens with a cause to advocate or idea to advance, who once depended on being allowed in to the sacred media centres on terms determined by the gatekeepers, can now evade these spaces and appeal for public attention within the networked public sphere. In areas of the world where hegemonic monopolies have come to feel entitled to control the terms of civic expression, the ubiquity of technologies of networked communication have had immense consequences: from China, where online communication through social networks such as *weibo* has enabled activists to counter the misinformation of the state media, to the Arab dictatorships in which street demonstrators came to rely upon digital networks as sources of civic coordination and safety, to the United States, where arrogant commercial media conglomerates have been hit by a generational migration to online sources of social knowledge. (Of course, this is not a matter of the substitution of one media form by another, but a challenge that carries with it empirically observable consequences for the terms of publicness and the capacity of elites to manage flows of information and communication).

With this shift towards a more dispersed and diffuse space of publicness, something very important has happened to politics. Traditionally, the greatest obstacle to collective action has been the high cost of coordination. This has been especially disempowering for the poorest and most marginalized in society (in truth, most people) because they lacked the resources needed to find and access people who shared their interests and values. With the Internet, political content circulates via technologies that facilitate large and relatively coherent networks. Network power has strong potential to transcend barriers to political coordination, afford opportunities for movements that do not comprise traditional political participators (that is, the wealthiest and most educated) and do not organize in the hierarchical fashion of modernist politics. As Bennett and Segerberg (2012, p. 753) have put it in their superb account of 'the logic of connective action',

> Technology-enabled networks of personalized communication involve more than just exchanging information or messages. The flexible, recombinant nature of DNA makes these web spheres and their offline extensions more than just communication systems. Such networks are flexible organizations in themselves, often enabling coordinated adjustments and rapid action aimed at often shifting political targets, even crossing geographic and temporal boundaries in the process.

Here again, just as I was not arguing earlier that new communication networks have somehow displaced old mass-media centres, I do not wish to suggest that new connective movements are now the dominant form of political coordination, supplanting long-standing models of institutional affiliation. The extent and impact of the shift in forms of collective action will differ across cultural contexts and are clearly both fast-moving and incomplete. What we can say about this is that the terms of publicness, once clear, are now fractured; that conceptions of the public sphere that emphasize places of assembly rather than the circulation of ideas appear to lack freshness or currency; and that some of the most energetic and innovative changes in political communication that we have witnessed in recent times have fallen outside the bubble within which long-standing entanglements between politicians and journalists have resided. To study political communication in the early 21st century calls for sensitivity to circuits of symbolic diffusion that transcend the boundaries of the early Habermasian model of the public sphere.

Not only has the logic of public connection changed, but also with it has emerged scope for more eclectic modes of public expression. As the generic solemnity of the rationalistic public sphere gives way to new ways of speaking in public, the 'mysterious power of intersubjectivity' that Habermas ascribes to the public sphere begins to assume a new feel and sound. The potential spaces of intersubjective discourse and recognition that have emerged in recent years seem to be closer to the ground, lighter to the common touch, less culturally prescriptive and more open to the bricolage of everyday conversation. While scholars have produced sophisticated accounts of emergent structures of political opportunity (Bimber et al., 2012; Tufekci and Wilson, 2012; Coleman, 2012; Bennett and Segerberg, 2012), less attention has been paid to the consequences of these changes for the character and quality of public communication (for exceptions, see Graham, 2008 and 2010; Graham and Hajru, 2011). Contemporary political discourse is caught between an established code for speaking in public about public issues and a less restrictive amenableness to the words, tone and pitch of quotidian inter-action. The three traditional actors in the theatre of politics – political elites, journalistic intermediaries and citizens – are all finding it neces-sary to change their game in the light of new ways of attracting public attention, producing political meaning and facilitating democratic inter-action between institutions claiming to speak for the people and the people themselves (Gurevitch et al., 2009). Authoritative voices have to find new ways to affirm their legitimacy, often by invoking claims to an authentic relationship with the lifeworld; journalists, once used to being *the* storytellers, are adapting to a new role as curators and translators of competing narratives; and citizens, long used to being both periph-eral spectators and relentless complainers, are having to work through the ethical responsibilities of interactive political presence. Running across all of these adaptive manoeuvres is a growing (though under-articulated) normative rejection of the belief that 'freedom to think as you will and to speak as you think' entails being bound by expressive shackles. Democratic discourse begins to feel less like a foreign language that must be learned by stuttering outsiders before they can be taken seriously. Indeed, an emerging and defining feature of democratic sensi-bility is an assertion of the right to enter public space on terms that are not predetermined by cultural elites.

A defence of democratic passion

Whitelaw's inelegant reference to 'stirring up apathy' points to an anxiety that has long underpinned and undermined liberal democ-racy. The assumption here is that democracy – meaning the primacy of citizens' values and preferences in all matters that affect them – can only be made to work if it is tempered by deterrents against the imagined cultural excesses of volatile and vulgar public emotion. When political commentators lament the wave of touchy-feely sentiment in modern politics; when proponents of deliberation demand that public discussion should only be taken seriously when personal feelings are politely repressed; when policy wonks insist that, unlike 'public opinion', they are guided by the facts alone; and when facile critics of online talk express exasperation with the noisy, messy, fragmented cross-talk of social networks, they are not articulating settled norms about what democratic expression should be like, but advocating a particular view that emerged in late 18th and 19th century Europe with a view to tempering the improvisational energy of emergent democratic citizenship. From its outset, liberal democracy was founded on an implicit balance between the principle of constitutional equality and a cultural disdain for the tastes and feelings of the majority. This has never been a normatively tenable or politically sustainable tension. Hovering between managerial democracy, which only ever pretends to regard all human feeling as worthy of respect, and cultural democracy, which seeks legitimacy on the basis of a consummate faith in uncoerced feeling, the form of liberal democracy that became established in the West during the 20th century was always transitory; a holding operation by which the transgressive energy of the public could be kept in check and the institutional ethos of cultural elitism could accommodate the inconvenience of electoral accountability.

The democratic project, if it is to mean anything, is based upon the promise that people can collectively, self-consciously and autonomously determine their social destinies. In order for that promise to be realized, the scope for cultural and intellectual transgression must be more or less unlimited; that is to say, no proposition about society can be ruled out of bounds; no language or mode of expression deemed unacceptable or inadmissible; no pleasure dismissed as irredeemably vulgar; no deliberative inferences curtailed by foundational dogmas. Democracy, in this sense, is the most powerful emancipatory project that human beings have ever undertaken. But as this project came to be translated into the codes of political rule, it became deeply entangled in a chain of paradoxes. On the one hand, democracy appears to entail an equality of voice; nobody has the right to shout me down because they are better than me. On the other hand, most media institutions are based on an ethos of shouting down, with volume control adjusted to levels of wealth ownership. On the one hand, the normative claim that the public will is sovereign is fundamental to democratic rhetoric. On the other hand, actually existing democratic states seem impotent in the face of global forces and institutions that are neither accountable nor controllable. On the one hand, democracy is committed to the opening up of debate – expanding the range of voices and values upon which decisions are founded; broadening the political agenda to reflect the diversity of lived experience; creating spaces in which words can make a difference. On the other hand, there is a pervasive frustration about the ways in which power evades public control, leaving citizens feeling like spectators upon the policies and decisions that affect them. On the one hand, the constitutional claim is that all citizens are equal in the political realm (if nowhere else). On the other hand, there is the manifest reality that, while no vote is worth more than another, some voters are worth much more than others.

One of the political affordances of the new publicness is that the taken-for-grantedness of these contradictions are more easily questioned and, when challenged, publicized. Democracy assumes vivid and plausible reality when those who have been told that they have nothing to say – nothing worth hearing – that their voices are only capable of emitting noise – begin to refuse their scripts and feel free to speak out of turn. Very often, when people speak in such a fashion, the first response of the complacently included is to put them down as being overly emotional. They are urged to control their passions. But the interruptive force of democratic passion lies in its refusal to acknowledge or respect the prescribed cultural absences that characterize the po-faced public sphere.

Part V

The Past, Present and Future of Political Communication

18
Jay Blumler: A Founding Father of British Media Studies

James Curran

Introduction

Jay Blumler was a pioneer researcher into the media before media studies became part of the British university repertoire. He was an institution builder, as the director of the Leeds University Centre for Television Research – the progenitor of the University of Leeds' celebrated Institute of Communications Studies – and as a co-founder of the influential *European Journal of Communication*, established in 1984. However, his principal claim to fame is that his publications, spanning half a century, have influenced the development of media studies both in Britain and internationally.

Three aspects of Blumler's background are worth highlighting since they have a bearing on the nature of the influence he has exerted. A political science graduate from Antioch University, Blumler was familiar with pioneering US communications studies. When he prepared for his interview for the post of the Grenada Television Research Fellow at the University of Leeds in 1963, he turned instinctively to the standard overview of US media effects research (Klapper, 1960).[1] One key way in which Blumler influenced the development of British media studies was to import insights from the United States.

Second, Jay Blumler was – and remains – a committed social democrat. The son of radical parents, he travelled to the London School of Economics in 1947 to do postgraduate research under the supervision of Harold Laski, a leading theoretical exponent of radical pluralism (Hirst, 2005) and chairman of the British Labour Party in the 1945 general election. Blumler then went on to teach for 14 years at Ruskin College, the worker and adult education institution affiliated to Oxford University. During this period, Blumler became a Labour Party activist and intellectual, aligned with the Gaitskellite wing of the party. Blumler's strongly held ethical social democratic outlook emphasised social solidarity, public deliberation and the pursuit of a wider public interest above private interests. These values shaped his work, and led him to become a leading exponent of a centre-left tradition of political communication research.

Third, Blumler is a citizen of two nations. He is an expatriate American who has lived in Britain for much of his adult life, and married a British woman. Yet, he retains strong ties to the United States, speaks with a soft American accent, and in the latter part of his career combined a post at Maryland University with that at Leeds. This dualism encouraged him to resist the national introversion of media research in both Britain and America, and to adopt a comparative approach that was profoundly influential.

The best way to examine Blumler's place in the formation of British media studies is to consider selectively some of his key publications. Situating these in the context of their time helps to illuminate both their intellectual provenance and wider significance. We will begin with Blumler's first book published in 1968, seven years before the first 'media studies' degree was introduced in Britain.

Audience power

An academic legend has grown up that the once popular perception of media audiences as dupes was only demolished by cultural studies reception research in the 1980s (for example, Morley, 1992). In fact, this perception was debunked in Britain by Jay Blumler and his associates long before. They were drawing in turn upon a rich tradition of American audience research extending back to a brilliant (and elegantly written) study of the media's influence on the 1940 Presidential election (Lazarsfeld et al., 1944).

However, this corpus of American work was not widely known in Britain during the 1960s. Instead a celebrated book by the American journalist, Vance Packard, called *Hidden Persuaders*, which invoked an alarming picture of the conditioning impact of subliminal messages embedded in advertising, and of the omnipotence of new political public relations techniques, was still being lauded in Britain (Packard, 1957/1967). Another more crafted and insightful work, Richard Hoggart's *The Uses of Literacy*, which portrayed a hyper-commercialized, candyfloss media as culturally depriving and emotionally enfeebling, was then the best known treatise on the media (Hoggart, 1957). Both books, and others like them, reflected a widespread belief in the all-pervasive power of the media.

Blumler's first book, co-authored with Denis McQuail, was implicitly a riposte to this conventional view (Blumler and McQuail, 1968). Based on a panel study of Yorkshire voters who were interviewed three times during the 1964 general election, it showed that exposure to campaign communications on television consolidated rather than changed voting intentions. Television's most significant influence was an increase in awareness of policy issues, and a small improvement in the perception of the Liberal party and its leader, especially among those with only a limited interest in following the campaign. But the general impression conveyed by Blumler and McQuail's study was that the British electorate was partisan, not much interested in politics and difficult to influence.

This was the second British electoral study to reveal the limited power of television. A panel study in two constituencies during the 1959 general election had also concluded that television had increased political knowledge but had only a modest influence on political attitudes and voting (Trenaman and McQuail, 1961). In broadly reaching the same conclusions, Blumler and McQuail were subverting with powerful evidence the myth that television had the power to brainwash the public.

But while Blumler was being iconoclastic in a British context, he was being faithful to American academic orthodoxy. Indeed, the book that had helped Blumler to secure his job at Leeds (Klapper, 1960) offered a magisterial overview of this orthodoxy. Its central thesis is that, in general, people selectively attend to, make sense of, and retain media information in line with their prior beliefs, which are shaped primarily by their social networks and early socialisation. The media are not usually a direct cause of attitudinal change but 'function[s] among and through a nexus of mediating factors and influences' (Klapper 1960, p. 8). The media, in this view, generally reinforce rather than convert.

Blumler and McQuail (1968, p. 5) explicitly invoked Klapper's assessment, as did other American studies supporting the view that the media have limited persuasive influence. Studies not cited by Blumler and McQuail also reached a similar verdict during this period. Thus an overview of studies of the impact of the televised presidential debates between Nixon and Kennedy in 1960 showed that most Democrats thought that Kennedy had won, whereas most Republicans believed Nixon had been the victor (Katz and Feldman, 1971, p. 727 ff.) – a view different from the scorecard of journalists at the time who commented negatively on Nixon's tendency to sweat and look shifty.

In effect, Blumler and his colleagues showed that what was seemingly true of the United States also applied to Britain. Blumler was later to challenge this minimal media effects perspective. But before we come to this, it is worth looking at Blumler's championship of another strand of US research.

Audience pleasure

There was a strange convergence between left and right onslaughts on popular culture in Britain and America during the 1950s and 1960s (for example, Rosenberg and White, 1957). A left-wing critique which argued that the industrialization and commercialization of culture was impoverishing meshed with a right-wing critique which contended that increasing market influence was eroding social hierarchy. The two critical traditions were synthesized in an influential conception of a media-dominated, atomized, homogeneous 'mass society' (Bramson, 1961; McQuail, 1969).

For social democrats like Blumler and his collaborator, Denis McQuail, this disdain for popular culture sounded uncomfortably like scorn for the people they identified with. In a joint study, they argued that popular TV viewing should not be dismissed as mere escapism, or written off as 'shallow, undemanding and trivial' (McQuail et al., 1972, p. 140). They pointed out that the American investigator Hilda Herzog (1944) had discovered that radio listening was an interactive process in which the same soaps had a different appeals to different people. This insight, they suggested, should provide a cue for reassessing TV viewing.

Their reappraisal concluded with the results of their small-scale, quantitative study of TV quiz show fans in Leeds. This revealed that what people brought to their viewing strongly influenced what they got out of it. Some sat back and enjoyed the excitement of TV quiz contests; others actively competed against TV contestants in a self-rating process; still others (drawn disproportionately from those with limited education) viewed quiz shows as the equivalent of attending night school; and some from all these groups enjoyed chatting about these shows with their friends. What this revealed, argued the authors, is a 'diverse and overlapping pattern of motive and satisfaction' (McQuail et al., 1972, p. 143) that lofty critics of popular TV viewing overlooked.

The 1944 Herzog study that McQuail et al. cited was part of a consumer uses and gratifications tradition that had flourished in 1940s and 1950s America,[2] only to subside by the 1960s. Thus, uses and gratifications research had featured prominently in a famous anthology of the field in the mid-1950s (Schramm, 1954), only to be dropped in a second edition issued much later (Schramm and Roberts, 1971). Blumler and Elihu Katz (1974) resuscitated this dying American legacy by mobilising communications scholars in Europe and America to undertake new research, or to comment on old work, on audience uses of the media. This initiative gave rise to a landmark edited volume, cited in over 1000 publications (Google Scholar, 2014).

With characteristic openness that characterized Blumler's and Katz's lifelong readiness to engage in intellectual debate, they commissioned an attack on uses and gratifications research written by Philip Elliott (1974). Uses and gratifications research was often underpinned, Elliott argued, by a flawed functionalist understanding of inherent wants and needs, and usually excluded wider considerations of power and ideology (Elliott, 1974). In the event, his critique was more attuned to the radical drumbeat of British media research during the 1970s than to the editors' quantitative approach to exploring media uses and gratifications. Blumler and Katz's initiative faltered, save in the United States.

However, the underlying ideas that informed their championship of uses and gratifications research – their concern to explore the nature of audience pleasure, their view of audiences as active or at least interactive, and their stress on the socially situated and diverse nature of audience uses of the media – had a wider resonance. These ideas were imaginatively developed in a succession of cultural studies books exploring the dynamics of media use, pleasure and identity, most notably in an exploration of subcultural style (Hebdige, 1979), watching soap opera (Ang, 1985), and reading romantic fiction (Radway, 1987).

It has become the convention to view these studies as a major advance because they tended to pay more attention to content, and brought to bear a wider intellectual frame of reference, than uses and gratifications research (for example, Morley, 1992). While this judgement is broadly correct, it is inclined to overstate the new work's originality. To take but one example, Roger Silverstone's (1994) argument that the ritualized watching of television imparts a sense of order, continuity and social connection is a widely cited 'new' insight of cultural studies. In fact, it broadly restates what Bernard Berelson (1949) had found in a uses and gratifications study of newspaper reading, though with the important difference that Berelson's study was based on empirical evidence.

Something important was gained through Blumler's championship of the declining tradition of uses and gratifications research. Old insights and concerns were rediscovered; new ones were developed (most notably, Katz et al., 1973); and a new tradition of enquiry into media reception was helped into being, even if it liked to cock a snoop at its forebear (for example, Ang, 1989, p. 103 ff).

Reconceptualising media power

Blumler thus entered the field by importing insights from American research which revealed audience manipulation of the media, and the multiple satisfactions that people derive from commercial culture. This orthodoxy fitted readily into an uncritical view of the role of the media in capitalist society. But for a social democrat like Blumler, its implications were double-edged. On the one hand, this orthodoxy affirmed the popular power of the people, and illuminated the imaginative life of media audiences – all grist to the mill of a centre-left academic identifying with ordinary citizens. On the other hand, it seemed to register very little concern about the shortcomings of the media, and very little grounds for thinking that any such shortcomings might matter.

This encouraged Blumler to pick a quarrel with the intellectual tradition he was importing. Even in his first book, he was anxious to work against the grain of US orthodoxy by making as much as he could of data registering some degree of television influence (for example, Blumler and McQuail, 1968, pp. 197–207), even though most of his data in fact pointed the other way.

However, he persevered in seeking to revise the minimal effects model of the media. His next attempt was a before-and-after investigation of the impact of media coverage of the investiture of Prince Charles in 1969, based on a small quota sample of Leeds inhabitants. The media's coverage was so extensive, noted Blumler and his co-authors, that 84% of respondents said that they had discussed the event with someone else (Blumler et al., 1971, p. 164). Did this a typical media event change anything?

Their fine-grained analysis concluded that it did. They showed that below the level of widespread support for the monarchy were feelings of ambiguity expressed in contradictory conceptions of what the monarchy should represent, and how it should function, that was a response to the historic shift from a traditional monarchy to a secular democracy. Although media coverage of the investiture did not change attitudes towards the Queen, it encouraged a more positive view of Prince Charles. Crucially, it also gave rise to a shift in the way in which the monarchy was viewed, encouraging both heightened awareness of, and increased acceptance of, the formal role of the monarchy. In this way, argued the authors, media coverage encouraged people to savour the grandeur of the monarchy (and its links to a proud past), with diminished class and democratic resentment. The monarchy was strengthened, conclude the authors, through a televised ritual of rededication and reconciliation that made for a more secure foundation of support.

Shortly afterwards, Blumler and McLeod (1974) undertook an electoral study, notable for the more sophisticated statistical techniques it deployed. It revealed that frequency of media exposure influenced the level of turnout among young voters (though not older ones) in the 1970 British general election. Here was further evidence of a media effect that mattered since differential turnout can affect election outcomes.

This was followed by an ambitious study which, before the era of emails, must have been a nightmare to organize. It took the form of a comparative investigation into the role of television, in nine countries, in the first direct election to the European Parliament in 1979 (Blumler, 1983a), based on an examination of television regulation, interviews with TV journalists and party spokespersons, a content analysis of TV election coverage, and a post-election survey.

This was a landmark study because comparative media research was then in its infancy (about which more will be said in a moment). Among the study's many findings, one is especially relevant in terms of Jay Blumler's battle against the minimal effects orthodoxy. The amount of television coverage of the election campaign and the level of support for the European community were found to be key drivers determining election turnout. Thus, Germany, with extensive TV coverage of the election and favourable attitudes towards the European project, had the highest turnout. Britain, with the least TV coverage and negative attitudes towards the European community, had the lowest (Blumler, 1983b).

The next step in Blumler's revisionist campaign was the writing of an overview essay with Michael Gurevitch about 'the political effects of mass communication'. This presented an eloquent narrative of the field that proclaimed the emergence of a 'new look' (Blumler and Gurevitch, 1982, p. 245). The old minimal effects model was wrong, argued the authors, because politics had changed. Throughout the West, there was cumulative evidence of declining party loyalty and increasing electoral volatility. People were more amenable to media persuasion because they were less anchored to stable political allegiances. The rise of television – a bipartisan medium of political communication – had also exposed audiences to more information that challenged their beliefs, in contrast to partisan newspapers. Selective attention was consequently a less effective barrier against media influence.

More important still, fresh evidence of media influence was emerging because the nature of media effects had been reconceptualised. The old orthodoxy was founded on a narrow focus on media persuasion, usually in terms of changing public opinion and voting intentions. But new studies, argued Blumler and Gurevitch, had investigated a broader range of potential effects in terms of strengthening or weakening the motivation to vote, influencing what people think about ('agenda-setting'), shaping images of society ('cultivation differential'), and promoting or weakening trust in public institutions. These more varied approaches had revealed results that demonstrated the power of the media.

In the event, Blumler and Gurevitch's championship of the new revisionism won the day. Subsequent studies confirmed that the media influence what some people think about, and also what they think is important (McCombs, 2014). Experimental studies also showed that television could influence frameworks of understanding of public events and political issues (for example, Iyengar, 1991; Philo, 1990). And there is now a large literature revealing myriad ways in which the media matter. For example, strong public service television systems support a higher level of public affairs knowledge, and contribute to a smaller knowledge gap between the advantaged and disadvantaged, than strongly commercial TV systems (Curran et al., 2009; Aalberg and Curran, 2012; Soroka et al., 2013).

However, it is now being argued that the growth in the number of TV channels and the rise of the Internet is leading to increased audience selection of news sources on the basis of partisan preferences, and that this is strengthening selective exposure as a protective audience shield (Bennett and Iyengar, 2008, among others). But this is a qualification (especially applicable in polarized societies like the United States) rather than a rebuttal of Blumler's 'new look'. The pendulum has swung not back to where it was, but merely part of the way.

Political communication theorist

In the 1970s and 1980s, media research was organized almost entirely in terms of work undertaken within the nation state. This gave rise to a number of recurring distortions: the projection of America as a microcosm of the world (for example, Lichtenberg, 1990), soaring meta-theory delineating the role of the media in society irrespective of national difference (for example, Althusser, 1984), and parochial short-sightedness in which researchers failed to see the wood for the trees (for example, Hetherington, 1985). While these distortions persisted, they became less prominent as a consequence of the increased awareness of comparative difference that developed within media studies.

One of Jay Blumler's most important contributions was to foster comparative media research. This had enjoyed a brief vogue during the 1950s and 1960s, usually linked to a Cold War/modernization thesis (for example, Siebert et al., 1956, and Pye, 1963). Comparative media research then fell into decline when this tradition lost authority. Blumler's European election study (Blumler, 1983a), already mentioned, marked a key moment of revival and was followed by other comparative studies in which he was involved (Blumler and Nossiter, 1991a; Semetko et al., 1991 and Blumler et al. 1992a).

Among other things, Blumler distinguished between three different types of public service television organisation in Western Europe. These were classified in terms of autonomy from the state, strong state influence, or the incorporation of diverse political representation (Blumler and Thoveron, 1983, p. 10). Subsequently, Blumler proposed a typology of six different broadcasting systems in the world (Blumler and Nossiter, 1991b, p. 407). His work was part of the process in which differences between media systems began to be more adequately mapped.

In addition to initiating projects, Blumler was also an effective cheerleader. He wrote two celebratory essays with Michael Gurevitch, similar to their 'new look' effects essay, that set out the achievements of comparative media research (Blumler and Gurevitch, 1990; Gurevitch and Blumler, 2004). A central theme of the second essay was that the comparative approach had rendered visible things that had seemed invisible before. Blumler also used his year as president of the International Communications Association to promote comparative media research, resulting in an edited book (Blumler et al., 1992). The tradition that Blumler worked hard to foster finally took off with the publication of Hallin and Mancini's landmark *Comparing Media Systems* (2004a). Comparative media research is now an established sub-field generating its own compendious handbook (Esser and Hanitsch, 2012a).

The second significant contribution that Jay Blumler made as a media theorist was to propose, with Michael Gurevitch, an overview model of the media as part of a 'political communication system' (something that was clearly linked to Blumler's comparative research). They argued that this model should take account of 'linkages' between political and media institutions in terms of state control/media autonomy, the level of partisanship and media-political elite integration, viewed in relation to audience orientations and the political culture of society. This would provide a key, they contended, to understanding the media's role in supporting or weakening citizen engagement and political partisanship, and of the structuring of political agendas. Underlying this conception was a social systems theory that assumed 'a set of input-output relationships that bind its constituent elements in a network of mutual dependencies' (Gurevitch and Blumler, 1977, p. 287).

This model was revised on successive occasions (Blumler and Gurevitch, 1996, 2000, and 2005, among others) by being elaborated in more complex ways, and updated to take account of major developments like media expansion, globalisation, and the rise of political public relations. The tenor of the model's presentation also changed with an increasing emphasis on the dysfunctional consequences of the political communications system.

However, the more complicated and ambitious the model became, the more its 'system' claims (the notion that changes in the interrelationship between components of the political communications system lead to adaptive changes in the rest of the system) became more elusive. Despite expansion, the model did not expand enough. It understated the role of civil society,[3] something that Blumler (2014) implicitly conceded. And while recognising the more 'porous' nature of contemporary politics, it never properly addressed the centrality of entertainment as a form of political communication – a blind spot that is part of the political studies tradition (Curran, 2011).

But if the specificities of Blumler and Gurevitch's model-building are open to challenge, it had the merit of providing a platform for making sense in an insightful way of changes in political communications systems. It also provided an antidote to the drive towards ever greater specialization of political communications research (reflected in the journal *Political Communication*, founded in 1991). It forced people to think about and debate the interconnections between media and politics in a wider context. Indeed, Blumler and Gurevitch's systems approach can be viewed as being a parent, or at least godparent, of the current debate about 'mediatization' (exemplified in political communications by Esser and Stromback, 2014).

The third way that Jay Blumler contributed as a theorist was to monitor changes in the British media system, and reflect on their wider implications. He and associates undertook ethnographies of BBC reporting during every general election campaign between 1966 and 2001. This revealed an oscillation in the balance of power between broadcasters and politicians. Broadcasters were subordinate to politicians during the 1950s, but became increasingly autonomous during the 1960s. In the subsequent period, politicians adapted by developing increasingly professionalized, media-centred election strategies that adjusted to television news values, while seeking to advance their electoral objectives. Television journalists reacted to this attempted manipulation by exposing the electoral and public relations strategies of political parties, as a way of reasserting their journalistic autonomy.

By the 1990s, argued Blumler and his colleagues, a mutual accommodation had been reached between politicians and broadcast journalists that served both. However, this détente, Blumler argued, was not in the wider public interest. It led to increased centralisation of control both within broadcasting and political organisations that excluded dissenting voices. It led to a PR-driven form of political discourse, reflected in shrinking television sound bites, which failed to serve the informational needs of democracy. It also generated journalistic disdain, and an increased focus on the 'game' rather than the substance of politics, which fostered public cynicism. This was in sharp contrast to an earlier era when broadcast journalists felt obliged to report fully on election campaigns, almost irrespective of their ratings appeal, as part of their sacerdotal duty to serve democracy, and when political parties had not yet invested heavily in the professionalization of political advocacy (Blumler and Gurevitch, 1995; Blumler, et al., 1996; Blumler and Gurevitch, 2002; Blumler, 2014).

While being a critic, Jay Blumler remained a passionate supporter of public service broadcasting. With William Dutton, he wrote a scathing analysis of the market-based development of British cable television in the 1980s, viewing it as a programme, economic and policy failure (Dutton and Blumler, 1988). Mounting attacks on the public ownership and regulation of television, and his examination of the functioning of the United States broadcasting market (1986), led Blumler to restate and develop a defence of public service regimes. Their function, he argued, is to support commitment to high standards and investment in quality children's programmes, innovative drama and informative current affairs and other content that the market tends not to foster. In these ways, public service broadcasting helps to 'deepen the expression of experience about the human and social condition' and assist 'society in all its parts to bind, reconnect and commune with itself' (Blumler, 1989, pp. 87–8).

The rise of the Internet invited further reflection. With Stephen Coleman, Blumler argued that the deliberative deficit of the political communication system, the fragmentation of public life, and increasing public disengagement from politics could be offset by the development of the Internet within a progressive policy framework (2008). The Internet, they point out, has created a shared space for peer-to-peer and many-to-many interactive exchange between citizens. It also offers a means by which citizens, and a constellation of networks, can communicate to different levels and centres of governance. But the Internet's potential to enrich democracy, they warn, is vulnerable. Consequently, a publicly funded agency needs to be established, 'charged with promoting, publicising, regulating, moderating, summarising and evaluating the broadest and most inclusive range of online deliberation', and with 'facilitating public deliberation between government at its various levels and the dispersed networks which constitute the contemporary communicative landscape' (ibid., p. 172 and p. 183). Its overriding objective should be to forge an effective 'civic commons in cyberspace' (ibid., p. 169).

This recommendation runs counter to the current neo-liberal consensus in favour of an Internet free of public intervention (save in relation to national security, protection of minors, defamation and intellectual property). In an act of heresy, Coleman and Blumler are imagining how the Internet can best serve the public, just as their reformist predecessors – the architects of public service broadcasting – did the same in relation to radio and television technology.

Retrospect

In brief, Jay Blumler shaped media studies by importing the insights of American communications research into Britain, and by being a leading participant in overthrowing its minimal effects consensus. He was also a pioneer of comparative media research, an exponent of an influential, totalizing conception of the political communications system, an insightful, critical observer of changes in British media and politics, and an eloquent media reformist. Starting as a caterpillar in the essentially administrative cast of American effects research, he flourished as a progressive butterfly, pollinating different areas of media research.

Blumler should be viewed also as a leading figure among a pioneering group of social scientists – recruited from psychology, sociology, anthropology, economics and political science – who founded a social science strand within British media studies.[4] This remained a minority strand because a humanities-based cultural studies tradition became dominant in the British version of media studies. But this minority strand has extended the range of media research, deployed effective tools of analysis, and kept open channels of communication between media research and new developments in the social sciences. Without it, British media studies would be enormously impoverished.

Blumler's place in the history of media studies is defined not only by his publications, institution building, and development of a distinctive tradition of research. His kindness, love of debate, enthusiasm for media research, encouragement of others (including people of different political and intellectual dispositions than himself) and irrepressible geniality are all reasons why he is regarded with such affection. These are qualities that helped to make him a dynamic presence in the building of a new academic subject. They are also frontier virtues, from a pioneer era, that should be cherished and preserved.

Notes

1. Conversation with Jay Blumler on 21 November 2014, on leaving an inaugural lecture.
2. Incidentally, this ancient essay is well worth reading.
3. This model also played down social conflict, a theme that is not salient in the ethical tradition that Blumler comes out of.
4. This pioneer group includes Jeremy Tunstall (anthropology), Dennis McQuail (history/sociology), Michael Gurevitch and Colin Seymour-Ure (both political science), Hilde Himmelweit (psychology), and James Halloran (sociology and economics).

19
'Values Are Always at Stake': An Interview with Jay G. Blumler

Katy Parry and Giles Moss

Normative perspective: democracy and citizenship

> One of the questions you often raise in research seminars is about the normative position of the speaker. Is it essential for media and communications researchers to have a clear normative stance? Why is it so important in your view?

I'm not sure whether it's essential, but I certainly think it is desirable and important. And that's because values are at stake in our subfield of the communication discipline. I think one can see that at four different levels. First of all, there is the civic level itself. On the one hand, there is the Schumpeterian view that democracy should pivot on competition between two teams of would-be political leaders for the votes of citizens. Now, that was not just an observation of how democratic politics was being conducted on the part of Schumpeter and others who followed him (often described as a 'realist' view of democracy), but it was also normative for him. At one point, Schumpeter even maintained that for politics to work well, there should be restraint on the part of citizens from trying to do more than choose between competing leaders (Schumpeter, 1942). Well, of course, that stands in opposition to the participatory view of democracy, especially as outlined by Carole Pateman (1970), who argued that a worthwhile democratic process should encourage, enable and involve more wide-ranging forms of citizen participation. So that's just a simple example of how values are at stake at the civic level.

Then, at the level of media organization, I guess we have the contrast between public service broadcasting and commercially organized broadcasting. These, too, are normative. Obviously, public service broadcasting is normative: it's set up to pursue certain ideals. And the supporters of commercial broadcasting are not just, all of them, guys who want to make a fast buck. Many of them do believe that this is the best way in which to provide materials for consuming audience receivers.

Then, there's the level of political journalism, hit off perhaps by the distinction between a kind of sacerdotal status as against a much more pragmatic one.

And then finally, the fourth level: communication research itself entails an old distinction between critical and administrative communication research. This contrast is thoroughly normative, really, because the administrative research idea was that scholars should help the media to do their jobs better and critical communication research aimed to expose the inadequacies of media provision. So it's normative at that level, too.

Your own normative perspective appears connected to democracy and citizenship, but these terms, as you know, are highly contested. How would you characterize your own view of democracy and citizenship?

My point of departure for democratic citizenship is the ideal of what I would call 'collective self-determination'. The notion of self-determination is often applied to an individual's passage through life. They are self-determining if they know what they're trying to do and if they can assess the environment in terms of the available opportunities and the possible difficulties of pursuing whatever they would like to do and are not determined by external pressures which undermine their self-determination. That's how I understand personal self-determination, and I think that's collectively applicable when we come to the ideal of democratic citizenship. The realization of this ideal is a *more-or-less* matter, rather than an *either-or* matter. So we can have more or less manifestations of citizenship, democracy, etc. Of course, the pursuit of such an ideal almost inevitably has to struggle against powerful countervailing forces in any polity or society. So you've got your ideals, you've got the countervailing forces, and there is sometimes a terrible struggle. But it does seem to me also, at times, that democratic impulses turn out to be hearteningly resilient and even enduring.

I think my outlook on democratic citizenship has three implications for the role of communication in democracy. We need

1. the provision of valid information to satisfy the surveillance needs of citizens in a democracy.

2. the provision of what I'll call 'meaningful choice', so that citizens can have before them the main options at policy levels between different ways of dealing with current issues and problems – a criterion which I think is very badly served by media-based communication in present-day circumstances, where so much in the way of the framing of key political issues is almost monolithic. (I mean, you can see it in the whole way in which the policy responses to the financial crisis have been filtered by the media: 'deficit reduction, deficit reduction, deficit reduction'. The alternatives to that are not there on the table, really, except amongst some intellectuals.)

3. inclusiveness. The aim of public communication should be one in which the experiences, the issues, the problems of all sectors of a polity are included in media-based communication – and all voices are included.

Have your views about democracy and citizenship changed over time?

That is very interesting. When I came to Leeds and I looked at how television was becoming the prime political communication medium, I thought 'Aha, we've got a liberal pluralist democracy, and we've got television reaching more and more people, dispensing information around, awakening them to more things; we've got party broadcasts during campaigns, news coming up into the picture as well'. This encouraged me to think of political democracy and communication and democracy as pivoting on three things: provision of relevant information, accountability mechanisms, and opportunities for people to participate in politics if they wished to do so. Looking back, I guess that I situated this perspective in a sort of paradigm of political communication organization which was relatively top-down. So there were active communicators – mainly politicians, officials and their aides and journalists – and there was a body of audience receivers. Okay, the audience could do other things, but, in the main, they were a body of receivers, so it was a kind of pyramidal view, if you like, of the political communication system.

I think my views have evolved – rather than changed on the whole – and developed in perhaps two main ways, due mainly to the advent of the Internet and digital communication and also to my collaboration with Stephen Coleman here – I mean, that was a real influence on the evolution of my thought. So, what are the two ways? Well, first of all, I'm going to call it the desirability of trying to bat down political stratification: up here are the really knowledgeable, involved, influential actors, and down there in the abyss are the ignorant, the apathetic and so on. Somehow the need to try to do one's best to diminish political stratification. So I think that's one thing I became somehow more aware of. And there was the implication from that of the desirability of fostering navigable avenues of meaningful exchange between citizens and decision takers, through the Internet, in part.

Secondly, there has been the addition to my corpus of democratic values the value of deliberation. That wasn't in my consciousness in the old days, and certainly that's come to the fore as a means of furthering citizen understanding and improving political decision taking. But here again, deliberation should be treated as an ideal. In the book I wrote with Stephen Coleman called *The Internet and Democratic Citizenship* (2009), we argued that we shouldn't be talking about establishing a *deliberative democracy*, but instead pursuing a *'more' deliberative democracy*. Like democratic citizenship, deliberation is an ideal; you can have more or less of it.

How does your view of democracy and citizenship connect with your long attachment to socialist politics?

They are intimately connected both normatively and intellectually. By normatively, I mean that for me, socialism is inconceivable without democracy. I just don't see any chance of advancing socialist ideals in any enduring way without it. Intellectually, well, you know, that's my own history. I came to this country from the US as a sort of ordinary progressive Democrat, but I got introduced to a really impressive body of ethical socialists, some of whom had escaped from Nazi Germany, having developed quite a philosophically grounded conception of ethical socialism. And I just realized how philosophically non-grounded my position as a New Deal Democrat was. Nothing against New Deal Democrats, but there wasn't the philosophic basis, in the way that this group seemed to have achieved. They based their ethical socialist position on three ideals: freedom, in a self-determining sense; equality, and not just in a social mobility sense; and fellowship, in the sense of the need in all organization to think in terms of people's relations with each other in a positive manner. And these were socialist ideals. I was very closely associated with them and was on the editorial board of their monthly journal.

You have stressed in your work the importance of connecting academic research to policy and practical recommendations. Why is this important in your own view? And are there any compromises that need to be made in order to do this?

In my view, the answer to the first question is so obvious. Because if one takes the kind of normative stance that I have done, and also if one maintains that values are always at stake in how political communication is organized – what it produces, how it impinges on ordinary people, and so on – then surely you've got to want to try and have some influence on policy. Otherwise, what the hell is the point of it?

But you've asked about compromising. I don't think it is a matter of compromising, but it is a matter of having to find ways of relating your ideals and what follows from them to social reality. So that you don't just develop ideas within your own thought processes, but try to understand what's going on out there in terms of possible channels for furthering your ideals. This entails trying to understand the mentalities of significant practitioners in the political communication field so that you can seek ways of getting across to them the importance of the kinds of things you feel political communication should stand for and do.

Methodological perspectives

You've completed a wide range of empirical studies focusing on different aspects of media and communication: producers, texts, audiences, and policy and regulation. Can you tell us something about the general methodological tenets that have informed your empirical work?

First of all, I don't think of myself as an echt-methodologist. I've met or seen in the literature one or two echt-methodologists, and I shy away from them – but maybe that's my limitation rather than theirs. At any rate, I don't think of myself as having a rounded methodological perspective. But I have worked with a number of specific methodological tenets. I'll just list some of them. One is 'horses for courses': choose the methods which are most suited to your research purposes, and these can properly differ according to differences in your purposes. Now, I suppose that almost immediately brings in the unending debate between quantitative and qualitative approaches to communication research, much of which – though not all of which – I think of as pointless. I think it only has a point if one is trying to identify the particular virtues and advantages, and the things one can get out of quantitative methods and likewise out of qualitative methods, rather than thinking of them as somehow superior over here and inferior over there. That's horses for courses.

Of course, methodological rigour is highly desirable, but never perfectly achievable. You know, I think one has got to be realistic about that because if someone comes along and sees someone else's really good work but also seems to think the methods they have adopted have not been perfect, then the critique could be, somehow, overly negative.

When one is approaching a research topic, try in advance to specify some expectations of what might be likely to come out at the findings end when you've applied your methods. Because if you've got advance expectations in relation to research outcomes, then you've got a real basis for trying to figure out why there may have been disparities between those expectations and the results.

Be alert to what's going on in the actual wider world in your sphere of research interest and not just be alert to what's going on in the relevant literature. I think quite a few academics tend to be very alert to what's going on in the literature – and naturally so, that's fine – but then get so wrapped up in that that they're insufficiently alert to what is going on in the outer real world that is relevant to what they want to think and theorize about. And that's especially important in the political communication field because it's so continually in flux. A good example of that in my own case is how I reacted when I was employed part-time at the University of Maryland in the 1980s to how the Reagan administration had determined to relate to the American news media. Reagan had a corps of communication consultants around him who had developed strategic views on how, for example, journalistic agenda-setting should be mastered and about the efficacy of negative campaigning. We tend to think of negative campaigning nowadays as just part and parcel of the system, but prior to the 1980s, its practice was typically incidental – maybe frequently incidental – but only incidental. In the case of the Reagan administration, it became systematic. 'Hey, wait a minute' – I thought, recalling the famous four theories of the press (Siebert et al., 1956): 'Here's a fifth theory of the press'. I called it a Machiavellian theory of the press, and then an increasingly elaborated analysis of the modern publicity process spilled out of all that for me (Blumler, 1990).

On the subject of comparative political communication research, Mancini writes in this volume that even in the 'age of the world-wide web, each media system is still affected by the local culture, by the national language and by all those cultural symbols that still characterize cultural production'. Would you agree that we can still effectively conduct comparative media systems studies in the age of the Internet and the more abundant, multi-channel media landscape that we have now?

Three thoughts occur to me here. First of all, Mancini's absolutely right in recognizing that local cultural specificities keep coming up when scholars try to undertake really good pieces of comparative research. For example, in our nine-nation study of the role of television in the first European Parliamentary elections of 1979, we approached it in a really comparative spirit, and we did get comparative findings out of it, but we referred in the concluding chapter to what I called 'spatio-temporal noise' (Blumler, 1983). There's a whole page in which I listed all the specifics of that campaign that couldn't be incorporated into a comparative perspective, but that were particular to different countries' approaches to the campaign. Barbara Pfetsch, a very fine German scholar, has recently published a nine-country study exploring the cultures that are involved in politician-journalist relations and interactions (Pfetsch, 2014). Here also she spells out a whole host of what she calls contingent conditions – as distinct from comparatively differentiating conditions – that emerged from her study. But those contingent elements don't negate the value of comparative research because the case for such research rests on the fact that there are things you cannot know about political communication unless you can get to grips with the role of contextual systemic factors impinging on phenomena at other levels, which, in turn, you cannot get to grips with unless you can compare different systems. So the case for comparative research is still as strong as ever, but one has got to be more circumspect in terms of what will eventually come out of it.

Secondly, I think that there are four different ways in which one can conceive of and undertake comparative communication research. The first is to have a very large vessel into which one pours as many research locales as one can, assuming one can find investigators who are willing to work with you in those locales and that there's some data you can collect in those locales. That's probably the most often used form of comparative research. Secondly, there's side-by-side comparativism. Somebody does a study of, let's say, political communication in Finland and says 'But, you know, I don't think this works quite like that in Germany'. This is impressionistic side-by-side comparativism. Then, there's hand-me-down comparativism. That's more rigorous than these other two. It involves resort to a typology of how different systems are organized and run, like the Hallin and Mancini typology (2004a), for example, and then tries systematically to see whether phenomena are different in, say, the Liberal Democratic model, the Polarized Pluralist model or the Democratic Corporatist model. Of course, it's possible that when you conduct comparative research that way, you shed more light on the typology categories than on the phenomena, if the phenomena aren't best investigated through the categories of that typology. Lastly, there's creative theorizing, whereby one tries to identify the dimensions of systemic organization that might impact on phenomena at other levels, pinning it down to specified, formulated dimensions that might be operative. The study that Holli Semetko, Michael Gurevitch, David Weaver and I did (1991), comparing the sources of campaign agendas in Britain and the US in the 1980s, was of that kind.

> Early on in your career, you pointed to the problem of 'fact starvation' (1964) in media and communication research and of the illusions of 'grand theory'. Meanwhile, critics accused you of giving 'too modest a role to theory' (Garnham 1979) in your own research. How do you look back at those debates today?

Well, I still adhere to my scepticism about grand theories' often overblown claims. Grand theory can be pursued at such a stratospheric level that the readiness to be involved in real empirical spade work gets lost. Alternatively, if the 'grand theorist' does undertake empirical research, it may be confined to certain bounded forms of enquiry, mainly designed to confirm the validity of the original view. That has been a basis of my critiques of so-called critical theory, much of which, in the 1960s and 1970s especially, displayed the shortcomings of 'grand theory'. I also think that grand theory can sometimes encourage scholarly overconfidence, buttressed by what I would call 'in-camp group think', and I think it may also foster unproductive, polarized divisions between different positions. But nowadays, fortunately, scholarly debate in our field, though still vigorous, is less polarized and is waged more temperately and with greater mutual understanding.

However, there is some justice in Nicholas Garnham's criticism of my scholarship. I do not regard myself as a theoretician of political communication, although I am certainly not a hard-nosed positivist! Instead I think of myself as a conceptualizer, who strives for holistic understandings of an evolving political communication system that can be empirically grounded and advanced.

Public service broadcasting: challenges and future prospects

You wrote in the 1980s about the importance of public service broad-casting, but also about how its position was 'vulnerable'. What do you think about the pressures facing public service broadcasting and how public service broadcasters might best respond?

Again, I think I've got three points to try to make on this. First of all, I think the reference in my 1992 book to values of public service broad-casting that were vulnerable to the pressures that were being imposed on them has been amply confirmed – and I think perhaps more fully confirmed than even today's public service broadcasters might realize. In that 1992 analysis, there is a specification of five main values that I then regarded as intrinsic to public service broadcasting. I know that if you were to read those characterizations now you'd think, 'Gee, they're out of date, aren't they?' Not totally out of date, but somehow belonging to a lingering past, still to some extent influential and acted upon, but no longer adequate to characterize how public service broadcasting is conducted today (Blumler, 1992a).

Then, another way I've looked at it can be found in that publication based on the research that Stephen Coleman and I and others did on the 2010 televised election debates. There is a chapter in it in which I try to say something about trends over time in the civic dimension of public service broadcasting and in which I refer to a 'diminution and dilution' of its civic mission (Coleman et al., 2011). If you think about it in those ways, there's been a hell of a lot of such diminution and dilution, which was clearly shown by the results of the last piece of ethnographic research which Michael Gurevitch and I did at the BBC during the 2001 general election campaign (Blumler and Gurevitch, 2002). We evidently witnessed at that time a transition from the grand civic mission of the BBC – especially when an election campaign was ongoing – to something that was much more mixed. The public service broadcasting influence was still there, but it was situated differently. The amount of campaign coverage was reduced; the editors of the news programmes were very concerned to ensure that their coverage of the campaign was 'newsy' (that was a word one of them used): in other words, they didn't want their news coverage to come across as if special, but rather as part and parcel of what news was and should be like. There was an almost total remoulding of political news as essentially prag-matic – sacerdotalism was out. The Corporation's substantial corps of specialist correspondents was used less prominently in 2001 than in the previous campaign. There was a greater sense of the news and current affairs outfit being in greater competition for status and resources with the other parts of the broadcasting organization, especially those to do with entertainment. And particularly marked and important here, there was a newly emergent concern among the people involved in covering the 2001 campaign to find ways to attract the attention of the audience to what they were going to report, something that was much more salient to them, much more prominent in their minds, than in previous campaigns we had observed (every single one from the 1979 election onward, actually). So in all those respects, you can see how graphically and demonstrably, the civic mission of this great public service broadcaster was changing and diminishing – or at least was in some tension with many other impulses.

So we then come on to the question of how public service broadcasting might or should be strengthened to deal with present-day circumstances. And that is a truly difficult question because it seems to me that tackling it in isolated bits and pieces isn't going to be any good. You can see that on the political side of the system's responses to the crisis of disengagement. As if allowing petitions supported by 150,000 signatures to be debated one day in the House of Commons is going to restore trust, engagement, connection! But that's the way in which things are tending to be approached now: 'OK, let's let people register to vote on polling day itself, or let's have primary elections in constituencies'. These won't cut the mustard! In the mid-1970s, with the cooperation of the three main political parties and the two main broadcasting organizations, Michael Gurevitch, Julian Ives and I conducted a major enquiry into how television had covered election campaigns up till that point and what options there might be for change in how it might cover election campaigns in the future (Blumler et al., 1978). The recommendations we made of the latter kind were relatively comprehensive. Taken together, they were conceived to be transformative, but though considered by representatives of the major political parties and discussed with us, they weren't adopted. And then of course there's the notion of a 'civic commons in cyberspace' (2009) that Stephen Coleman and I have advocated. What a great idea! But I haven't noticed any attempts to generate that. So bits and pieces won't work. Full-scale transformation won't work. Somehow one's got to try and find some approach that is sufficiently transformative to have an effect, but not so transformative that it can't be adopted. I don't know what that would be, but I think that's what's needed. And maybe there are a few opportunities ahead for trying to work out something like that. There is, for example, the Charter Review of the BBC. There is, for example, the possibility of trying to work out good ideas that might have some broad scope for making better, more civic-oriented connections, between Internet-based or online-based political communication and mainstream-based political communication. For example, how about tackling the long-established triad of the BBC's aims – educate, inform, entertain – and rework them – reword them – to incorporate some of those political communication aims that I mentioned much earlier in our conversation? A revamping of the aims of public service broadcasting might be something worthwhile to try for.

In the UK, the phone-hacking scandal, Leveson enquiry and current political-media stalemate on a new form of press regulation have soured discussions on the public interest role of journalism and tainted notions of press freedom. Is there now room for optimism following this 'critical juncture' (see Stanyer, this volume) in journalism, for the UK and beyond?

No, I am not optimistic. After all, Michael Gurevitch and I declared that there was a crisis of public communication way back in 1995 (Blumler and Gurevitch, 1995), and if you think about what's been going on since then, all sorts of additional forces have been generating an even worse crisis of public communication. So that's been – I won't spell them out – but if that is a fair way of looking at what's been happening over time then that doesn't give grounds for optimism because those are powerful trends, and they've hit the system even harder from a standpoint of citizenship and democracy as we've been discussing it. But, as against that, I think – and this hasn't come up in our discussion so far – that there are what might be called civic resources in the prevailing system which if built upon effectively and imaginatively, might give one grounds not for optimism but hope. I'm not sure I can spell them out well, but I do think that such resources do exist. First of all, there is that almost primal need for information, enabling a surveillance of whatever is happening in the political environment which might matter to oneself at a given time. I think that's primal, including the need for political information to be reliable and trustworthy and available accessibly and available for batting the breeze about things with other people. I think that's a hard and fast element in the system. So if one could find better ways of catering for that reliably, accessibly, in a trustworthy way and so on, then that would be what I would call a civic resource that could be built upon. Then, despite all the nasty things I seem to have been saying about journalism,

I recognise that a sense of vocation infuses many of its practitioners as well, and if one could find ways of building on and making more influential the elements of a journalistic vocation, however one might characterize them, that would be another civic resource. And then as the wording of your question has suggested, something of a civic resource may inhere in the much greater round-the-houses awareness that has emerged recently of the things that are pretty bad about unsavoury journalistic practice which should no longer be tolerated. And although it seems frustrating that, even with Leveson, one hasn't yet been able to really do something about it, maybe the book isn't entirely closed on that, and maybe that's another civic resource. So these are, I think, three examples of what I would call civic resources, why we shouldn't give up hope, though we shouldn't be pie-in-the-sky optimistic.

Finally, if you could embark on a fully funded, ideal research project starting tomorrow, what would be the key questions for that research?

My ideal would be to undertake a present-day Herbert Gans (1979)! Do you know what I mean? A programme of ethnographic observation research within media, and especially journalistic organizations: to try to find out from the inside how they are now relating to all the newer cumulative pressures that are impinging on their work. Not just the viability pressures, but also how they are responding to the challenges to the civic adequacy of their performance. If one could do that in Gans's way – well, he spent two years, and he did this in four major media outlets, didn't he, two commercial TV networks and two news magazines – if one could do that, over time, trying to ascertain both through observation and interviews how these guys are trying to shape their materials in relation to all these pressures, that would be my ideal project.

Bibliography

Aalberg, T. and Curran, J. (eds) (2012) *How Media Inform Democracy: A Comparative Approach* (New York: Routledge).

Adorno, T. W. (1941a) 'On Popular Music' in *Studies in Philosophy and Social Science*, 1X(1), 17–48.

———. (1941b) 'The Radio Symphony' in Lazarsfeld, P. F. and Stanton, F. N. (eds) *Radio Research* (New York: Duel, Pearce and Sloan), 110–39.

———. (1945) 'A Social Critique of Radio Music', *Kenyon Review*, 11(2/Spring), 208–17.

———. (1969) 'Scientific Experiences of a European Scholar in America' in Fleming, D. and Bailyn, B. *The Intellectual Migration* (MA: Harvard University Press).

——— and Horkheimer, M. (1977) 'The Culture Industry: Enlightenment as Mass Deception' in Curran, J. et al. (eds) *Mass Communication and Society* (London: Edward Arnold), 349–383.

Agarwal, S., et al . (2012) 'Networked Organization in Occupy Protests: A Multi-Methods Approach to Big Twitter Data'. Paper presented at the Oxford Internet Institute Big Data Conference, Oxford, 20–21 September.

Agrawal, A. and Chadha, S. (2005) 'Corporate Governance and Accounting Scandals', *Journal of Law and Economics*, 48(2), 371–406.

Albæk, E., van Dalen, A., Jebril, N. and de Vreese, C. (2013) *Political Journalism in Comparative Perspective* (New York: Cambridge University Press).

Aitamurto, T. (2013) 'Balancing Between Open and Closed: Co-creation in Magazine Journalism', *Digital Journalism,* 1(2), 229–51.

Alexander, J. (1981) 'The Mass Media in Systemic, Historical, and Comparative Perspective' in Katz, E. and Szecsko, T. (eds) *Mass Media and Social Change* (London and Beverly Hills: Sage), 17–51.

Almond, G. and Verba, S. (1966) *The Civic Culture, Political Attitudes and Democracy in Five Nations* (London and Beverly Hills: Sage).

Almond, G. and Powell, B. (1966) *Comparative Politics* (Boston: Little, Brown and Company).

Altheide, D. L. and Snow, R. P. (1979) *Media Logic* (Beverly Hills, CA: Sage).

Althusser, L. (1984) *Essays on Ideology* (London: Verso).

Anderson, B. (2006) *Imagined Communities: Reflections on the Origin and Spread of Nationalism* (London: Verso Books).

Ang, I. (1985) *Watching 'Dallas'* (London: Methuen).

———. (1989) 'Wanted: Audiences. On the Politics of the Empirical Audience' in Seiter, E., Borchers, H., Kreutzner, G., Warth, E. (eds) *Remote Control* (London: Routledge), 96–116.

———. (1990) *Desperately Seeking the Audience* (London: Routledge).

Arbaoui, B. (2014) 'Transformations of Television Systems: Implications for Media Content, Political Parties and Political Attitudes', PhD. diss., University of Amsterdam.

Asp, K. (1990) 'Medialization, Media Logic and Mediarchy', *Nordicom Review,* 11(2), 47–50.

Asp, K and Esaiasson, P. (1996) 'The Modernization of Swedish Campaigns: Individualization, Professionalization, and Medialization' in Swanson, D. L. and Mancini, P. (eds.) *Politics, Media, and Modern Democracy. An International Study of Innovations in Electoral Campaigning and Their Consequences* (Westport, CT: Praeger), 73–90.

Bakker, P. (2012) 'Aggregation, Content Farms and Huffinization: The Rise of Low Pay and No Pay Journalism', *Journalism Practice,* 6(5–6), 627–37.

Ball, T. (2003) 'Freedom of Choice: Public Service Broadcasting and the BBC' in Franklin, B. (ed.) *Television Policy, The MacTaggart Lectures* (Edinburgh: Edinburgh University Press), 255–64.

Barnett, S. (2002) 'Will a Crisis in Journalism Provoke a Crisis in Democracy?' *The Political Quarterly* 73(4), 400–408.

—— and Docherty, D. (1991) 'Purity of Pragmatism: Principles and Practice of Public Service Broadcasting' in Blumler, J. G. and Nossiter, T. (eds) *Broadcasting Finance in Transition: A Comparative Handbook* (Oxford: Oxford University Press), 23–40.

Barnett, S., Ramsey, G. N., and Gaber, I. (2012) *From Callaghan to Credit Crunch: Changing Trends in British Television News 1975–2009* (London: University of Westminster).

Barnhurst, K. G. (2000) 'Political Engagement and the Audience for News: Lessons from Spain', *Journalism & Communication Monographs,* 2(1), 6–61.

Bastiansen, H. (2008) 'Media History and the Study of Media Systems', *Media History,* 14(1), 95–112.

Bauman, Z. (2000) *Liquid Modernity* (Cambridge UK: Polity Press).

BBC (2012) 'Leveson Inquiry: Police Reveal Likely Victim Numbers', *BBC News,* 6 February, accessed online at http://www.bbc.co.uk/news/uk-16905465, date accessed 28 June 2014.

Beam, R. A. , Weaver, D. A., and Brownlee, B. J. (2009) 'Changes in Professionalism of U.S. Journalists in the Turbulent Twenty-First Century', *Journalism & Mass Communication Quarterly,* 86(2), 277–98.

Beck, U. (1992) *Risk Society: Towards a New Modernity* (London: Sage).

Benkler, J. (2006) *The Wealth of Networks: How Social Production Transforms Markets and Freedom* (New Haven: Yale University Press).

Bennett, W. L. (1998) 'The Uncivic Culture: Communication, Identity, and the Rise of Lifestyle Politics', *Ithiel de Sola Pool Lecture,* American Political Science Association, published in *P.S.: Political Science and Politics,* 31, 41–61.

——. (2008) 'Changing Citizenship in the Digital Age' in Bennett, W. L. (ed.) *Civic Life Online* (Cambridge: M.I.T. Press), 1–24.

——. (2012) 'The Personalization of Politics: Political Identity, Social Media, and Changing Patterns of Participation', *The Annals,* 644, 20–38.

Bennett, W. L. and Entman, R. M. (eds) (2001) *Mediated Politics: Communication in the Future of Democracy* (Cambridge, Cambridge University Press).

——. and Iyenger, S. (2008) 'A New Era of Minimal Effects? The Changing Foundations of Political Communication', *Journal of Communication,* 58, 707–31.

——. and Segerberg, A. (2012) 'The Logic of Connective Action: Digital Media and the Personalization of Contentious Politics', *Information, Communication & Society,* 15(5), 739–68.

————. (2013) *The Logic of Connective Action: Digital Media and the Personalization of Contentious Politics* (New York: Cambridge University Press).

Bennett, W. L., Segerberg, A. and Walker, S. (2013) 'Organization in the Crowd'. Paper presented at the Meeting of the European Consortium for Political Research, Mainz, Germany, 11–16 March.

Benson, R. and Neveu, E. (2005) 'Introduction: Field Theory as a Work in Progress' in Benson, R. and Neveu, E. (eds) *Bourdieu and the Journalistic Field* (Cambridge and Malden: Polity), 1–27.

Berelson, B. (1949) 'What "Missing the Newspaper" Means' in Lazarsfeld, P. and Stanton, F. (eds) *Communication Research*, 1948–9 (New York: Duel, Sloan and Pearce), 111–129.

Berners-Lee, T. , Hall, W., Hendler, J. A., O'Hara, K., Shadbolt, N. and Weitzner, D. J. (2006) 'A Framework for Web Science', *Foundations and Trends in Web Science*, 1, 1–134.

Best, S. and Engel, B. (2011) 'Alter und Generation als Einflussfaktoren der Mediennutzung' ('Age and Generation as Factors in Media Use'), *ARD/ZDF Media Perspectiven*, 6, 525–42.

Bevir, M. (2011), 'Governance as Theory, Practice, and Dilemma' in Bevir, M. (ed.) *The SAGE Handbook of Governance* (London: Sage), 1–16.

Bimber, B. (2003) *Information in American Democracy: Technology and the Evolution of Political Power* (New York: Cambridge University Press).

Bimber, B., Flanagin, A. and Stohl, C. (2012) *Collective Action in Organizations: Interaction and Engagement in an Era of Technological Change* (New York: Cambridge University Press).

Bingham, A. (2007) '"Drinking in the Last Chance Saloon": The British Press and the Crisis of Self-regulation, 1989–95', *Media History*, 13(1), 79–92.

Biocca, F. A. (1988) 'The Breakdown of the Canonical Audience' in Anderson, J. (ed.) *Communication Yearbook 11* (Newbury Park, CA: Sage), 127–32.

Blair, T. (2007) 'Speech to Reuters on the Media'. *BBC News*, 12 June. Accessed 14 June 2014. http://news.bbc.co.uk/1/hi/uk_politics/6744581.stm.

Blondheim, M. and Liebes, T. (2009) 'Television News and the Nation: The End?' *Annals of the American Academy of Political and Social Science*, 65(September), 182–95.

Blumer, H. (1946/1961) 'The Crowd, the Mass, and the Public' in Schramm, W. (ed.) *The Process and Effects of Mass Communication* (Urbana: University of Illinois Press), 363–79.

————. (1948) 'Public Opinion and Public Opinion Polling', *American Sociological Review*, 13(5) 542–9.

Blum-Kulka, S. and Liebes, T. (1999) 'Peres Versus Netanyahu: Television Wins the Debate' in Coleman, S. (ed.) *Televised Election Debates: International Perspectives* (London: Palgrave Macmillan), 66–92.

Blumler. J. G. (1964) 'British Television: The Outlines of a Research Strategy', *British Journal of Sociology*, 15(3), 223–33.

————. (1969) 'Producers' Attitudes towards the TV coverage of an Election' in Halmos, P. (ed.) *The Sociological Review Monograph*, 13.

————. (1970) 'The Political Effects of Television' in Halloran, J. (ed.) *The Effects of Television* (London: Panther).

————. (1978) 'Purposes of Mass Communication Research: A Transatlantic Perspective', *Journalism Quarterly* 55/Summer, 219–230.

————. (1979) 'The Role of Theory in Uses and Gratifications Studies', *Communication Research,* 6(9), 9–36.

————. (1981) 'Mass Communication Research in Europe: Some Origins and Prospects' in Wilhoit, G. C. and de Bock, H. (eds) *Mass Communication Review Yearbook, Volume 2* (Beverly Hills, CA: Sage Publications), 37–49.

————. (ed.) (1983a) *Communicating to Voters. Television in the First European Parliamentary Elections* (London: Sage).

————. (1983b) 'Communication and Turnout' in Blumler, J. G. (ed.) *Communicating to Voters* (London: Sage).

————. (1983c) 'Communication and Democracy: The Crisis beyond and the Ferment within', *Journal of Communication* 33(3), 166–173.

————. (1986) 'Television in the United States: Funding Sources and Programme Consequences' in *Research on the Range of and Quality of Broadcasting Services* (London: HMSO).

————. (1989) 'Multi-Channel Television in the United States: Policy Lessons for Britain', *Markle Foundation Report* (mimeo).

————. (1990) 'Elections, the Media and the Modern Publicity Process' in Ferguson, M. (ed.) *Public Communication: The New Imperatives. Future Directions for Media Research* (London: Sage), 101–13.

————. (ed.) (1992a) *Television and the Public Interest: Vulnerable Values in West European Broadcasting* (London: Sage).

————. (1992b) 'Public Service Broadcasting before the Commercial Deluge' in Blumler, J. G. (ed.) *Television and the Public Interest: Vulnerable Values in West European Broadcasting* (London: Sage), 1–21.

————. (1998) 'Wrestling with Public Interest in Organized Communications' in Brants, K., Hermes, J. and van Zoonen, L. (eds) *The Media in Question* (London: Sage), 51–63.

————. (2011a) 'Foreword – The Two Legged Crisis of Journalism' in Franklin, B. (ed.) *The Future of Journalism* (London: Routledge), xv–xvii.

————. (2011b) 'Voter's Responses to the Prime Ministerial Debates: A Rock of (Future?) Ages' in Coleman, S. (ed.) *Leaders in the Living Room: The Prime Ministerial Debates of 2011: Evidence, Evaluation, and Some Recommendations* (Oxford: RISL), 35–55.

————. (2011c) 'In Praise of Holistic Empiricism' in Brants, K. and Voltmer, K. (eds) (2011) *Political Communication in Postmodern Democracy. Challenging the Primacy of Politics* (New York: Palgrave), ix–xii.

————. (2012) 'Foreword' in Esser, F and Hanitzsch, T. (eds) *Handbook of Comparative Communication Research* (London: Routledge), xi–xiii.

————. (2014) 'Mediatization and Democracy' in Esser, F. and Stromback, J. (eds) *Mediatization of Politics* (Basingstoke: Palgrave Macmillan), 31–41.

————. (forthcoming) 'The Shape of Political Communication' in Kenski, K. and Jamieson, K. H. (eds) *Handbook of Political Communication* (Oxford: Oxford University Press).

Blumler, J. G., Brown, J. R., Ewbank, A. J. and Nossiter, T. J. (1971) 'Attitudes to the Monarchy: Their Structure and Development during a Ceremonial Occasion', *Political Studies,* 19(2), 149–71.

Blumler, J. G. and Coleman, S. (2010) 'Political Communication in Freefall: The British Case – and Others?' *The International Journal of Press/Politics,* 15(2), 139–54.

Blumler, J. G. and Gurevitch, M. (1975) 'Towards a Comparative Framework for Political Communication Research' in Chaffee, H. S. (ed.) *Political Communication: Issues and Strategies for Research* (Beverly Hills, CA: Sage), 165–193.

——. (1982) 'The Political Effects of Mass Communication' in Gurevitch, M, Bennett, T., Curran, J. and Woollacott, J. (eds) *Culture, Society and the Media* (Methuen: London), 236–267.

——. (1990) 'Comparative Research: Extending the Frontier' in Swanson, D. and Nimmo, D. (eds) *New Directions in Political Communication* (Newbury Park, CA: Sage) reprinted in Blumler, J. G. and Gurevitch, M. (1995) *The Crisis of Public Communication* (London and New York: Routledge), 73–85.

——. (1995) *The Crisis of Public Communication* (London and New York: Routledge).

——. (1996) 'Media Change and Social Change: Linkages and Junctures' in Curran, J. and Gurevitch, M. (eds) *Mass Media and Society*, 2nd edn (London: Arnold), 177–203.

——. (2000) 'Rethinking the Study of Political Communication' in Curran, J. and Gurevitch, M. (eds) *Mass Media and Society*, 3rd edn (London: Arnold), 155–172.

——. (2001) 'Americanization Reconsidered: UK-US Communication Comparisons across Time' in Bennett, W. L. and Entman, R. M. (eds) *Mediated Politics: Communication in the Future of Democracy* (Cambridge: Cambridge University Press), 380–403.

——. (2002) 'Public Service in Transition?: Campaign Journalism at the BBC' in Bartle, J., Mortimore, R. and Atkinson, S. (eds) *Political Communication* (London: Cass), 215–35.

——. (2005) 'Rethinking the Study of Political Communication' in Curran, J. and Gurevitch, M. (eds) *Mass Media and Society* (London: Hodder Arnold), 104–21.

Blumler, J. G., Gurevitch, M. and Ives, J. (1978) *The Challenge of Election Broadcasting* (Leeds: Leeds University Press).

Blumler, J. G. and Katz, E. (eds) (1974) *The Uses of Mass Communications: Current Perspectives on Gratification Research* (Beverly Hills, CA: Sage).

Blumler, J. G. and Kavanagh, D. (1999) 'The Third Age of Political Communication: Influences and Features', *Political Communication*, 16(3), 209–30.

Blumler, J. G., Kavanagh, D. and Nossiter, T. J. (1996) 'Modern Communication versus Traditional Politics in Britain: Unstable Marriage of Convenience' in Swanson, D. and Mancini, P. (eds) *Politics, Media and Modern Democracy* (Westport, CT: Praeger), 49–73.

Blumler, J. G. and McLeod, J. (1974) 'Communication and Voter Turnout in Britain' in Leggatt, T. (ed.) *Sociological Theory and Survey Research* (Beverly Hills, CA: Sage), 265–312.

Blumler, J. G., McLeod, J. M. and Rosengren, K. E. (1992) (eds) *Comparatively Speaking* (Newbury Park, CA: Sage).

Blumler, J. G., McLeod, J. M. and Rosengren, K. E. (1992) 'An Introduction to Comparative Communication Research' in Blumler, J. G. et al. (eds) *Comparatively Speaking: Communication and Culture across Space and Time* (Newbury Park, CA: Sage), 3–18.

Blumler, J. G. and McQuail, D. (1968) *Television in Politics: Its Uses and Influence* (London: Faber and Faber).

Blumler, J. G. and Nossiter, T. (1991a) *Broadcasting Finance in Transition* (Oxford: Oxford University Press).

——. (1991b) 'Broadcasting Finance in Transition Broadcasting; An International Comparison' in Blumler, J. G. and Nossiter, T. (eds) *Broadcasting Finance in Transition* (Oxford: Oxford University Press), 405–426.

Blumler, J. G. and Thoveron, G. (1983) 'Analysing a Unique Election: Themes and Concepts' in Blumler, J. G. (ed.) *Communicating to Voters* (London: Sage), 3–24.

Bork, R. H. (1971) 'Neutral Principles and Some First Amendment Problems', *Indiana Law Journal*, 47(1), 1–35.

Bourdieu, P. (1999) *On Television* (New York: Free Press).

Bösch, F. and Frei, N. (2006) Die Ambivalenz der Medialisierung. Eine Einführung' in Bösch, F. and Frei, N. (eds) *Medialisierung und Demokratie im 20. Jahrhundert* (Göttingen: Wallstein), 7–23.

Boudon, R. (1972) 'An Introduction to Lazarsfeld's Philosophical Papers' in Lazarsfeld, P. F. *Qualitative Analysis, Historical and Critical Essays* (Boston: Allyn and Bacon), 410–27.

Bramson, L. (1961) *The Political Context of Sociology* (Princeton, N.J.: Princeton University Press).

Brants, K. and Krasnoboka, N. (2001) 'Between Soundbites and Bullets. The Challenges and Frustrations of Comparing Old and New Democracies' in Zassoursky, Y. and Vartanova, E. (eds) *Media for the Open Society* (Moscow: IKAR Publisher), 281–306.

Brants, K. and van Praag, Ph. (2006) 'Signs of Media Logic. Half a Century of Political Communication in the Netherlands', *Javnost/The Public*, 13(1), 27–41.

Brants, K. and Voltmer, K. (eds) (2011) *Political Communication in Postmodern Democracy. Challenging the Primacy of Politics* (New York: Palgrave).

The Broadcasting Research Unit (1985) *The Public Service Idea in British Broadcasting: Main Principles* (Luton: John Libbey).

Butsch, R. (2000) *The Making of American Audiences: From Stage to Television 1750–1990* (Cambridge: Cambridge University Press).

—— and Livingstone, S. (eds) (2013) *Meanings of Audiences: Comparative Discourses* (London: Routledge).

Capella, J. N. and Jamieson, K. H. (1997) *The Spiral of Cynicism* (New York: Oxford University Press).

Carlyle, T. (1905) *On Heroes: Hero Worship and the Heroic in History*, Repr. of the Sterling Edition of Carlyle's Complete Works (Teddington, Middlesex: The Echo Library).

Carpentier, N. (2009) 'Participation Is Not Enough: The Conditions of Possibility of Mediated Participatory Practices', *European Journal of Communication*, 24(4), 407–20.

Carpini, M. (1996) *What Americans Know about Politics and Why It Matters* (New Haven: Yale University Press).

Carvajal, M., García-Avilés, J. A. and González, J. L. (2012) 'Crowdfunding and Non-Profit Media: The Emergence of New Models for Public Interest Journalism', *Journalism Practice*, 6(5–6), 638–47.

Castells, M. (2001) *The Internet Galaxy* (Oxford: Oxford University Press).

——. (2009) *Communication Power* (Oxford: Oxford University Press).

——. (1996/2010) *The Rise of the Network Society*, 2nd ed. (Chichester, UK: John Wiley & Sons).

————. (2012) *Networks of Outrage and Hope: Social Movements in the Internet Age* (Cambridge, UK: Polity Press).

Chadwick, A. (2013) *The Hybrid Media System: Politics and Power* (Oxford UK: Oxford University Press).

Chambers, S. (2003) 'Deliberative Democratic Theory', *Annual Review of Political Science*, 6, 307–26.

Chouliaraki, L. and Blaagaard, B. (2013) 'Cosmopolitanism and the New News Media', *Journalism Studies*, 14(2), 150–5.

Christians, C., Glasser, T. L., McQuail, D., Nordenstreng, K. and White, R. A. (2009) *Normative Theories of the Media. Journalism in Democratic Societies* (Urbana: University of Illinois Press).

Clarke, J., Newman, J., Smith, N., Vidler, E. and Westmarland, L. (2007) *Creating Citizen-Consumers: Changing Publics and Changing Public Services* (London: Sage).

Cole, P. (2008) 'Compacts' in Franklin, B. (ed.) *Pulling Newspapers Apart; Analysing Print Journalism* (London: Routledge), 183–191.

Coleman, R., McCombs, M., Shaw, D. and Weaver, D. (2009) 'Agenda Setting' in Wahl-Jorgensen, K. and Hanitzsch, T. (eds) *The Handbook of Journalism Studies* (New York and London: Routledge), 147–60.

Coleman, S. (ed.) (2011) *Leaders in the Living Room: The Prime Ministerial Debates of 2010: Evidence, Evaluation and Some Recommendations* (Oxford: RISJ).

————. (2012) 'The Internet as a Space for Policy Deliberation' in Fischer, F and Gottweis, H. (eds) *The Argumentative Turn Revisited: Public Policy as Communicative Practice* (Durham and London: Duke University Press), 149–179.

———— and Blumler, J. G. (2009) *The Internet and Democratic Citizenship: Theory, Practice and Policy* (Cambridge: Cambridge University Press).

Coleman, S., Blumler, J. G. and Steibel, F. (2011) 'Media Coverage of the Prime Ministerial Debates' in Coleman, S. (ed.) *Leaders in the Living Room: The Prime Ministerial Debates of* 2011: *Evidence, Evaluation, and Some Recommendations* (Oxford: RISL), 17–34.

Corner, J. (1991) 'Documentary Voices' in Corner, J. (ed.) *Popular Television in Britain: Studies in Cultural History* (London: British Film Institute), 42–59.

Couldry, N., Livingstone, S. and Markham, T. (2010) *Media Consumption and Public Engagement: Beyond the Presumption of Attention*, 2nd edn (Basingstoke: Palgrave Macmillan).

Curran, J. (2011) *Media and Democracy* (London: Routledge).

Curran, J., Iyengar, S., Lund, A. B. and Salovaara-Moring, I. (2009) 'Media Reporting, Public Knowledge and Democracy: A Comparative Study', *European Journal of Communication*, 24(1), 5–26.

Curran, J. and Seaton, J. (2009) *Power without Responsibility*, 7th edn (Abingdon: Routledge).

Cushion, S. (2012) *The Democratic Value of News: Why Public Service Media Matter* (Basingstoke: Palgrave MacMillan).

———— and Lewis, J. (2009) 'Towards a "Foxification" of 24 Hour News Channels in Britain? An Analysis of Market Driven and Publicly Funded News Coverage', *Journalism: Theory, Practice and Criticism*, 10(2), 131–53.

———— and Thomas, R. (2013) 'The Mediatization of Politics. Interpreting the Value of Live Versus Edited Journalistic Interventions in U.K. Television News Bulletins', *International Journal of Press/Politics*, 18(3), 360–80.

Dahlgren, P. (1995) *Television and the Public Sphere* (London: Sage).

———. (2003) 'Reconfiguring Civic Culture in the New Media Milieu' in Corner, J. and Pels, D. (eds) *Media and the Restyling of Politics* (London: Sage), 151–70.

Danziger, J. N., Dutton, W., Kling, R. and Kraemar, K. (1982) *Computers and Politics* (New York: Columbia University Press).

Davies, N. (2008) *Flat Earth News* (London: Chatto and Windus).

Dayan, D. (2001) 'The Peculiar Public of Television', *Media, Culture & Society*, 23, 751–73.

——— and Katz, E. (1994) *Media Events: The Live Broadcasting of History* (Cambridge: Harvard University Press).

Deans, J. (2012) 'BBC News Cuts – at a Glance', *The Guardian*, 27 March, accessed online at http://www.guardian.co.uk/media/2012/mar/27/bbc-news-cuts1, date accessed 4 January 2014.

Dearing, J. W. and Rogers, E. M. (1996) *Agenda-Setting* (Thousand Oaks, CA: Sage Publications).

Deibert, R., Palfrey, J., Rohozinski, R. and Zittrain, J. (eds) (2008) *Access Controlled* (Cambridge, MA: MIT Press).

de Sola Pool, I. (1983) *Technologies of Freedom* (Cambridge, MA: Harvard Press).

de Vreese, C. H. (2003) 'Television Reporting of Second-Order Elections', *Journalism Studies*, 4(2), 183–98.

Donovan, M. (1995) 'The Politics of Electoral Reform in Italy', *International Political Science Review*, 16(1), 47–64.

Downey, J., Mihelj, S. and König, T. (2012) 'Comparing Public Spheres: Normative Models and Empirical Measurements', *European Journal of Communication*, 27(4), 337–53.

Downie, L. and Schudson, M. (2010) *The Reconstruction of American Journalism*. Accessed 7 January 2013. http://www.journalism.columbia.edu/system/documents/1/original/Reconstruction_of_Journalism.pdf.

Drew, D. and Weaver, D. H. (1991) 'Voter Learning in the 1988 Presidential Election: Did the Debates and the Media Matter?', *Journalism Quarterly*, 68(1,2), 27–37.

———. (1998) 'Voter Learning in the 1996 Presidential Election: Did the Media Matter?' *Journalism & Mass Communication Quarterly*, 75(2), 27–37.

———. (2006) 'Voter Learning in the 2004 Presidential Election: Did the Media Matter?' *Journalism & Mass Communication Quarterly*, 83(1), 27–37.

Dutton, W. H. (1999) *Society on the Line: Information Politics in the Digital Age* (Oxford and New York: Oxford University Press).

———. (2005) 'The Internet and Social Transformation: Reconfiguring Access' in Dutton, W. H., Kahin, B. and O'Callaghan, R. (eds) *Transforming Enterprise* (Cambridge, MA: MIT Press), 375–97.

———. (2007) 'Through the Network (of Networks) – the Fifth Estate', Inaugural Lecture, Examination Schools, University of Oxford, 15 October. Accessed 28 June 2014 http://webcast.oii.ox. ac.uk/?view=Webcast&ID=20071015_208.

———. (2009) 'The Fifth Estate Emerging through the Network of Networks', *Prometheus*, 27, 1–15.

——— and Blank, G. (2011) *The Next Generation Users: The Internet in Britain* (Oxford: Oxford Internet Institute, University of Oxford).

——— and Blumler, J. G. (1988) 'The Faltering Development of Cable Television in Britain', *Political Studies*, 9(4), 279–303.

—— and Eynon, R. (2009) 'Networked Individuals and Institutions', *The Information Society*, 25, 1–11.

—— and Shepherd, A. (2006) 'Trust in the Internet as an Experience Technology', *Information, Communication and Society*, 9, 433–51.

Dutton,W. H., Shepherd, A. and di Gennaro, C. (2007) 'Digital Divides and Choices Reconfiguring Access' in Anderson, B. et al. (eds) *Information and Communication Technologies in Society* (London: Routledge), 31–45.

Earl, J. and Kimport, K. (2011) *Digitally Enabled Social Change; Activism in the Internet Age* (Cambridge, MA: M.I.T Press).

Easton, D. (1953) *The Political System. An Inquiry into the State of Political Science* (New York: Alfred Knopf).

Eliasoph, N. (1998) *Avoiding Politics: How Americans Produce Apathy in Everyday Life* (Cambridge: Cambridge University Press).

Elliott, P. (1974) 'Uses and Gratifications Research: A Critique and a Sociological Alternative' in Blumler, J. G. and Katz, E. (eds) *The Uses of Mass Communications: Current Perspectives on Gratifications Research* (Beverly Hills, CA: Sage), 249–68.

Elmelund-Praestekaer, C. (2011) 'Does Mediatization Change MP-Media Interaction and MP Attitudes towards the Media? Evidence from a Longitudinal Study of Danish MPs', *International Journal of Press/Politics*, 16, 382–403.

Elstein, D. (1991) 'The Future of Television: Market Forces and Social Values' in Franklin, B. (ed.) *Television Policy, The MacTaggart Lectures* (Edinburgh: Edinburgh University Press), 147–56.

Esser, F. (2008) 'Dimensions of Political News Cultures: Sound Bite and Image Bite News in France, Germany, Great Britain and the United States', *International Journal of Press/Politics*, 13(4), 401–28.

Esser, F. and Hanitzsch, T. (eds) (2012a) *Handbook of Comparative Communication Research* (London: Routledge).

——. (2012b) 'On the Why and How of Comparative Inquiry in Communication Studies' in Esser, F. and Hanitzsch, T. (eds) *Handbook of Comparative Communication Research* (London: Routledge), 3–22.

Esser, F., Strömbäck, J. and de Vreese, C. H. (2012) 'Reviewing Key Concepts in Research on Political News Journalism: Conceptualizations, Operationalizations, and Propositions for Future Research', *Journalism*, 12(2), 139–43.

Esser, F. and Stromback, J. (2014) (eds) *Mediatization of Politics* (Basingstoke: Palgrave Macmillan).

Evans, M. (2006) 'George Cross for Iraq War hero', *The Times*, 24 March, p. 17.

Eveland Jr, W. P., Hayes, A., Shah, D.V. and Kwak, N. (2005) 'Understanding the Relationship between Communication and Political Knowledge: A Model Comparison Approach Using Panel Data', *Political Communication* 22(4), 423–446.

Eyre, R. (1999) 'Public Interest Broadcasting: A New Approach' in Franklin, B. (ed.) *Television Policy, The MacTaggart Lectures* (Edinburgh: Edinburgh University Press), 219–28.

Fico, F., Lacy S., Wildman, S.S., Baldwin, T, Bergan, D. and Zube, P. (2013) 'Citizen Journalism Sites as Information Substitutes and Complements for United States Newspaper Coverage of Local Governments', *Digital Journalism*, 1(1), 136–52.

Fiske, J. (1987) *Television Culture* (London: Methuen).

——. (1992) 'Audiencing: A Cultural Studies Approach to Watching Television', *Poetics*, 21(4), 345–59.

Franklin, B. (1997) *Newszak and News Media* (London: Arnold).
———. (2001) *British Television Policy: A Reader* (London: Routledge).
———. (2005a) *Television Policy, The MacTaggart Lectures* (Edinburgh: Edinburgh University Press).
———. (2005b) 'McJournalism, The Local Press and the McDonaldization Thesis' in Allan, S. (ed.) *Journalism: Critical Issues* (Maidenhead: Open University Press), 137–50.
———. (2011a) *The Future of Journalism* (London: Routledge).
———. (2011b) 'Sources, Credibility and the Continuing Crisis of UK Journalism' in Franklin, B. and Carlson, M. (eds) *Journalists, Sources and Credibility; New Perspectives* (New York: Routledge), 90–106.
———. (2012) 'The Future of Journalism: Developments and Debates', *Journalism Studies*, 13(5–6), 663–81.
———. (2013) *The Future of Journalism: Developments and Debates* (London: Routledge).
Fraser, N. (1990) 'Rethinking the Public Sphere: A Contribution to the Critique of Actually Existing Democracy', *Social Text*, 25/26, 56–80.
Gallie, W.B. (1956) 'Essentially Contested Concepts', *Proceedings of the Aristotelian Society*, 56, 167–98.
Gamson, W. (1992) *Talking Politics* (Cambridge: Cambridge University Press).
Gandy, O. (1982) *Beyond Agenda Setting; Information Subsidies and Public Policy* (New York: Ablex).
Gans, H. (1979) *Deciding What's News* (New York: Vintage).
Garnham, N. (1979) 'Politics and the Mass Media in Britain: The Strange Case of Dr Blumler', *Media, Culture & Society*, 1979, 1(1), 23–34.
———. (1999) 'Information Politics: The Study of Communicative Power' in Dutton, W. H. (ed.) *Society on the Line* (Oxford and New York: Oxford University Press), 77–8.
Gibson, O. (2007) 'Murdoch Wants Sky News To Be More Like Rightwing Fox', *The Guardian*, 24 November. Accessed 4 January 2013. http://www.guardian.co.uk/media/2007/nov/24/bskyb.television.
Giddens, A. (1991) *Modernity and Self Identity: Self and Society in the Late Modern Age* (Stanford: Stanford University Press).
Google Scholar (2014) Citations for 'Blumler, J. G. and Katz, E. (1974) (eds) *The Uses of Mass Communications* (Beverly Hills: Sage)'. Accessed 7 June 2014. http://scholar.google.co.uk/scholar?hl=en&q=jay+blumler&btnG=&as_sdt=1%2C5&as_sdtp.
Gouldner, A. W. (1982) *The Dialectic of Ideology and Technology: The Origins, Grammar, and Future of Ideology* (New York: Oxford University Press).
Graber, D. A. (1988) *Processing the News: How People Tame the Information Tide*, 2nd edn (New York: Longman).
———. (1993) 'Political Communication: Scope, Progress, Promise' in Finifter, A. W. (ed.) *Political Science: The State of the Discipline* (Washington, DC: American Political Science Assoc.), 305–32.
———. (2003). 'The Media and Democracy: Beyond Myths and Stereotypes', *Annual Review of Political Science*, 6, 139–160.
Graham, T. (2008) 'Needles in a Haystack: A New Approach for Identifying and Assessing Political Talk in Non-Political Discussion Forums', *Javnost-The Public*, 15(2).

——. (2010) 'The Use of Expressives in Online Political Talk: Impeding or Facilitating the Normative Goals of Deliberation?' in Tambouris, E., Macintosh, A. and Glassey, O. (eds) *Electronic Participation* (Berlin, Heidelberg and New York: Springer), 26–41.

—— and Hajru, A. (2011) 'Reality TV as a Trigger of Everyday Political Talk in the Net-Based Public Sphere', *European Journal of Communication*, 26(1), 18–32.

Greenslade, R. (2012) 'Report in Danger of Gathering Dust', *British Journalism Review*, 23(3), 20–6.

The Guardian (2012a) 'David Cameron Statement in Response to the Leveson Inquiry Report', 29 November 2012. Accessed 24 June 2014. http://www.theguardian.com/media/2012/nov/29/leveson-inquiry-david-cameron-statement.

The Guardian (2012b) 'The BBC, Trust and Jimmy Savile Survey – The Full Report', 17 December 2012. Accessed 4 January 2013. http://www.guardian.co.uk/media/interactive/2012/dec/17/bbc-trust-jimmy-savile-survey.

Gunter, B. (2005) 'Trust in the News on Television', *Aslib Proceedings: New Information Perspectives*, 57(5), 384–97.

Gurevitch, M. and Blumler, J. G. (1977) 'Linkages between the Mass Media and Politics: A Model for the Analysis of Political Communication Systems' in Curran, J., Gurevitch, M. and Woollacott, J. (eds) *Mass Communication and Society* (London: Edward Arnold), 270–90.

——. (1990a) 'Comparative Research: The Extending Frontier' in Swanson, D. L. and Nimmo, D. (eds) *New Directions in Political Communication: A Resource Book* (Newbury Park: Sage), 305–25.

——. (1990b) 'Political Communication Systems and Democratic Values' in Lichtenberg, J. (ed.) *Democracy and the Mass Media: A Collection of Essays* (Cambridge: Cambridge University Press), 269–89.

——. (2004) 'State of the Art of Comparative Political Communication Research: Poised for Maturity?' in Esser, F. and Pfetsch, B. (eds) *Comparing Political Communication: Theories, Cases, and Challenges* (Cambridge, UK: Cambridge University Press), 325–43.

Gurevitch, M., Coleman, S. and Blumler, J. (2009) 'Political Communication: Old and new media relationships', *The ANNALS of the American Academy of Political and Social Science*, 625(1), 164–81.

Habermas, J. (1962/89) *The Structural Transformation of the Public Sphere* (Cambridge, MA: MIT Press).

——. (1981/87) *The Theory of Communicative Action. Lifeworld and System: A Critique of Functionalist Reason,* T. McCarthy, trans. vol. 2. (Cambridge: Polity).

——. (1984) 'The Public Sphere: An Encyclopedia Article', *New German Critique*, Autumn, 49–55.

——. (1996). *Between Facts and Norms*, W. Rehg, Trans. (Cambridge: PolityPress).

——. (2004). 'Public Space and Political Public Sphere – The Biographical Roots of Two Motifs in My Thought', *Commemorative Lecture, Kyoto*, 11.

Habermas, J., Lennox, S. and Lennox, F. (1964/1974) 'The Public Sphere: An Encyclopaedia Article', *New German Critique*, 3, 49–55.

Hall, S. (1980) 'Encoding/Decoding' in Hall, S., Hobson, D., Lowe, A. and Willis, P. (eds) *Culture, Media, Language* (London: Hutchinson), 128–38.

Hallin, D. and Mancini, P. (2004a) *Comparing Media Systems: Three Models of Media and Politics* (Cambridge: Cambridge University Press).

——. (2004b) 'Americanization, Globalization, and Secularization: Understanding the Convergence of Media Systems and Political Communication' in Esser, F. and Pfetsch, B. (eds) *Comparing Political Communication. Theories, Cases, and Challenges* (Cambridge: Cambridge University Press), 25–45.

——. (2012a) *Comparing Media Systems Beyond the Western World* (Cambridge: Cambridge University Press).

——. (2012b) 'Conclusion' in Hallin, D. and Mancini, P. (eds) *Comparing Media Systems Beyond the Western World* (Cambridge: Cambridge University Press), 278–304.

Hamilton, E. (2010), CEO of Swedish Public Television, 'Debatt', *Dagens Nyheter*, 27 October. Accessed 22 July 2013. http://www.dn.se/debatt/svt-har-problem-med-att-na-tittarna-mellan-25-och-55/.

Hamilton, J. and Lawrence, R. (2012) *Foreign Correspondence* (London: Routledge).

IPPR (Institute for Public Policy Research) (2009) *Mind The Funding Gap*. 7 January 2013. http://www.ippr.org/publications/55/1689/mind-the-funding-gapthe-potential-of-industry-levies-for-continued-funding-of-public-service-broadcasting.

Hardin, R. (2013) 'Government without trust', *Journal of Trust Research* 3(1), 32–52.

Hardy, J. (2012) 'Comparing Media Systems' in Esser, F. and Hanitzsch, T. (eds) *The Handbook of Comparative Communication Research* (New York and London: Routledge), 185–206.

Hebdige, D. (1979) *Subculture* (London: Methuen).

Herzog, H. (1941) 'On Borrowed Experience' in *Studies in Philosophy and Social Science*, 1X(1), 65–95.

——. (1944) 'What Do We Really Know about Daytime Serial Listeners?' reprinted in Schramm, W. (ed.) (1954) *The Process and Effects of Mass Communication* (Urbana: University of Illinois), 36–47.

Hetherington, A. (1985) *News, Newspapers and Television* (Basingstoke: Macmillan).

Himmelweit, H.T., Oppenheim, A. N and Vince, P. (1958) *Television and the Child* (Oxford: Oxford University Press).

Hirst, P. (2005) (ed.) *Pluralist Theories of the State* (London: Routledge).

Hjarvard, S. (2008a) 'The mediatization of religion: A theory of the media as agents of religious change' in *Northern Lights: Film & Media Studies Yearbook* (Bristol: Intellect), 9–26.

——. (2008b) 'The Mediatization of Society. A Theory of the Media as Agents of Social and Cultural Change', *Nordicom Review*, 29, 105–34.

Hodierne, R. (2009) 'Is There Life After Newspapers?' *American Journalism Review*, February/March. Accessed 26 March 2013. http://www.ajr.org/article.asp?id=4679.

Hogan, J. and Doyle, D. (2007) 'The Importance of Ideas: An A Priori Critical Juncture Framework', *Canadian Journal of Political Science*, 40(4), 883–910.

Hoggart, R. (1957) *The Uses of Literacy* (London: Chatto and Windus).

Holtz-Bacha, C. (1990) 'Videomalaise Revisited: Media Exposure and Political Alienation in West Germany', *European Journal of Communication*, 5(1), 73–85.

Høst, S. (2010) 'Hvordan blir vi oppdatert? Kontakt med forskjellige nyhet-skilder 1994–2009' ('How are we updated? Contact with different news sources 1994–2009'), *Norsk medieforskerlags konferanse 2010, Ålesund* (Association of Norwegian Media Researchers, conference in Ålesund 2010), Prekonferanse 27 October.

Inglehart, R. (1997) *Modernization and Post-Modernization: Cultural, Economic and Political Change in 43 Societies* (Princeton: Princeton University Press).

Iyengar, S. (1991) *Is Anyone Responsible?* (Chicago: University of Chicago Press).

Jamieson, K. H. and Birdsell, D. S. (1988) *Presidential Debates: The Challenge of Creating an Informed Electorate* (New York: Oxford University Press).

Jankowski, N. W. and Wester, F. (1991) 'The qualitative tradition in social science inquiry: Contributions to mass communication research' in Jensen, K. B. and Jankowski, N. W. *A Handbook of Qualitative Methodologies for Mass Communication research* (London: Heinemann), 44–74.

Jansson, A. (2002) 'Spatial phantasmagoria: The mediatization of tourism experience', *European Journal of Communication*, 17, 429–43.

Jay, M. (2010) *The Virtues of Mendacity: On Lying in Politics* (Charlottesville, VA: University of Virginia Press).

Jeřábek, H. (2012) 'Six Examples of Collaboration Between Paul F. Lazarsfeld and Robert K. Merton' in Haas, H., Jeřábek, H. and Petersen, T. (eds) *The Early Days of Survey Research and their Importance Today* (Wienna: Braumuller).

Johnson, D. R., Crawford, S. P. and Palfrey Jr, J. G. (2004) 'The Accountable Net: Peer Production of Internet Governance', *Virginia Journal of Law and Technology*, 9. Accessed 20 June 2014. http://ssrn.com/abstract=529022.

Johnstone, J. W. C., Slawski, E. J. and Bowman, W. W. (1976) *The News People* (Urbana: University of Illinois Press).

Jones, B. D. and Baumgartner, F. R. (2012) 'From There to Here: Punctuated Equilibrium to the General Punctuation Thesis to a Theory of Government Information Processing', *The Policy Studies Journal*, 40(1), 1–19.

Karp, J. A., and Banducci, S. A. (2008) 'Political Efficacy and Participation in Twenty-Seven Democracies: How Electoral Systems Shape Political Behaviour', *British Journal of Political Science* 38(2), 311–34.

Katz, E. (1996) 'Viewers' Work' in Hay, J., Wartella E. and Grossberg, L. (eds) *The Audience and its Landscape* (Boulder: Westview), 9–22.

——. (2006) 'Rediscovering Gabriel Tarde', *Political Communication*, 23(3), 263–70.

—— and Feldman, J. J. (1962) 'The Kennedy-Nixon Debates: A Survey of the Surveys', *Studies in Public Communication*, 4(Autumn), 127–63.

—— and Feldman, J. J. (1971) 'The Debates in the Light of Research: A Survey of Surveys' in Schramm, W. and Roberts, D. (eds) *The Process and Effects of Mass Communication*, 2nd edn (Urbana: University of Illinois).

Katz, E., Gurevitch, M. and Haas, H. (1973) 'On the Use of Mass Media for Important Things', *American Sociological Review*, 38, 164–81.

Keen, A. (2007) *The Cult of the Amateur: How Today's Internet is Killing Our Culture* (New York: Doubleday).

Kenski, K, and Stroud, N.J. (2006) 'Connections between Internet Use and Political Efficacy, Knowledge, and Participation', *Journal of Broadcasting & Electronic Media* 50(2), 173–192.

Kepplinger, H. M. (2002) 'Mediatization of Politics: Theory and Data', *Journal of Communication*, 52, 972–86.

———. (2007) 'Reciprocal Effects: Toward a Theory of Mass Media Effects on Decision Makers', *Press/Politics*, 12(2), 3–23.

Kernell, S. (1986) *Going Public: New Strategies of Presidential Leadership* (Washington, D.C.: Cq Press).

Kevill, S. (2002) *Beyond the Soundbite: BBC Research into Public Disillusion with Politics* (London: BBC).

Kinsley, M. (2009) 'Life After Newspapers', *The Washington Post*, 6 April, p. A15.

Klapper, J. (1960) *The Effects of Mass Communication* (New York: Free Press).

Kleinsteuber, H. (2001) 'Habermas and the Public Sphere: From a German to a European Perspective', *Javnost/The Public* 8(1), 95–108.

Klingler, W. (2008) 'Jugendliche und ihre Mediennutzung 1998–2008' ('Young People and their Media Use 1998–2008'), *MediaPerspektiven*, 12, 625–34.

Köcher, R. (2009) 'Die schleichende Veränderung der Gesellschaft', in Institut für Demoskopie Allensbach GmbH (eds) *Allensbacher Jahrbuch der Demoskopie 2003–2009 Band 12* (Berlin, New York: DeGruyter Saur), 433–36.

Kosterlitz, J. (2008) 'A Nonprofit Model for News', *National Journal*, 15 November. Accessed 1 April 2009. http://www.nationaljournal.com/njmagazine/print_friendly.php?ID=nj_20081112_7923.

Kovach, B. and Rosenstiel, T. (2001) *The Elements of Journalism* (New York: Crown Publishers).

Kraidy, M. (2011) 'Globalizing Media and Communication Studies: Thoughts on the Translocal and the Modern' in Wang, G. (ed.) *De-Westernizing Communication Research: Altering Questions and Changing Frameworks* (London: Routledge), 50–7.

Kranich, N. (2004) *The Information Commons: A Policy Report* (New York: Democracy Program, Brennan Center for Justice, NYU School of Law). Accessed 24 June 2014. www.fepproject.org/policyreports/InformationCommons.pdf.

Kriesi, H. (ed.) (2012) *Political Communication in Direct Democratic Campaigns. Enlightening or Manipulating?* (New York: Palgrave).

Krotz, F. (2007) 'The Meta-Process of "Mediatization" as a Conceptual Frame', *Global Media and Communication*, 3(3), 256–60.

Lang, K. and Lang, G. E. (1953) 'The Unique Perspective of Television and its effect: A Pilot Study', *American Sociological Review*, 18, 2–12.

———. (1968) *Politics and Television* (Chicago: Quadrangle Books).

Latour, B. (2005) *Reassembling the Social: An Introduction to Actor-Network-Theory* (Oxford: Oxford University Press).

Lazarsfeld, P. F. (1969) 'An Episode in the History of Social Research: A Memoir' in Fleming D. and Bailyn B. (eds), *The Intellectual Migration: Europe and America, 1930–1960* (Cambridge, MA: Harvard University Press), 270–337.

———. (1972) *Qualitative Analysis: Historical and Critical Essays* (Boston: Allyn and Bacon).

Lazarsfeld, P. F., Berelson, B. and Gaudet, H. (1944) *The People's Choice* (New York: Duell, Sloan and Pearce).

Lazarsfeld, P. F. and Merton, R. K. (1948) 'Mass Communication, Popular Taste and Organized Social Action' in Bryson, L. (ed.) *The Communication of Ideas: A Series of Addresses* (New York: Harper & Row), 95–118.

Leveson, The Right Honourable Lord Justice (2012) *An Inquiry into the Culture, Practices and Ethics of the Press: Executive Summary* (Norwich: The Stationary Office).

Lichtenberg, J. (ed.) (1990) *Mass Media and Democracy* (New York; Cambridge University Press).

Livingstone, S. (1990) *Making Sense of Television: The Psychology of Audience Interpretation* (Oxford: Pergamon Press).

———. (ed.) (2005a) *Audiences and Publics: When Cultural Engagement Matters for the Public Sphere* (Bristol: Intellect Press).

———. (2005b) 'In Defence of Privacy: Mediating the Public/Private Boundary at Home' in Livingstone, S. (ed.) *Audiences and Publics: When Cultural Engagement Matters for the Public Sphere* (Bristol: Intellect Press), 163–85.

———. (2009) 'On the Mediation of Everything: ICA Presidential Address 2008', *Journal of Communication*, 59(1), 1–18.

———. (2010) 'Giving People a Voice: On the Critical Role of the Interview in the History of Audience Research', *Communication, Culture & Critique*, 3(4), 566–71.

———. (2012) 'Exciting Moments in Audience Research – Past, Present and Future' in Bilandzic, H., Patriarche G. and Traudt, P. (eds) *The Social Use of Media: Cultural and Scientific Perspectives on Audience Research*, ECREA Book Series (Bristol: Intellect), 257–74.

Lloyd, J. (2004) *What the Media Do to Our Politics* (London: Constable & Robinson Limited).

Luhmann, N. (2000) *The Reality of the Mass Media* (Stanford: Stanford University Press).

Lundby, K. (2009) 'Media Logic: Looking for Social Interaction' in Lundby, K. (ed.) *Mediatization: Concepts, Changes, Consequences* (New York: Peter Lang), 101–19.

Lunt, P. and S. Livingstone (2012) *Media Regulation: Governance and the Interests of Citizens and Consumers* (London: Sage).

MacAloon, J. J. (1984) 'Olympic Games and the Theory of Spectacle in Modern Societies' in MacAloon, J. J. (ed.) *Rite, Drama, Festival, Spectacle: Rehearsals Toward a Theory of Cultural Performance* (Chicago: Chicago University Press), 241–80.

Machill, M. and Beiler, M. (2009) 'The Importance of the Internet for Journalistic Research; A Multi-Method Study of the Research Performed by Journalists Working for Daily Newspapers, Radio, Television and Online', *Journalism Studies*, 10(2), 178–203.

Mancini, P. and Hallin, D. (2012) 'Some Caveats about Comparative Research in Media Studies' in Semetko, H. A. and Scammell, M. (eds) *Sage Handbook of Political Communication* (London: Sage), 509–17.

Mazzoleni, G. (2008) 'Mediatization of Society' in Donsbach, W. (ed.) *International Encyclopedia of Communication* (Malden, MA: Blackwell), 3052–5.

——— and Schulz, W. (1999) '"Mediatization" of Politics: A Challenge for Democracy?' *Political Communication*, 16, 247–61.

McChesney, R. (2000) *Rich Media, Poor Democracy: Communication Politics in Dubious Times.* (New York: New Press).

———. (2007) *Communication Revolution: Critical Junctures and the Future of Media* (New York: The New Press).

——— and Nicholls, J. (2010) *The Death and Life of American Journalism: The Media Revolution That Will Begin the World Again* (Philadelphia: Nation Books).

McCombs, M. E. (2004) *Setting the Agenda: The Mass Media and Public Opinion* (Malden, MA: Polity Press).

———. (2014) *Setting the Agenda*, 2nd edn (Cambridge: Polity).

——— and Shaw, D. L. (1972) 'The Agenda-Setting Function of Mass Media', *Public Opinion Quarterly*, 36(2), 176–87.

McCombs, M. E., Shaw, D. L. and Weaver, D. H. (eds) (1997) *Communication and Democracy: Exploring the Intellectual Frontiers in Agenda-Setting Theory* (Mahwah, NJ: Erlbaum).

McHugh, D. and Parvin, P. (2005) *Neglecting Democracy: Participation and Representation in 21st Century Politics* (London: Hansard Society).

McQuail, D. (1969) *Towards a Sociology of Mass Communication* (London: Collier-Macmillan).

———. (1994) *Mass Communication Theory. An Introduction* (London: Sage).

———. (1997) *Audience Analysis* (London: Sage).

———. (2010) *McQuail's Mass Communication Theory*, 6th edn (London: Sage).

McQuail, D., Blumler, J. G. and Brown, J. R. (1972) 'The Television Audience: A Revised Perspective' in McQuail, D. (ed.) *Sociology of Mass Communications* (Harmondsworth: Penguin).

Meinhof, U. H. (2005) 'Audiences and Publics: Comparing Semantic Fields across Different Languages' in Livingstone, S. (ed.) *Audiences and Publics: When Cultural Engagement Matters for the Public Sphere* (Bristol: Intellect Press), 213–38.

Merton, R. K., Fiske, M. and Curtis, A. (1946) *Mass Persuasion: The Social Psychology of a War Bond Drive* (New York: Harper and Bros).

Meyrowitz, J. (1985) *No Sense of Place: The Impact of Electronic Media on Social Behavior* (New York: Oxford University Press).

Micheletti, M. (2003) *Political Virtue and Shopping* (New York: Palgrave).

Mills, W. C. (1959) *The Sociological Imagination* (New York: Oxford University Press).

Minow, N. N. and LaMay, C. L. (2006) *Inside the Presidential Debates: Their Improbable Past and Promising Future* (Chicago: Chicago University Press).

Mitchell, D. (1964) *The Dream Machine*. ATV Denis Mitchell.

Morgan, D. L. (1988) *Focus Groups and Qualitative Research* (Newbury Park: Sage Publications).

Morley, D. (1992) *Television, Audiences and Cultural Studies* (London: Routledge).

Morrison, D. E. (1978) 'Kultur and Culture. T. W. Adorno and Paul F. Lazarsfeld', *Social Research*, 45(2), 331–55.

———. (1998) *The Search for a Method: Focus Groups and the Development of Mass Communication Research* (Luton: University of Luton Press).

Morozov, E. (2011) *The Net Delusion: How Not to Liberate the World* (London: Penguin Books).

Murdoch, J. (2009) *The Absence of Trust: The MacTaggart Lectures*, Edinburgh International Television Festival, 28 August. Accessed 3 January 2013. http://image.guardian.co.uk/sys-files/Media/documents/2009/08/28/JamesMurdochMacTaggartLecture.pdf.

Murdoch, R. (1989) 'Freedom in Broadcasting' in Franklin, B. (ed.) *Television Policy: The MacTaggart Lectures* (Edinburgh: Edinburgh University Press), 131–8.

Mutter, Alan D. (2011) 'Newspaper Job Cuts Surged 30% in 2011', *Newsosaur*. Accessed 26 March 2013. http://newsosaur.blogspot.de/2011/12/newspaper-job-cuts-surged-30-in-2011.html.

Mutz, D. C. (2006) *Hearing the Other Side: Deliberative Versus Participatory Democracy* (New York: Cambridge University Press).

———. and Reeves, B. (2005) 'The New Videomalaise: Effects of Televised Incivility on Political Trust', *American Political Science Review*, 99(1), 1–15.

Nel, F. and Westlund, O. (2012) 'The 4C's of Mobile News: Channels, Conversation, Content and Commerce', *Journalism Practice*, 6(5–6), 744–53.

Nelson, W. (2010) 'The Historical Mediatization of BMX-Freestyle Cycling', *Sport in Society: Cultures, Commerce, Media, Politics*, 13, 1152–69.

Neuberger, C. and Nuernberg, C. (2011) 'Competition, Complementarity or Integration? The Relationship between Professional and Participatory Media' in Franklin, B. (ed.) *The Future of Journalism* (London: Routledge), 235–48.

Newman, N., Dutton, W. H. and Blank, G. (2012) 'Social Media in the Changing Ecology of News: The Fourth and Fifth Estates in Britain', *International Journal of Internet Science*, 7(1), 6–22.

Nielsen, R. (2012) *Ten Years that Shook the Media World: Big Questions and Big Trends in International Media Developments* (Oxford: Reuters Institute for the Study of Journalism).

Nisbet, R. A. (1966) *The Sociological Tradition* (New York: Basic Books).

Norris, P. (2009) 'Comparative Political Communications: Common Frameworks or Babelian Confusion', *Government and Opposition*, 44(3), 321–40.

———. (2011) *Democratic Deficit* (Cambridge: Cambridge University Press).

OECD (2010) *The Evolution of News and the Internet*, June. Accessed 27 March 2013. http://www.oecd.org/sti/ieconomy/45559596.pdf.

Ofcom (2009) 'Public Service Broadcasting', *Annual Report 2009*. Accessed 22 July 2013. http://stakeholders.ofcom.org.uk/binaries/broadcast/reviews-investigations/psb-review/psbrpt.pdf.

O'Malley, T. and Soley, C. (2000) *Regulating the Press* (London: Pluto Press).

Outhwaite, W. (ed.) (1996) *The Habermas Reader* (Cambridge: Polity).

Packard, V. (1957/1967) *Hidden Persuaders* (Harmondsworth: Penguin).

Parsons, T. (1952) *The Social System* (New York: The Free Press).

Pateman, C. (1970) *Participation and Democratic Theory* (Cambridge and New York: Cambridge University Press).

Patterson, T. E. (1993) *Out of Order* (New York: Alfred A. Knopf).

PBS (Public Broadcasting System) (2012) 'PBS and Member Stations Are Named #1 in Public Trust and an "Excellent" Use of Tax Dollars for Ninth Consecutive Year', *PBS.org*. Accessed 10 June 2014. http://www.pbs.org/about/news/archive/2012/pbs-most-trusted/.

Peleg, A. and Bogoch, B. (2012) 'Removing Justitia's Blindfold: The Mediatization of Law in Israel', *Media, Culture and Society*, 34, 961–78.

Perez-Pena, R. (2008) 'Web Sites That Dig for News Rise as Watchdogs', *The New York Times*, 18 November, p. A1 of the New York edition.

——— and Arango, T. (2009) 'They Pay for Cable, Music and Extra Bags. How About News?' *The New York Times*, 8 April, p. B1 of the New York edition.

Peters, H. P., Heinrichs, H., Jung, A., Kallfass, M. and Petersen I. (2008) 'Medialization of Science as a Prerequisite of its Legitimization and Political

Relevance' in Cheng, D. et al. (eds) *Communicating Science in Social Contexts: New Models, New Practices* (Berlin: Springer Netherlands), 71–92.

Pew Research Center (2013) *The State of the Media 2013*. Accessed 27 March 2013. http://stateofthemedia.org/2013/overview-5/.

Pfetsch, B. (2014) *Political Communication Cultures in Europe: Attitudes of Political Actors and Journalists in Nine* Countries (New York: Palgrave Macmillan).

Phillips. A. (2010) 'New Sources and Old Bottles' in Fenton, N. (ed.) *New Media, Old News: Journalism and Democracy in the Digital Age* (London: Sage), 87–101.

———. (2011) 'Transparency and the New Ethics of Journalism' in Franklin, B. (ed.) *The Future of Journalism* (London: Routledge), 289–98.

Philo, G. (1990) *Seeing and Believing* (London: Routledge).

Pickard, V. (2011) 'The Battle Over the FCC Blue Book: Determining the Role of Broadcast Media in a Democratic Society, 1945–48', *Media, Culture and Society*, 33(2), 171–91.

Plasser, F. and Lengauer, G. (2008) 'Television Campaigning Worldwide' in Johnson, D. W. (ed.) *Handbook of Political Management* (London: Routledge), 253–71.

Plasser, F., Pallaver, G. and Lengauer G. (2009) 'Die (Trans-)Nationale Nachrichtenlogik in Mediendemokratien. Politischer TV-Journalismus im Wahlkampf zwischen Transatlantischer Konvergenz und Nationaler Divergenz' ['The (Trans)National News Logic in Media Democracies. Political TV Journalism in Election Campaigns between Transatlantic Convergence and National Divergence'] in Marcinkowski, F. and Pfetsch, B. (eds) *Politik in der Mediendemokratie [Politics in Mediated Democracy]* (Wiesbaden, Germany: VS Verlag), 174–202.

Powell, J. (2010) *The New Machiavelli: How to Wield Power in the Modern World* (London: Bodley Head).

Preston, P. (2009) 'The Curse of Introversion' in Franklin, B. (ed.) *The Future of Journalism* (London: Routledge), 13–21.

Prior, M. (2007) *Post-Broadcast Democracy: How Media Choice Increases Inequality in Political Involvement and Polarizes Elections* (New York: Cambridge University Press).

Putnam, R. D. (2000) *Bowling Alone: The Collapse and Revival of American Community* (New York: Simon & Schuster).

Putnam, L. L. and Nicotera, A. M. (eds) (2009) *Building Theories of Organization: The Constitutive Role of Communication* (New York: Routledge).

Pye, L. (ed.) (1963) *Communications and Political Development* (Princeton: Princeton University Press).

Radway, J. (1987) *Reading the Romance* (London: Verso).

Reith, J. (1925) *Personality and Career* (London: George Newnes).

Rosenberg, B. and White, D. (eds) (1957) *Mass Culture* (New York: Free Press).

Roudakova, N. (2011) 'Comparing Processes. Media, "Transitions" and Historical Change' in Hallin, D. and Mancini, P. (eds) *Comparing Media Systems Beyond the Western World* (Cambridge: Cambridge University Press), 246–277.

Russell, J. (2012), 'KONY 2012', Invisible Children YouTube. Accessed 27 March 2013. http://www.youtube.com/watch?v=Y4MnpzG5Sqc.

Sabbagh, D. (2012) 'Jimmy Savile Row: Newsnight Emails Spark "Crisis" at BBC', *The Guardian*, 22 October. Accessed 4 January 2013. http://www.guardian.co.uk/media/2012/oct/21/bbc-emails-jimmy-savile.

Sampson, A. (1996) 'The Crisis at the Heart of Our Media' *British Journalism Review*, 7(3), 42–56.

Scheuch, E. (1990) 'The Development of Comparative Research: Towards Causal Explanations' in Oyen, E. (ed.) *Comparative Methodology: Theory and Practice in International Social Research* (London, Newbury Park and New Delhi: Sage).

Schillemans, T. (2012) *Mediatization of Public Services: How Organizations Adapt to News Media* (Frankfurt: Peter Lang).

Schramm, W. (ed.) (1954) *The Process and Effects of Mass Communication* (Urbana: University of Illinois).

―――― and Roberts, D. (1971) (eds) *The Process and Effects of Mass Communication*, 2nd edn (Urbana: University of Illinois).

Schrøder, K. C. (2013) 'Audiences as Citizens: Insights from Three Decades of Reception Research' in Parameswaran, R. (ed.) *Audience and Interpretation – Volume IV, The International Encyclopedia of Media Studies* (Oxford: Blackwell), 510–34.

Schudson, M. (1995) *The Power of News* (Cambridge: Harvard University Press).

―――――. (1997) 'Why is Conversation Not the Soul of Democracy?' *Critical Studies in Mass Communication*, 14, 297–307.

―――――. (1998) *The Good Citizen: A History of American Civic Life* (New York: The Free Press).

Schulhofer-Wohl, S. and Garrido, M. (2009) 'Do Newspapers Matter? Evidence from the Closure of *The Cincinnati Post*', *Princeton University Discussion Papers in Economics*, 236(March), 1–20.

Schulz, W. (2004) 'Reconstructing Mediatization as an Analytical Concept', *European Journal of Communication*, 19, 87–101.

Schumpeter, J.A. (1942) *Capitalism, Socialism and Democracy* (London and New York: Allen and Unwin).

Seltz, H. and Yoakam, R. D. (1962) 'Production Diary of the Debates' in Kraus, S. (ed.) *The Great Debates: Kennedy v. Nixon, 1960* (Bloomington: Indiana University Press), ch. 5, 73–126.

Semetko, H. A., Blumler, J. G., Gurevitch, M., Weaver, D. H, Barkin, S. and Wilhoit, G. C. (1991) *The Formation of Campaign Agendas: A Comparative Analysis of Party and Media Roles in Recent American and British Elections* (Hillsdale, NJ: Lawrence Erlbaum).

Sennett, R. (1992) *The Fall of Public Man* (New York and London: WW Norton & Company).

Shafer, J. (2009) 'Democracy's Cheat Sheet? It's Time to Kill the Idea that Newspapers are Essential for Democracy', *Slate.com*, 27 March. Accessed 10 June 2014.   http://www.slate.com/articles/news_and_politics/press_box/2009/03/democracys_cheat_sheet.html.

Shaw, D. L., Hamm, B. J. and Terry, T. C. (2006) 'Vertical Versus Horizontal Media: Using Agenda-Setting and Audience Agenda-Melding to Create Public Information Strategies in the Emerging Papyrus Society', *Military Review*, November-December 2006, 13–25.

Sherman, J W. (1978) *Scandal and Reform: Controlling Police Corruption* (Berkley, CA: University of California Press).

Shils, E. (1970)'Tradition, Ecology, and Institution in the History of Sociology', *Daedalus*, 99(4), 760–825.

Shiratori, R. (1995) 'The Politics of Electoral Reform in Japan', *International Political Science Review*, 16(1), 79–94.

Siebert, F., Peterson, T. and Schramm, W. (1956) *Four Theories of the Press* (Urbana: University of Illinois Press).

Silverstone, R. (1994) *Television and Everyday Life* (London: Routledge).

———. (2002) 'Complicity and Collusion in the Mediation of Everyday Life', *New Literary History*, 33, 761–80.

Smythe, D. (1995) 'On the Audience Commodity and its Work' in Boyd-Barrett, O. and Newbold, C. (eds) *Approaches to Media: A Reader* (London: Arnold), 222–8.

———. (1981) *Dependency Road: Communications, Capitalism, Consciousness, and Canada* (Norwood, NJ: Ablex).

Sombart, W. (1927) *Der moderne Kapitalismus. Dritter Band. Das Wirtschaftsleben im Zeitalter des Hochkapitalismus. Erster Halbband.* (München und Leipzig: Duncker & Humblot).

Son, Y. J. and Weaver, D. H. (2006) 'Another Look at What Moves Public Opinion: Media Agenda Setting and Polls in the 2000 U.S. Election', *International Journal of Public Opinion Research*, 18(2), 174–97.

Soroka, S., Andrew, B. Aalberg, T., Iyengar, S., Curran, J., Coen, S., Hayashi, K., Jones, P., Mazzoleni, G., Rhee, J. W., Rowe, D. and Tiffen, R. (2013) 'Auntie Knows Best? Public Broadcasting and Public Affairs Knowledge', *British Journal of Political Science*, 43(4), 719–39.

Stanyer, J. (2013) *Intimate Politics: Publicity, Privacy and the Personal Lives of Politicians in Media Saturated Democracies* (Cambridge: Polity Press).

Starr, P. (2009) 'The End of the Press: Democracy Loses its Best Friend', *The New Republic*, 4 March, 28–35.

Stelter, B. (2010) 'Honoring Citizen Journalists', *New York Times*, 21 February. Accessed 6 May 2013. http://www.nytimes.com/2010/02/22/business/media/22polk.html?_r=0.

Sternvik, J. (2010) 'Ungas Nyhetskonsumtion – I En Foranderlig Nyhetsvarld' ('Young People's News Consumption in a Changing News World') in Holmberg, S. and Weibull, L. (eds) *Nordisk Ijus*, SOM Institute, Gotherberg University, 369–79. Accessed 22 July 2013. http://www.som.gu.se/om_som/Kontakt/soren_holmberg/publikationer/.

Sunstein, C. R. (2007) *Republic.com 2.0* (Princeton, NJ: Princeton University Press).

Swanson, D. (1992) 'Managing Theoretical Diversity in Cross-National Studies of Political Communication' in Blumler, J. G., McLeod, J. M. and Rosengren, K. E. (eds) *Comparatively Speaking: Communication and Culture Across Space and Time* (Newbury Park, London and New Delhi: Sage), 19–34.

Swanson, D. L. and Mancini, P. (eds) (1996a) *Politics, Media and Modern Democracy: An International Study of Innovations in Electoral Campaigning and their Consequences* (Westport, CT: Praeger).

———. (1996b) 'Patterns of Modern Electoral Campaigning and Their Consequences' in Swanson, D. L. and Mancini, P. (eds) *Politics, Media, and Democracy: An International Study of Innovations in Electoral Campaigning and Their Consequences* (Westport, CT: Praeger), 247–78.

Swanson, D. L. and Nimmo, D. (eds) (1990) *New Directions in Political Communication* (London: Sage).

Tan, Y. and Weaver, D. H. (2007) 'Agenda-Setting Effects among the Media, the Public, and Congress, 1946–2004', *Journalism & Mass Communication Quarterly*, 84(4), 729–44.

———. (2009) 'Local Media, Public Opinion, and State Legislative Policies: Agenda Setting at the State Level', *International Journal of Press/Politics*, 14(4), 454–76.

Thompson, J. B. (1995) *The Media and Modernity: A Social Theory of the Media* (Stanford: Stanford University Press).

———. (2000) *Political Scandal: Power and Visibility in the Media Age* (Cambridge: Polity).

Trenaman, J. and McQuail, D. (1961) *Television and the Political Image* (London: Methuen).

Tufekci, Z. and Wilson, C. (2012) 'Social Media and the Decision to Participate in Political Protest: Observations from Tahrir Square', *Journal of Communication*, 62(2), 363–79.

Tulis, J. K. (1987) *The Rhetorical Presidency* (Princeton, NJ: Princeton University Press).

Turow, J. (1992) *Media Systems in Society: Understanding Industries, Strategies, and Power* (London: Constable).

van Cuilenburg, J. and McQuail, D. (2003) 'Media Policy Shifts: Towards a New Communications Policy Paradigm', *European Journal of Communication*, 18(2), 181–207.

van Noije, L., Kleinnijenhuis, J. and Oegema, D. (2008) 'Loss of Parliamentary Control Due to Mediatization and Europeanization: A Longitudinal and Cross-Sectional Analysis of Agenda Building in the United Kingdom and the Netherlands', *British Journal of Political Science*, 38, 455–78.

von Hippel, E. (2005) *Democratizing Innovation* (Cambridge, MIT Press).

Weaver, D. H. (1977) 'Political Issues and Voter Need for Orientation' in Shaw, D. L. and McCombs, M. E. (eds) *The Emergence of American Political Issues: The Agenda-Setting Function of the Press* (St. Paul, MN: West Publishing Company), 107–19.

———. (1991) 'Issue Salience and Public Opinion: Are There Consequences of Agenda-Setting?' *International Journal of Public Opinion Research*, 3(1), 53–68.

———. (1998) *The Global Journalist: News People Around the World* (Cresskill, NJ: Hampton Press).

———. and Drew, D. (1995) 'Voter Learning in the 1992 Presidential Election: Did the "Nontraditional" Media and Debates Matter?' *Journalism & Mass Communication Quarterly*, 72(1), 7–17.

———. (2001) 'Voter Learning and Interest in the 2000 Presidential Election: Did the Media Matter?' *Journalism & Mass Communication Quarterly*, 78(4), 787–98.

Weaver, D. H., Beam, R. A., Bradlee, B. J., Voakes, P. S. and Wilhoit, G. C. (2007) *The American Journalist in the 21st Century* (Mahwah, NJ: Lawrence Erlbaum).

Weaver, D. H., Graber, D., McCombs, M. E. and Eyal, C. H. (1981) *Media Agenda-Setting in a Presidential Election: Issues, Images, and Interest* (New York: Praeger).

Weaver, D. H., McCombs, M. E. and Spellman, C. (1975) 'Watergate and the Media: A Case Study of Agenda-Setting', *American Politics Quarterly*, 3(4), 458–72.

Weaver, D. H., McCombs, M. E. and Shaw, D. L. (2004) 'Agenda-Setting Research: Issues, Attributes, and Influences' in Kaid, L. L. (ed.) *Handbook of Political Communication Research* (Mahwah, NJ: Erlbaum), 257–82.

Weaver, D. H. and Wilhoit, G. C. (1986) *The American Journalist: A Portrait of U.S. News People and Their Work* (Bloomington: Indiana University Press).

———. (1996) *The American Journalist in the 1990s: U.S. News People at the End of an Era* (Mahwah, NJ: Lawrence Erlbaum).

Weaver, D. H. and Willnat, L. (2012) *The Global Journalist in the 21st Century* (New York and London: Routledge).

Westlund, O. (2013) 'Mobile News: A Review and Model of Journalism in an Age of Mobile Media', *Digital Journalism*, 1(1), 6–21.

Williams, B. A. and Delli Carpini, M. X. (2011) *After Broadcast News: Media Regimes, Democracy and the New Information Environment* (New York: Cambridge University Press).

Williams, K. (2010) *Read All About It! A History of the British Newspaper* (London: Routledge).

Wolf, A. (2010) *News Kind of Comes to Me….Young Audiences, Mass Media, and Political Information*, Master's Thesis, Berlin School of Creative Leadership, March.

Wolton, D. (1995) 'Les contradictions de la communication politique', *Hermès*, 17–18, 107–26.

YouGov (2011) *The Sunday Times Survey Results*, 7–8 July. Accessed 6 January 2013. http://cdn.yougov.com/today_uk_import/yg-archives-pol-st-results-08-100711.pdf.

Zaller, J. (2001) *A Theory of Media Politics: How the Interests of Politicians, Journalists and the Citizens Shape the News* (Chicago: University of Chicago Press).

Index

Printed and bound by CPI Group (UK) Ltd, Croydon, CR0 4YY